A PRELUDE

BOOKS BY EDMUND WILSON

EDMUND WILSON

A Prelude

Landscapes, Characters and Conversations
from the Earlier Years of My Life

FARRAR STRAUS AND GIROUX
NEW YORK

Copyright © 1967 by Edmund Wilson

All rights reserved

Library of Congress catalog card number 67–15011

"Lieutenant Franklin" copyright 1936 by
Harcourt, Brace & Co., copyright renewed 1964,
Edmund Wilson

Except for the illustrations, the contents of this book
appeared in *The New Yorker*

First printing, 1967

Published simultaneously in Canada by Ambassador
Books, Ltd., Rexdale, Ontario

Printed in the United States of America

CONTENTS

Illustrations appear following pages 88 and 152

First Trip to Europe
1908

In the summer of 1914, I began keeping a notebook, which eventually turned into something like a journal —though it never became for any length of time a day-by-day diary. I never noted the weather or recorded everything that I did but only aimed to catch *sur le vif* things that struck me as significant or interesting. This volume is a first instalment. At this stage, my notations were scrappy, and I have had to fill them in with something in the nature of reminiscences. Later on, I came to develop this chronicle on a very much larger scale, and even to some extent to organize it in the form of episodes that consisted of interwoven elements of experience. It is unlikely that very much more than this volume, with perhaps a second volume, can be published till after my death.

Of the two short stories included here, *The Death of a Soldier* first appeared in book form in *The Undertaker's Garland,* written in collaboration with John Peale Bishop, and *Lieutenant Franklin,* in *Travels in Two Democracies.* In the notebooks, I have corrected punctuation and spelling, and have occasionally corrected the style in order to remedy some intolerable clumsiness. I do not much recommend for its interest the 1908 diary of my first trip to Europe, but I am printing it for the sake of completeness, and because it provides me with a pretext for explaining certain family matters.

"My Trip Abroad"
Edmund Wilson Jr.
Red Bank N.J.
Presented
By
Miss Margaret
Edwards

[Margaret Edwards, about my own age, was at that time my closest friend in Red Bank. I shall tell more about her later. The diary, bound in leather, that she gave me when I was going away, had "My Trip Abroad" stamped on the cover.

I crossed with my family on the North German Line *König Albert*. At the dock, I bought a riddle-book, which must have been British. Two of the riddles, because of their badness, have remained in my mind ever since: "Why is a needy pauper like a man getting down a pork pie from the top shelf?" Answer: "Because he is a pore creature." "What is the difference between a beggar and the Tsar of Russia?" Answer: "The Tsar issues manifestoes, and the beggar manifests toes without his shoes." This joke-book is forever embedded in the memory of my first excitement at going to Europe.

On the boat was William Randolph Hearst, of whose sinister reputation I had been constantly hearing and reading. He resembled the caricatures I had seen of him. Tall and stooping, gray-eyed and gray-faced, he walked the deck by himself.]

May 8, 1908 [My birthday. I was thirteen]
The Azore Islands

In the afternoon we passed three of the Azores. First we passed Fayal, then Peko. On Peko is Mount Peko 7613 ft. high, the top of which is in the clouds. After that we saw San Jorge, which was very beautiful.

On the tops of the hills we could see palm trees. The houses were nearly all white with red roofs and there were a great many windmills, which looked like large pinwheels. From San Jorge a man in uniform, the American consul and some Portuguese came out to the ship to get the mail, which was lowered to them while the captain talked to the consul, who wore an eyeglass, through a megaphone.

The people on the Azores are mostly Portuguese (because the islands are owned by Portugal) and are very clean. So clean that some emigrants from the Azores were not allowed to mix with the others, but were given a place by themselves.

The islands themselves are very uneven and mountainous and seem to be surrounded by high cliffs, on which the waves dash very high.

A lady told us she had three sons who had never seen the Azores, all boys.

We passed St. Michael at 4 o'clock in the morning.

May 11th, 1908
Gibraltar

Today we stopped at Gibraltar. The rock looked exactly like the advertisement for the Prudential Life Insurance Company. [In those days, it was pronounced *advértisement*, as it is in England, but I now call it *advertízement* and spell it with a z.]

When we first landed there, a lot of men and boys crowded around us selling things.

We took a carriage and drove first to the Alameda Garden, where the flowers were beautiful and the cactus plants grew very large. Some were crab cacti, others looked like feet. Gibraltar is semi-tropical, and the fields are filled with wild poppies and other flowers. After this, we drove around the rock. The streets are filled with Moors, who have donkeys with packs slung over their backs, on both sides.

Then we drove through some of the streets and bought things. I bought a little clay bull, Sandy bought some stamps, and mother and Esther bought crazy little baskets. ["Sandy," Reuel B. Kimball, Jr., and Esther C. Kimball were my first cousins on my mother's side, the former fifteen months older than I, the latter, a little more than two years younger.]

After that, we went in some of the markets, where we bought some very good dates and baskets.

The Mediterranean looked very calm and we could see Africa and Spain across it.

May 11th, 1908
Spain
Linea

After Gibraltar we visited a Spanish village, we had to walk because carriages are not allowed inside.

The village was called Linea and we drove across the neutral ground to reach it.

A guide showed us around. Begging is allowed in Spain and a lot of bogus beggars came around us when we got out of the carriage.

The guide told us that there was a bull-fight every Sunday there.

After we had seen the village and bought some post-cards we came home.

May 15–19
Naples

We arrived at Naples Friday. Naples is a very dirty place, full of howling dagoes. We visited the Aquarium, which, though small, has many interesting fish, including several octopi which we watched a long time.

Saturday we went to Pompeii. And the day after to Capri. I was sick after that [the truth was that I was terribly scared at the prospect of a trip up Vesuvius; I pretended that I was ill and remained at the hotel in bed]—on Monday we saw the Naples Museum where all the best statuary from Pompeii and Herculaneum is. There were busts of all the Cæsars and a great many famous statues, including the statue of Hercules leaning on his club, the Venus de [Capua?], the Farnese Bull, the statue of Trajan which is in my history book, and others. After the statues, we saw the mosaics, which we liked best. There were mosaic altars and pictures, one of which was of different animals, one of which greatly resembled a skink. [Sandy and I thought we had made up this animal, which we often talked about, then were astonished to find it in the dictionary. Our skinks had ice-cream flavoring in their tails, which, when we drew them, appeared as cubic bulges.] Also there was a very large one of Alexander the Great. Then we saw the things taken from Pompeii, musical instruments, wall paintings, eggs, grain, olives, latches of doors and other things. The theater tickets were very interesting: there were skulls for dead heads, violins for orchestra seats, pigeons for the gallery and round things for the slaves and ordinary seats. There were also fishes no one knows about. In the next room was Pompeii in miniature, which we did not have time to examine because the guide told us that the museum closed in a few minutes. So we had to go away without seeing many of the best things. In Naples we bought a great many things.

May 16
Pompeii
   [I had prepared for this visit on the voyage over by reading *The Last Days of Pompeii,* which I found intolerably tedious. I was never even then susceptible of becoming engrossed in stories that were clumsily told and badly written, and I have never liked historical novels. *Ivanhoe,* which I also read at this time, bored me just as much.]

   When we first got to Pompeii, we got a very poor guide, but walked until we got to a little post-card store where a man telephoned for a guide. We ate our lunch while waiting for the guide to come and when he came we felt much better.

First he showed us the civil forum and the temple of Mercury, where there was a dining table. In the olden time, when the priests had eaten as much as they could, they leaned over and threw up in a trench where there was running water, and began all over again. We saw the public washing place, in which was the statue of the goddess of washing.

The temple of Isis and the temple of Apollo were very interesting. The temple of Apollo has a statue which was used as an oracle. After the people had paid to hear it speak, a priest would talk through a brass tube which went into the head of the statue and made it look as if it spoke.

The house of the Vettii was only excavated a little while ago. It had very beautiful wall paintings and the fountains were in such good condition that they would even play when turned on. Above the peristyle (which is what they used to call the garden which is in the middle of nearly every house) hung masks which used to have lights behind them. Then we saw the house of the golden cupids, which was only excavated a little while ago.

We also saw the cellars of the house of Diomed and the house of Glaucus or the house of the tragic poet, where there is a mosaic of a dog with the motto "Cave Canem" ("Beware of the Dog").

After a while we took two chairs which were carried by two men, which we took turns riding in. We finally came back very tired, the only drawback being that the chicken sandwiches were all hide [skin].

We also saw Virgil's tomb in Naples, but did not go to Herculaneum as we had planned.

May 17
Capri

The day after Pompeii, we went to Capri on the boat. On the way we passed Sorrento which looked very pretty. When we reached Capri, we first went to the Blue Grotto. The entrance is about 3 ft. high, so we had to lie down in the boat to get in. When we got in everything looked blue, the walls and the water, and anything put in the water turned a beautiful silvery blue.

After the Blue Grotto, we went back to the town of Capri, where we had a very good luncheon. After lunch we took a drive all around Capri.

We passed the Villa of Tiberius and we were going to another little village near Capri when we found it was time to go home.

The water looks all different colors from the shore at Capri.

[It ought to be explained at this point that our European summer was a joint expedition by the Kimballs, the Knoxes and the Wilsons. My Aunt Caroline, my Uncle Reuel's wife, had been a Knox, and her mother and my aunt's sister Adelaide were travelling with us as well as my aunt and uncle and their children, my two cousins, Esther and Sandy. There was a great deal of going and coming. We were rarely all together for long. Uncle Reuel and Aunt Caroline spoke German and Aunt Caroline French. Esther and Sandy had had a French governess and could get along in French. I was rather envious of them and declared that I did not want to learn French, but would perfect myself in German because it was a more virile language. (In later life, it turned out that German was the language that I was never able to learn

really well.) It was one of the jokes of the party that Mrs.
Knox claimed to speak Italian, which her family did not
believe. They would say, "When we get to Italy, Mother
will take care of everything."

Mrs. Knox, like my mother, was a sturdy example of
the American women of her generation: very dominating,
active and downright. Her husband, John Jay Knox, had
been Comptroller of the Currency for many years, then
the President of a New York bank. The Knoxes came
from Knoxsboro, New York, which is not very far from
Talcottville, where my mother's family had lived. I do not
know whether the two families had known one another
before they came to New Jersey and lived next door to
one another at Monmouth Beach; but both John Jay
Knox and my grandfather and his brother had gone to
Hamilton College, at Clinton, New York. Mrs. Knox had
acquired from her husband a considerable knowledge of
finance, and she kept up her ample establishment by an
adroit manipulation of the stock market. My father used
to give her advice, though he never bought stocks himself, since he regarded playing the market as a form
of gambling and hence immoral. After her husband's
death in the nineties, she built a big house at Seabright,
New Jersey. It had a huge room, with a grand piano and
French windows on three sides, and at the other end a
raised platform on which concerts were sometimes given.
Mrs. Knox was fond of music and had friends in the
professional musical world, whom she brought down from
New York and induced to perform. Above this stage was
a kind of balcony, from which she could peer down and
see what was going on below. Her household was a
special kingdom, self-contained and self-satisfied. Till her
youngest daughter married, two sons and two daughters
lived with her, and my uncle and aunt lived next door, so
that the whole thing composed a family unit, buried away

just off the Rumson Road on a kind of little alley called Hartshorn Lane. The Knox sons had vague jobs in New York, to which they would commute by steamboat, but I remember them as almost always at Seabright and always seeming dependent on their mother, as were also, a good deal of the time, a son-in-law and his Knox wife. They called each other by their childhood nicknames—Caroline was "Tibby," Adelaide "Raidy" and the third sister "Betty-Betty"—and they created such an atmosphere of intimacy that the men and girls whom they married might find themselves a little uncomfortable when they discovered that an effort was needed to accept the Knoxes on their own terms and to realize that they themselves could never quite be part of the clan. I always enjoyed seeing them, though everyone not a Knox was thus a kind of outsider. The young men, who would be drinking cocktails, would always be most charming and amusing when Sandy and I dropped in, and if we seemed to be smartly dressed, would address us as "Count" and "Lord Wilson," which latter was my pseudonym for the stories derived from the Sherlock Holmes and Raffles series that Sandy and I were writing. I remember that one of them, who had just bought a new suit, delighted me by showing it off in the poses of the figures in the clothing ads: "Spring Suitings for Young Men," etc. The tactless asperities of Mrs. Knox immediately became favorite family jokes. She had said on one occasion to a departing caller who stood and talked in the open screen door: "I'd rather have you come in again than the flies." When, in the twenties, I saw *The Cherry Orchard* performed by the Moscow Art Theater, it reminded me exactly of something I had known; but I could not identify this with the household of my Virginian relatives, who lived not in that kind of country house but in or near the University at Charlottesville. Then I remembered the

Knoxes: the same spirit of family cohesiveness, the same amiable frivolity and futility. It had, for example, been a joke for years that one of the young men had always been under the delusion that there were fish to be caught in a pond on the place but always came back empty-handed. I used to catch baby painted turtles there and keep them in pans of water for pets. The meadows behind the Knox place were full of daisies and black-eyed susans that grew in the long grass. The charm of this part of New Jersey is always today revived for me by Winslow Homer's little painting, called *In June*, of a girl in summer clothes lying in such a meadow, as the charm of the old Jersey Coast—the young women with their parasols on the sandy cliffs—is caught by him in his painting of Long Branch.

The temperament of my uncle Reuel Kimball—he will be described later on—did not lend itself to the Knox family tone, but he became an accepted institution, and would come over to play backgammon or bridge with them in the evenings. When the youngest daughter, Adelaide, married, her husband, André Chéronnet-Champollion, half-American but the great-grandson of the well-known Egyptologist who discovered the Rosetta Stone, turned out, to the discomfort of the Knoxes, entirely un-assimilable by them. He was a painter but quite affluent, much-travelled, very well-read and well-informed, and independent to the point of insolence. When the family and their visitors began their conversations and cocktails in the later afternoon, he would continue to sit reading with his back to them. They began by making fun of his mustache, whose shape he carefully preserved when in bed by a device that prevented its getting dishevelled and which they said was exactly like the Kaiser's; but he was soon making fun of them—he would mimic my Aunt Caroline teaching Esther ladylike manners—and could be extremely disconcerting when he resorted to a kind of clowning which I supposed he had picked up in youth in performing with the Hasty Pudding Club. I shall tell more about him later. Adelaide, whom he married not long after our trip, was by far the most attractive of the family. She was dark and extremely pretty—though "pretty" is not really suitable for so proud and so trenchant a personality. She was a great favorite with my father, for whom the rest of the Knoxes—"except the old lady"—were too light-weight and too worldly; and I was later to have for her the kind of admiration of a boy for an older woman completely beyond his reach that can only make him shy and awkward. I remember how much I was pleased by Adelaide's appreciation when I sang her a song from New York:

I'm the only star that twinkles on Broadway—
All the other stars are only shines they say.
I'm a public benefactress—
I'm a lady and an actress.
Why, I'm making Mrs. Leslie Carter's hair—turn—gray!
I remember when Belasco saw me play,
He threw up his hands and fainted dead away.
Charley Frohman's lost his reason
'Cause I've signed with him next season.
I'm the only star that twinkles—on—Broad-way!

Adelaide was quite unlike her conventional sister Caroline, who as a young girl, severely chaperoned, had studied music in Paris, and, with my mother, would scandalize Caroline in Europe by going out on the streets unescorted. Her ideas were, however, quite commonplace, and, in my conversation with her, I do not remember hitting off the least spark of response. Recalling that summer in Europe, I was to write about her years later,

when I heard that she was having a "breakdown" and had
been sent to a sanitarium:

> Her loved American laughter, male and clear,
> That rang so young in London or in Rome—
> A quarter century gone, my fortieth year—
> Is mute among those living ghosts at home.]

May 19
Rome

When we arrived in Rome we stayed at the Hotel
Royal. We noticed how clean it was, which was different
from Naples. One of the first things we saw was Saint
Peter's, which is the biggest church in the world. It is
very beautiful inside. We also saw the Coliseum and the
Baths of Caracalla, which were even more interesting.
When we first got there, we met Sandy's grandmother,
[his] Aunt Adelaide, Uncle John and Aunt Florence.
Sandy's Grandmother [Mrs. Knox] took us to the Capi-
tol to see the statue of Marcus Aurelius and the dying
gladiator. The same day she took us to see the Church of
the Cappuccini. Here when a monk dies he is buried in
earth brought from Jerusalem. After he has been there a
certain time, he is taken out and put in a niche in the
wall, and when the bones begin to fall apart, they are
used to decorate the walls and ceiling, which are covered
with designs of flowers and things all made of bones!

In the fountain of the Trevi we threw a penny and
made a wish and we are supposed to come back to Rome
again. [Here I express a hope that my pet dachshund is
"getting along all right" in my absence.]

Sandy and I found a puppet store where we bought a
lot of puppets at two cents each which we had lots of fun
with. It was somewhere here that we found out that

Sandy's Aunt Adelaide was engaged [to André Champol-
lion]. She got a letter, and the groom-to-be is going to
meet her in Venice or somewhere. We saw the Vatican,
where the Pope lives. It is full of picture galleries and has
a lot of famous statuary in it, which we enjoyed very
much. Besides this, we saw the Golden House of Nero
and drove out on the Appian Way to the catacombs,
which we were shown into by a Monk. We each took a
candle and went around through the dark passages.

We also saw two galleries, one of which contained the
statue of Apollo and Daphne. Apollo is pursuing her and
she is just turning into a tree. [I often returned to this
statue, which aroused my erotic imagination.]

One day we went out to Tivoli.

It is a very pretty place, with lots of waterfalls and
things.

The guide showed us the villa of some Bishop or
something which had a great many fountains. From there
we went to Hadrian's Villa. We had only time to see the
aquarium, the vomitory and several other choice things
before we came home.

We came home early because the next train was too
late, though Esther teased to come home late so she could
eat late dinner.

Florence

We only stopped at Florence for a few days, and we
got there just on a holiday. Nearly all the shops were
closed and men were all over the streets selling crickets in
little cages for good luck.

That afternoon Uncle Reuel took us to three moving
picture shows [one a film of Dante's *Inferno*]. The next
day everything was open, and we went to the galleries.
One was all most could stand, but Sandy, Uncle Reuel

and myself went to the Pitti gallery principally to see the Titian of the redheaded girl with nothing on but her hair. [This was my uncle's description of it—he thought we ought not to miss it.]

We saw in the first gallery several rooms filled with pictures of artists painted by themselves, from the oldest to the most modern. This was very interesting. We liked Florence very much, but we were glad to go on to Venice.

Sandy's Uncle John and Aunt Florence had left us in Rome. [These were Knoxes that I saw only rarely. John had tuberculosis, and they lived in some European health resort, where they were said to drink a great deal of champagne, as, I was told, TB sufferers tended to do. With their paleness and frailness and fine features, they seemed to me immensely distinguished, and their three daughters, so much quieter than we were, made upon me the impression of young royalties.]

Venice

At the station at Venice we were met by a gondola, which took us to the hotel. The next morning we went around in gondolas and went to the Square of St. Mark's. This is the public place and at one end of it are tall columns with the lion of St. Mark's and St. Theodore on an alligator on them. The cathedral of St. Mark's is also in the square, likewise the Doges' Palace and the great clock. This clock of course keeps Italian time with a dial of twenty-four hours. Every hour in the daytime two iron men on top strike the hour on a bell and a door opens below from which comes first Gabriel, who raises a horn to his lips, and afterwards several kings, all of which walk around the balcony into another door.

All night the hour is told by electric figures. The square is full of pigeons, which are so tame that they perch on your hands and hat to eat corn. These are the famous pigeons of Saint Mark's. One day we went out in a gondola to the Adriatic Sea, where we bathed. The Adriatic was full of little crabs that you had to be very careful about stepping on or annoying in any way.

Desdemona's house was pointed out to us as we went down the Grand Canal.

We also saw the Doges' Palace but did not have time to see it very thoroughly.

Murano

The same day we went bathing in the Adriatic, we took the hotel motor launch and went out to Murano, Burano and Torcello.

At Murano we went to the glass factory and watched them make glass. They made a goblet and a vase while we watched them and ended up with a bomb which was a large glass bubble burst.

At Murano we also saw them making pottery, which was interesting.

Burano-Torcello

From Murano we went to Burano, where the lace factories are. The lace there is all made by hand by little girls who at a certain age are all made to work on making lace.

We watched them for a while and then we bought some lace from them.

From here we went to Torcello, which was the last place.

At Torcello we went ashore, at least Aunt Carrie, Mother and I did while the rest stayed in the launch.

There was nothing at Torcello to see except an old church with lots of mosaic in it and an old well, which were interesting.

After this, soon we left Venice, where we also saw the Rialto.

But Sandy's Aunt Adelaide and Grandmother stayed behind to meet Mr. Champollion, and they were all to meet us again in Karlsbad.

Vienna

We got to Vienna just before a great holiday, the Emperor's birthday.

Vienna is a very beautiful city, though there is not much to see there. There are a great many fine shops there, which we went to.

One day Uncle Reuel took us out and we found a sort of small Coney Island, where we went to four or five moving-picture shows.

We left Vienna quite soon.

Karlsbad

We stayed in Karlsbad a month and enjoyed it very much there.

When we first came, we stayed at the Grand Hotel Pupp, but after a day we found a "Logis" on the hill called the Villa Victoria, Telegraf and König von England.

Mr. Geller, who owns the place, has a small Heinie dog called "Sleepfer." [Heinie was the name of my dachshund.] Karlsbad is full of Heinie dogs.

We used to go to tombolas every once in a while. Tombolas are like the game of lotto played on a large scale with prizes.

In Karlsbad they have a cracker about a foot in diameter called Karlsbader Oblaten, they are very good.

Every morning nearly we would go out to the Freundschaftssaal for breakfast, [where you ate in the open air].

While we were in Karlsbad we went to *The Geisha*, and the Karlsbader Orpheum twice.

We took several long drives, one out to the Engelhaus, which is an old ruined castle, and others to Giessüble, which is where the [Giessübler] water is bottled, and Hans Heiling, which is a very pretty place with a legend connected with it.

There is music all the time in Karlsbad, and at night Mr. Strauss came down and held a concert. We also drove to Marienbad in an auto.

[I have very pleasant memories of Karlsbad. It was the only place at which we stayed for any length of time. We walked up the little hills and skipped down them. We would save the oblaten paperbags and have an orgy of blowing them up and popping them—an amusement which we found, however, palled. When we were doing this once on a bench in a park, an official came up to us and told us that it was *verboten*. I was curious about the sometimes risqué jokes in the humorous weekly *Jugend*, which my Uncle Reuel enjoyed and did not hesitate to translate for us, and in the newsstands I saw exhibited a pamphlet on the cover of which Leopold of Belgium had been drawn with a huge beard that, on close scrutiny, was seen to be composed of the bodies of nude women. I read in a Tauchnitz edition Walter Scott's *Woodstock*, to which I had been attracted by the promise of spookiness suggested by the Woodstock ghost and by the lure of illicit love suggested by my having read that Henry II had kept Fair Rosamond there—not realizing that the novel took place in the seventeenth century—but which bored

me even more than *Ivanhoe*. Another Tauchnitz edition
was more rewarding: H. G. Wells's *Twelve Stories and a
Dream*. In Rome, we had gone to see the try-out, at
which the King had been present, of an Italian flying machine which was driven around a racetrack but which
hardly, if at all, got off the ground. Wells's dream was *A
Dream of Armageddon*, a vision of the flying machines of
the future, which ended with these words: " 'Nightmares,' he cried; 'nightmares, indeed! My God! Great
birds that fought and tore.' " This made an impression on
me. Blériot, a year later, flew across the English Channel.

My father joined us in Karlsbad. He had been suffering from his neurotic depression, and my Uncle Reuel, a
physician, had induced him to come to Karlsbad, with the
idea of making him relax. When he arrived, he told us of
having been waked on the train by an Austrian customs
officer with a mustache like a brigand, and other amusing
incidents of his journey. It was the first time, I think, that
he had been on the Continent, though he and my mother
had visited England. He laughed about these experiences
in a wild and almost hysterical way, as I had never known
him to do at home. Was it exhilaration at freedom from
his legal work, which often bored him, delight at rejoin-
ing his family? My uncle's remedy worked. He made my
father drink beer at the out-of-door cafés and listen to the
omnipresent waltz music. In these cafés there were orchestra conductors who were invariably advertized as
"Waltz Kings." The one mentioned in the diary was a
relative of Johann Strauss, perhaps his younger brother
Edward, who, I find, died in 1916. I always thought the
Merry Widow waltz and the *Waltz Dream* waltz pretty
banal, but I loved the *Silly Cavalier* and the *Vilya* songs
from the former and the *Piccolo* song from the latter.

But this regime of frequenting cafés which temporarily
restored my father proved fatal for my Uncle Reuel. He

and my father were the pillars of the family, highly successful in their respective professions. But my father had his hypochondria, and my Uncle Reuel spells of drinking that seemed to be equally neurotic. These spells came at very long intervals and were carefully planned ahead in a way that now seems to me curious. Uncle Reuel was a terrific worker. He was rather gruff and brusque but was loved by his patients, and I have heard a younger doctor who had known him at his hospital tell of his sometimes sitting up all night with a case that needed attention and appearing unshaved in the morning. His amusements were golf in summer and going to concerts in winter. I believe he cared little for social life. When my uncle had patients to attend to, my aunt, who was very much younger than he, would get young escorts to go to the concerts with her. On one occasion, feeling, in his study, a draught from the front door, my uncle went and shut it and returned to his reading, apparently without being aware that my aunt and her escort were saying goodbye at the threshold and that he had slammed the door in the young man's face. Sandy and I always found my uncle reading, no matter how late we came back from the theater. He kept up with the medical journals in a way that I was told was remarkable, and when he was done with them, he would read German literature. He said that Paul Heyse's prose was "like music." Eventually, he made the discovery of the naughty Viennese novels, and instead of inquiring about the play we had been to or otherwise making conversation when we dropped in upon him late in the evening, he would immediately, with unconcealed delight, translate for us the more risqué passages. But, as I say, this life of un-relieved application would sometimes be interrupted by carefully premeditated escapades. This occurred every two or three years. He would apparently brief his assistant, a much milder kind of man, whom he referred to as "the hairless Bingham"—he himself was thick-set and short, with a bristling square-cut mustache—and made sure that his patients would be properly cared for. Then he would disappear. I could never imagine where he went or what kind of companions he had: I don't remember ever seeing in his house any friend who seemed the least convivial. But when he was brought home, he would sometimes spend weeks in bed being de-alcoholized. I believe that the pressure of being forced to make money for my aunt's ever-expanding establishment had something to do with these aberrations. At any rate, his therapy for my father of making him a drinking companion betrayed him into one of his sprees. He made a trip alone to Prague, which he reported a beautiful city, and afterwards succumbed to drink and was for some time a serious problem. The Knoxes then left Karlsbad for Paris, where Adelaide's trousseau was bought.

My Aunt Caroline was, of course, sorely tried by all this, but I noticed no real friction between them. He had no secretary: she kept his accounts, in which she was assisted by her mother, who, as an expert in financial matters, would guide her in proportioning the amounts of the bills to the capacities of the patients. She dealt with my uncle's collapses with perfect restraint and dignity. Her life was a model of correctitude, which sometimes became oppressive. I remember that the Social Register was always in plain view somewhere. She played the violin in a small ladies' orchestra composed of her friends in Seabright and Rumson and read a book a week for a ladies "Discussion Club," without really, so far as I could see, caring much about either music or literature. She always had all the right opinions. She thought Bernard Shaw "a poseur," and when Sandy brought into the house the volume of Shaw's plays that contained *The*

Doctor's Dilemma, she thought it ought to be kept from my uncle for fear of offending his professional sensibilities. He got hold of the book, however, and was heard laughing heartily in his "office" over Shaw's satire on ephemeral medical fads. For years she would exclaim in horror over the dissonances of Richard Strauss and the anarchy of Debussy till they became so generally accepted that she was forced to admit their merit. When I discovered Wagner at college, and would come back from the Metropolitan full of excited enthusiasm, she would annoy me by her smug attitude that Wagner was a very old story and that it was boring to talk about him. She was goodlooking and very well-meaning, kindly and not always narrow-minded, but too unrelievedly preoccupied with doing the right social thing.

When we were staying in Karlsbad, my mother, who was already distressed by my neurotic father, was put under a further strain when my father came back to the pension one night and told her what was happening to her brother. There was little, by this time, in her life, in the way of human relations, which could really afford her much happiness; and, relatively young though she was, she suffered from deafness and gout. She had once lost her temper with me before my father had come, then afterwards apologized—which was unique in my relations with her and made an impression on me, for she was brusque and gruff like my uncle and her reprimands were always intended and not due to loss of control. In childhood, she would spank me with a silver-backed brush, which she would then complain had been dented, while my father, who never touched me and was incapable of the faintest brutality, would threaten without conviction that he would whip me "within an inch of your life." I was told by Sandy and Esther that their father, for purposes of discipline, would hang them headfirst over

the edge of the clothes-hamper and give them each "one
terrible swat."]

Nuremburg

Father, Sandy's Aunt Adelaide and Grandmother, also
Mr. Champollion, joined us in Karlsbad. And after a
while everyone left except Mother, Father, Uncle Reuel,
Sandy and myself. After a while we left, too, for Nuremburg.

Nuremburg is a very old city surrounded by a wall and
a moat, which no longer has any water in it.

At each of the four corners of the wall are towers.

Most of the toys are made in and around Nuremburg
and there are many toy shops there, which we visited.

The great sight in Nuremburg is the tower. As you go
in, you see a low wall on the edge of the moat, on which
are two marks of horse's feet, put there to show the place
where a robber chieftain (who was going to be put in the
Iron Maiden) had jumped off the wall into the moat and
escaped. He was afterwards recaptured and killed.

On the first floor of the tower are many torture machines. There are great wooden petticoats for drunkards
and gamblers, a confessor's chair full of spikes, masks for
scolding women, wooden collars for extravagant women, a
ducking machine for bakers who gave short weight, a
rack for stretching purposes, a wheel with a knife blade
on it which cut the victim up very small and very slowly,
a cradle full of spikes in which the victim was rocked to
death, a pear which when put in the mouth swells up to
four times its ordinary size, thus slowly cracking the
victim's head open, and a flute of iron which was fastened
to the fingers and mouths of musicians who played badly.

There were many other things such as racks, stocks,
thumbscrews, instruments for putting out the eyes and

pulling out the tongue, and a rack for women who fought which compelled them to hold their fists up in the air all the time, weights in the shape of cards and dice for gamblers and cheats, and a sword that had cut off 800 heads.

On the second floor is the Iron Maiden, a great iron cask with a woman's face. The victim is put inside and the door slowly shut. It is full of spikes inside, two of which put out his eyes. This is a very slow torture. When he stops yelling, he is let down into the river by a trap-door in the floor.

On the third floor are several prisons, one of which has the wax figure of the robber chieftain who jumped over the wall in it and is where he was imprisoned.

On the last floor are suits of armour, old chess and checker men, old playing cards, and many other antiquities.

We also saw the Albert Dürer house, the town hall and other interesting things.

Frankfurt

At Frankfurt we met the rest, who had gone to Dresden.

Frankfurt is a very fine city, and we were in a very fine hotel. We went to the Zoölogical Gardens and a circus which was very much like our Hippodrome, and several moving picture shows. We liked Frankfurt very much.

The Rhine—Cologne

We left Frankfurt for Mainz, where we took the boat to go down the Rhine to Cologne in.

We had a pleasant trip down the Rhine, which is lined on the bank by old ruined castles and castles which are not ruined. We passed the Lorelei rock and the Mouse-Tower of Bishop Hatto.

[I had the satisfaction of having been taught *Die Lorelei* by my Aunt Laura and of knowing Southey's poem about Bishop Hatto, which I had enjoyed as I usually did the imaginatively macabre. I remembered and hummed an old song:

> Be true to me, love, be true
> > Be ever, ever mine.
> When the war is o'er,
> We'll part no more
> > At Bingen on the Rhine.

There was a beautiful girl on the boat, who inspired in me romantic fantasies. She had long yellow hair, and I associated this with the Rheingold. I was to marry, thirty-eight years later, a blond and blue-eyed woman from the Rhineland. We must have passed, on our trip down the Rhine, Johannisberg, where her family lived. She would have been two years old then. I have derived from this event in connection with that memory—absurdly enough, no doubt—a romantic satisfaction at the realization of a youthful dream.]

————

At Cologne we visited the cathedral, and the church of St. Ursula, which is something like the church of the Cappuccini in Rome, having the bones of the eleven thousand virgins in it.

Cologne—Paris

There was very little to see in Cologne, and it was very dreary there so we soon left it. Nearly all the cologne is made in Cologne. We left for Paris and got there late at night.

————

[I stopped keeping my diary in Paris. There is very little fun in Paris for children from other countries. In France—unlike Germany and Italy—not much is provided to amuse the young. Our parents were always going to theaters and restaurants to which we could not be taken. I first heard then of the Tour d'Argent and its celebrated squeezed duck, and I was tantalized by posters all over the streets which said *"Tout nu"* and had a torso of a pretty woman, with nothing on but a fashionable hat. We were, however, taken to the Nouveau Cirque, where we saw the famous clown Chocolat, who had been sketched by Toulouse-Lautrec. He had been promised us as a great treat, but I found him disappointing. He must have been rather old by then. Sandy and I found a delightful restaurant in the Rue de Rivoli, where we would order the blown-up potatoes called *pommes de terre soufflées.* We wondered how it was done.

We made a brief stay in London. That was the summer when three, I think, of Somerset Maugham's plays were running at the same time, and I remember the poster for *Jack Straw,* in which the face of a man in evening clothes was half lit up by the match with which he was lighting a cigarette. We stayed at the Metropole, and my father was always amused by a waiter who exactly resembled the waiter William in *You Never Can Tell.* I eagerly bought *Punch,* which was still in its period of elaborately descriptive captions, and I visited the mummies in the British Museum. I saw the Maskelines' magic performance and bought some magic apparatus, which included the linking rings—an old trick that is easy to do but is still being performed by professionals.]

Family

In all my early life, before I went away to school, I was preoccupied with the members of my family as I imagine few young people can be today. The fact was that I knew almost nobody else, that my relatives were extremely varied and that most of them seemed to me interesting. I was surprised when, after college, a friend of mine spoke of the effort it had cost him to get away from the bleakness and dulness of his family, for my parents and my grandparents and my uncles and aunts had been the molding influences of my early life. The male members of the Wilson and Kimball families were mostly successful —or modestly able—preachers and lawyers and doctors, and I knew they had their doubts about me, and that in order to prove myself I should have to show that a writer could become a successful professional. I was much gratified the other day when a reviewer gave me this title.

I have already, in *A Piece of My Mind*, given some description of my father and, in a sketch called *At Laurelwood*, written of my Kimball grandparents and my Uncle Paul at Lakewood. But I should add here, to balance the Rumson end, some account of other members of the family. My Wilson grandfather and grandmother were from Newburgh on the Hudson and elsewhere in Orange

County. The first Wilson had come over from London-
derry in the eighteenth century, equipped, according to
the family legend, with nothing but a fishing-rod and a
silver onion watch. My grandmother was part Dutch. My
grandfather, Thaddeus Wilson, had a long incumbency
as minister of the Presbyterian Church in Shrewsbury,
New Jersey. He had graduated from the Princeton Theological Seminary, where his brother had previously
studied. But Andrew Wilson did not last at the Seminary.
Like the father of William and Henry James, he was
revolted by its fundamentalist doctrine and very soon gave
it up. I do not know how my grandfather got through.
He was certainly not a severe Calvinist. My father once
spoke of his tolerance, his unwillingness to blame anyone harshly. I never heard my grandfather preach. When
my parents went to church, they would leave me with my
grandmother, who would read me the Bible and instruct
me. She was said to have been handsome and, in her
limited way, was, I think, perhaps more "intellectual"
than my grandfather. She amused herself in the evenings
by going through the higher mathematics. I did not enjoy
my sessions with her, because she put moral pressure on
me, as nobody else did, and I stood very much in awe of
her; but they had for me a certain value because they
provided my only clue to what the old Calvinist religion
had been. My Virginian and Rumson cousins had been
brought up as Episcopalians, and my Wilson grandmother told me that Episcopalians were "worldly" people
—as the result of which, when I visited the Kimballs and
was taken to church at Galilee, New Jersey, I felt a little
of the thrill of doing something forbidden. The service,
like all services, was boring, but one did not have to
listen to a long Presbyterian sermon; and, on the part of
the congregation, there was a nuance of fashionable style
that one did not find in Shrewsbury. It was not till I was

very much older that I realized that my mother was entirely non-religious and that, after her father-in-law's death, she continued to go to his church because my father—without having, I think, much religion either—felt an obligation to support it. My great-great-grandfather Kimball, who had married a Mather and come from New England to upstate New York, had carried on the Mather tradition with an intemperance not wholly acceptable to the liberated New Englanders there who had emerged from their cramping communities and had the run of a vast country just settled. My great-grandfather, though not a preacher, continued in the dogma and the discipline of his father; but my grandfather, having suffered from it in youth, completely threw over this doctrine and the habits of living it imposed. As a physician, he had the scientific point of view, and none of his children, except perforce my mother, was ever known to go to church or to show the slightest interest in religion. It was one of my mother's fears that her funeral would be conducted by the local Presbyterian minister, and in one of her last illnesses, she refused to see this local minister. He sent her flowers in the hospital, but she had them given to the cook. When it got to the point in this country when people questioned and rebelled against Calvinism, it was rejected with a real detestation: no one who had been oppressed by it wanted ever to hear about it again. When my grandmother thought I was old enough, she began bringing pressure to bear on my mother to have me taught the Presbyterian catechism. My mother, however, was horrified when she examined the strictly orthodox catechism that I suppose my grandmother had given her, and found that it began by declaring that the non-chosen would be sent to eternal torment. She procured a modified catechism and had me learn the answers to a few of the early questions; but I never got beyond this, and she never tried to make me go further. She was able to tell my grandmother that I had been studying my catechism.

My mother and father, in that part of New Jersey, belonged to a kind of local gentry that seems to have been pitifully sparse: the people who had large farms and had been there since the eighteenth century, the doctors, the lawyers, the preachers, a military family, the Van Vliets. There were very few people that one could marry. I have been told that my father was in a desperate state of mind about getting my mother to marry him. I think that he must have been attracted by her positive, self-confident, determined nature, because he had been used to depending on the support of his mother's strong character. It should be noted that, in spite of her austere faith, she had always indulged her children. But my mother, I think, married my father only because there was no one else. Aside from their professional parents, they had nothing whatever in common, and the longer they were married, it seemed to me, the more they became estranged.

A more depressing illustration of the paucity of choices in that part of New Jersey was the marriage of my Aunt Laura Kimball. It was a kind of tradition in old-fashioned families that there had to be a spinster daughter who stayed at home and took care of the parents. With the Kimballs, this role fell to Laura. She had adored my grandfather to such a degree that she never quite recovered from his death. She continued to live with my grandmother, and they amused themselves by making trips together to Europe and to California. But, after my grandmother's death, it was impossible for Laura to live alone, and her life came to consist of a series of visits to her family and her friends. This became very painful. She would walk around our dining room, wringing her hands, and occasionally had fits of hysteria. She was by far the most literary of the Kimball children and one of my favorite relatives. I learned a good deal about books from her. She had the remnants of my grandfather's library and would give me volumes from time to time. For as long as I can remember, she had been courted by Charles Corlies, a former neighbor in Eatontown. He was the only eligible man for her, and he took her for a drive every Sunday afternoon and came to see her when she was staying at Talcottville, the village in upstate New York from which my mother's family came. He had even less in common with her sensitive poetic nature than my parents had with one another. His family, originally French, were an old one in that countryside. They had for generations owned a large farm, which, up to Charles's day, they had more or less profitably cultivated. But Uncle Charley—for he eventually married my Aunt Laura—had no taste or talent for farming. He was always having failures and fires, and his poultry yard was robbed with impunity. He was always deeply in debt. The place had an old stone smoke-house covered with red trumpet-vine, and a brook clogged with watercress. The house was a veritable museum of old-fashioned furniture and ornaments. Mrs. Corlies, Uncle Charley's mother, had made beautiful wax fruit, which was exhibited under bell-glasses, and curious pictures of Biblical scenes, put together from bits of paper and tinfoil. There was the only example I had ever seen of the formidable large-scale "parlor," which was kept with the shades pulled down on its great highboy and marble fireplace. The old Mr. Corlies survived, a taciturn and morose old man, of a kind that I had also seen at Talcottville, who resented the younger generation and was capable of blighting comments. It had been a sad blow to Uncle Charley that his father would not let him go to Princeton like the Kimball and Wilson boys, but had made him stay at home on the farm. He himself was not at all a bear like his father, but had the manners and dress of a country gentleman.

When my Aunt Laura finally yielded to the logic of her situation and married Charley Corlies, she had difficulty in adapting herself. There were the silent immovable presence of his father and her husband's reluctance to allow her to change any arrangements that had been sanctified by his mother. The two men had been living there so long by themselves that they hardly knew how to accept a woman. Nevertheless, one side of the house was remodelled, with more windows and a fireplace, and my aunt did her best to imbue it with some of the cheerfulness and brightness of my grandmother's house at Lakewood. She had an upstairs room to herself, in which she installed her books, which would never have fitted in with the antiquated library below, long entombed behind high glass doors. She now referred to herself deprecatingly as "a farmer's wife." She was too old to have children. I made a point of going over to see them, for I felt an obligation to my aunt, and I would find them, after the old man's death, sitting silent on the front porch, obviously at odds and with nothing to say to one another, while the darkness closed down on the country street on which they had no close acquaintances. Uncle Charley, who had no local friends and only one close cousin, who was married to a clergyman and came to see him every summer, seemed to relapse, as the years went on, more and more into a moroseness like his father's. My father was so depressed by this household that he gave them a Victor phonograph, which they put in the parlor on an old grand piano, where it seemed out of place and its music an intrusion. When their financial situation became even worse, they sold the highboy for a thousand dollars to the American Wing of the Metropolitan Museum. My aunt died before her husband, and he died not many years later in a state not much short of bankruptcy. All his and my aunt's property except some that he had left to his cousin—I think, the good old china and silver—was dismally sold at auction to satisfy Uncle Charley's creditors. My mother, to her pain, saw my grandmother's wedding dress sold, but rescued for me an object I had always admired: an elaborate model of a steamboat made in his boyhood with a jig-saw by Uncle Charley.

An example of the unfortunate consequences of marrying someone not eligible was provided by my Aunt Adeline. To the indignant disapproval of her brothers and the tragic distress of her father, she eloped with a man from Shrewsbury whom all her family looked down on and disliked. His family owned a certain number of acres, but they ran a slaughter-house, and this in itself would have been enough to put them beyond the pale. The curious thing is that at first her husband seems to have given my Aunt Adeline a very good time. He took her to Florida and Europe, and bought her many objects of luxury. Though when she talked about him later with her sisters, she referred to him as "the foul fiend," I always had the impression that her memories of him were rather tender. He abandoned her at some point, in any case, with four children and no means of support. My father arranged a divorce and got her a job teaching music in the Red Bank public school. The whole affair remained for me mysterious. I saw the husband only once, when he had come back to Shrewsbury to the Stilwell property, now about to be sold, in order to attend an auction of the family's remaining effects. He had a big white mustache and spoke with a lisp, and struck me as having once been the type of flashy unreliable adventurer. The children I knew well. Two of them—the boy and the eldest girl—had an allowance of artistic ambition and imaginative susceptibility that were not—except perhaps in Sandy—to be found to that degree in any others of my Kimball cousins. The boy, George Stilwell, was stage-struck from his earliest youth and used to make his sisters act with him in the basement in plays of his own creation. My father, who loved the theater, later got him a job with Charles K. Champlin, a former sign-painter and resident of Red Bank, who had built up a successful stock company that toured the provincial cities. He used to tell me of his playing the lead in *The Count of Monte Cristo*. In the scene that followed the shipwreck, he would have to crawl along on the stage, under the waves that were strips of cloth undulated by stagehands in the wings. George would stick his head up between them from time to time, and finally, with his lungs full of dust, arise as if on dry land and, restraining his coughs, splutter out: "My name is Monte Cristo, and the world is mine!" He pleased me by giving me some stage mustaches that were attached with blobs of wax. But he was in general something of a problem. He was a ham both off and on the stage, and the Rumson Kimballs dreaded his rare visits, when he would pay gallant compliments to Aunt Caroline and always address our Uncle Reuel as "sir," as if he were playing a role in some formal old-fashioned play. He later made himself a place in the company of Robert Mantell, the stock-company Shakespearean actor, in which he was, however, confined to very subordinate parts such as Paris in *Romeo and Juliet*—in such a role, he appeared quite handsome. His only real success, just before he died, was the result of a curious accident. Arthur Hopkins was then casting a sort of expressionist play called *Machinal*, in which a wife either murders or runs away from her husband. George was tried out by Hopkins and—not wholly, it would seem, by intention —made the husband so stupid and exasperating a figure that all the sympathy of the audience went to the wife, and George got excellent notices for a comic characterization.

The eldest of the Stilwell girls, Helen, was exceedingly handsome and clever. In my childhood, I found her fascinating because she was always willing to amuse me. She drew me dragons and other imaginary monsters, sang me English music-hall songs, read me Mrs. Gamp and Uncle Remus and amazed me by being able, after seeing a musical comedy, to come back and play the whole score by ear. She scandalized some of the family by living in New York as a "bachelor girl," which then required audacity. She made a living as a journalist both by writing and drawing, and eventually married Gene Carr, who was probably, as a draughtsman, the best comic-strip artist of his time. This, again, did not please the family, but was rather exciting to me, since I followed the "funny papers" with enthusiasm. Helen Stilwell had all the dominating drive which I associate with the women of my grandmother Kimball's family, and I think that she proved too much for Gene. He was small, high-strung and rather neurotic. He seems to have got on better with a second wife, for he lived with her to be seventy-nine. The next sister, Dorothy, was the one of the children most liked by my aunt's other relatives, who were embarrassed by George and disconcerted by Helen. My Aunt Adeline's two older brothers had outlawed her after her marriage and never willingly saw her again. But the pretty and well-behaved Dorothy was popular with everybody, and a favorite of my Uncle Paul, of whom I have written elsewhere, a fashionable doctor at Lakewood, New Jersey, with a great eye for pretty women. Dorothy married a civil engineer, with the kind of conventional good looks—broad shoulders and square-cut features—that one saw in the men's clothing advertizements, who had just graduated from Rutgers. This pair were then considered reliable, but they later followed the fashion of the twenties: got divorced and both married other people. The third of

the Stilwell sisters, though nearest my own age, was the
one with whom I had perhaps least in common. At one
point, she was considered in danger of becoming rather
out of hand, and my mother, with a view to discipline,
had her sent to a Catholic convent school. What Adeline
actually needed in order to fulfil herself was to see more
not less of the world, and when she later got the hang of
New York, she married a succession of wealthy men,
some of whom died and others of whom she divorced—
she was married five or six times—and was left a wealthy
woman. At one time, she had a broker's office, with a line
to the Stock Exchange, in which she handled her own
investments. Her prosperity was an excellent thing for
my aunt, who had been teaching music all those years
and sitting, among remnants of her early travels, in a
rather badly-kept house, taken care of by a bent old
Negro crone. This cook had a pet parrot, and my aunt—
strangely undismayed, I thought, in contrast to my har-
ried mother and my unfortunate Aunt Laura, by anything that happened to herself or her children—extracted
from her ménage and her vulgar neighbors a good deal of
jolly humor. Since her daughter was now in a position to
send her money and presents, she was no longer a poor
relation. These presents, although expensive, were sometimes quite inappropriate. One was a diamond bracelet,
which my aunt could hardly have had occasion to wear.
When somebody in the family asked her about it, she said
that she never wore it but carried it around in her bag,
"And Nelly knows about it." Nelly was my mother, who
liked to control the objects of her benefactions, and the
bracelet was a talisman of liberation.

I shall stop this family record here. I know how boring
and confusing it becomes to read about family connections. A whole other side of my early life I shall leave, in

this volume, untouched: my memories of upstate New York—Lewis and Oneida Counties—in which my mother's parents had lived and in which we spent every summer. This was something entirely distinct from, and by me much preferred to, New Jersey. It is one of the points of triangulation without which it would be impossible accurately to locate myself in the world in which I grew up. But I have touched on the subject elsewhere, and I hope to deal with it further in a book devoted to that region.

School and College Friends

I remember that, one afternoon when I was bicycling down Prospect Hill, at the foot of which our Red Bank house stood—it was just before I went away to school and must have been after our trip to Europe—I said to myself, "I'll eventually have friends with whom I'll have something in common." I was not, to be sure, without friends in Red Bank, but they were far from sharing my interests. Margaret Edwards, now Mrs. Walter Rullman—who gave me the "My Trip Abroad" diary—was the one I found most sympathetic. Her father had been a painter, and she herself had artistic ability and had been sent to a good boarding school. But at a given point, I was stopped from seeing very much of her and her sister by fear of the imputation of playing too much with girls and by her mother's tactless remark, "You're going to marry my daughter, aren't you?" My cousin Sandy had up to that time been my only really close companion. We were much together in the summer both in New Jersey and in Talcottville, and when the Kimballs were in New York during the winter, I would visit them in the holidays. In childhood, before we could write, we dictated stories to our Aunt Laura, who sewed them into little books. Thereafter, we wrote and illustrated a series called *The Adven-*

tures of Colonel Mellow, read more or less the same books, put on plays in a toy theater, made humorous phonograph records on wax cylinders by means of what was called a "recorder" and, with Esther, enacted charades. When the Fourth of July came round, we were much occupied with fireworks. In those days, one got fascinating catalogues which advertized rockets, "flowerpots" and other things, with such fancy names as Gerbes and Devil Among the Tailors. We would send for selections of these, and were very soon taking them apart and recombining their elements in order to see what would happen. We invented what we called a Pazazza—a name we had taken from the comic strip of the Katzenjammer Kids. It consisted of a flowerpot shell, into which we had put rocket and Roman candle balls with a certain amount of gunpowder, and, I think, red and green fire. It did not go off when we lit the fuse and, after waiting a long time, we eventually became so reckless as to stand over it and drop in matches. It suddenly erupted in our faces. Poor Sandy was worse injured than I. His father had to remove countless cinders from his eyes. I completely lost my eyelashes and eyebrows. But this turned out to be an advantage: my eyebrows before had been pink—I was redheaded—and scarcely discernible; but they now came in heavier and darker.

Through Sandy, I was made surreptitiously acquainted with Havelock Ellis's *Studies in the Psychology of Sex,* the circulation of which was at that time supposed to be restricted to members of the medical profession and which my uncle, as a doctor, had been able to acquire. I thus at an early age, when I had had no sexual experience, was already pretty thoroughly informed about the phenomena of sex, and the case histories in fine type at the back of the volumes became as familiar to me as at a somewhat earlier age, had been Andersen's fairy tales or the *Arabian Nights*. These volumes are never night-marish, as I afterwards found that Kraft-Ebbing was. The most outlandish of the "deviations" never results in hor-rors. The Vicar of Little Tiddlingham—I improvise—in spite of his misbehavior, remains Vicar of Little Tiddling-ham still; the versatile British officer—this is one of the actual histories—who tells of his exploits in many coun-tries and at the end gives a list, in order of preference, that extends through the vegetable and animal worlds and persons of both sexes, beginning with a humble melon and ending with "a woman, a friend and lady of my own class," never fails in his duty or forfeits his rank. The whole atmosphere of Ellis is reassuring.

When Sandy was staying with us in upstate New York, as he usually did in the summers, and my father would take us to Canada, he got on better with my father than I did. He always had something of the courtier, and my father liked to be admired. At the time he was Attorney General of New Jersey, Sandy made rather a point of referring to him as "the General." But Sandy was fifteen months older than I and went to prep school a year before I did, and this alienated us from one another. Before I went away myself, I resented the unfamiliar school slang that he brought back when I saw him in vacations. He was sent to St. Paul's and I to Hill. It was thought that Andover and Exeter, to which my father and uncles had gone, left the students too much on their own, and that Hill, which had in that period a great reputation, was better for the more sensitive and the less mature. In comparison with the seriousness of Hill, where they were always insisting on the importance of a high-minded object in life, and which was supposed to maintain such high standards that if you passed the Hill examinations, you could get into college with top grades, the products of St. Paul's that I saw at Princeton—including by that time Sandy—seemed to me rather frivolous. At Princeton, in different years and belonging to different clubs, we saw little of one another. With his usual easy urbanity, he gave me on my arrival, a little briefing, explaining, for example, that, in introducing friends to one another, I should always refer to them as "Mister" rather than give them their Christian names. But, in general, we did little more than greet one another on the campus.

When I myself went away to school, I did find congenial and interesting friends. My first year was rather difficult, as first years at school are likely to be. My room-mate and I had been assigned to the same room because his father and mine had been classmates at Princeton, and we were not at all suited to one another. My marks were so bad that I was not allowed to go home for a weekend, when I had set my heart on getting away to my family from the unfamiliar pressures of school and to seeing the young people race sleighs on the thoroughfare from Shrewsbury to Red Bank. My introduction to Hill had, besides, begun with an unpleasant incident. My mother, with characteristic lack of tact, had called me "Bunny" when she brought me on and, at a first get-together in my rooming-house, this was taken up by the boys. I tried to fight everybody who did this, but was outnumbered, and the house-master broke it up. I have been saddled with this nickname all my life. When I later asked my mother why she had called me that, she gave me the even more embarrassing explanation that she used to say about me as a baby that, with my black eyes, I "looked just like a plum-bun."

But in the spring of that first year, I had a story printed in the school magazine. I later became an editor, and the editors and contributors of the *Hill School Record* had a stimulating effect on one another and were encouraged by the highly intelligent masters. We had hilarious meetings in one of the classrooms. In my Fifth and my Sixth Form years, I was having so good a time at school that I hated to go home for the holidays and spent a large part of the summers visiting my friends. This continued after I got to college. The atmosphere in Red Bank was oppressive. My poor father was usually absent, in eclipse in some sanitorium for what were then called "neurasthenics"—he did not even come to my college graduation—and though I felt very sorry for my mother, I found it terribly difficult to talk to her, partly because she was deaf and partly because we had so little to talk about. On my journeys back to Red Bank, I used to make notes of topics about which I could communicate with her. One of my most desolating memories is a spell I had to spend at Red Bank when my father was at home with a nurse and my mother was taking a vacation from him. He would talk about nothing but his ailments and would ask—an impossible question—whether I thought that his career was finished. One had very little success in attempting to divert him to anything else. When, in the part of upstate New York from which she had come, I met this nurse not long ago, after not having seen her since then, and she reminded me of our previous acquaintance, the pang of revulsion I felt made me realize how completely I had blotted this experience from my mind. I seem to have accepted every invitation that gave me an excuse to be somewhere else, and when there was nobody available to visit—one summer when my parents had gone abroad in the hope that travel would again revive my father—I spent a solitary interval at Talcottville, where I bicycled and read and went every afternoon for a swim in Sugar River.

Since I have given already in *The Triple Thinkers,* in a memoir called *"Mr. Rolfe,"* some general account of the

Hill School, I shall limit myself here to brief notes on the various milieux which I discovered with attentive interest in the course of these visits to my friends. As I have said, I had known hitherto almost no one but the members of my own family, and such marginal persons as surrounded these in their habitats of Red Bank, Seabright, Rumson, Lakewood, Shrewsbury, Eatontown and Talcottville. My first intimation of the fact that there existed other self-contained worlds had occurred when my mother took me on one of her annual March holidays to Atlantic City. I made the acquaintance there of a family of amusing children who were staying at the same hotel and took part in an entertainment—I recited *Paul Revere's Ride*—which we gave in the basement for the grown-ups. It was revealed at some point to my little companions that I came from Red Bank, New Jersey, and they ran at once to their mother. "Never mind," I heard her say. "He may be a very nice boy even if he doesn't come from Philadelphia." This seemed to me strange at the time for I had never known Philadelphians, but I later on learned that to be one excludes almost everyone else. I had never known anyone in New York except the Kimballs and the children of their friends, and when I began to meet other New Yorkers, I came to realize that the Kimballs moved only in a limited circle, which, outside the Knox family connections, seemed mostly to consist of the families of my uncle's medical colleagues. Their relations with the Jews first revealed to me the peculiar and uncomfortable paradoxes of the then Jewish-Gentile relations. Several of the well-known Jewish families were friends as well as patients of my uncle's, and they often entertained the Kimballs, inviting them to their concerts and other affairs. The Kimball children were forbidden to make jokes about Jews—of the kind about which, at that time, the Jewish readers of *Life,* then a humorous weekly, some-

times wrote to protest, since the Jewish characters in
these jokes were invariably made to talk like Weber and
Fields. But Aunt Caroline used to complain that she could
not repay this hospitality because she could not invite
people to meet their Jewish friends. I remember she once
told me that one of them was one of the most attractive
men she had ever known, and it was evident to me that
these cultivated Jews were so far superior to many of
their neighbors as to overcome her natural snobbishness.
When I came later to know some of them in New York, I
saw that they constituted a strong intermarried group of
well-to-do and well-educated families, often active in
public affairs—a sort of Jewish counterpart to the world
of old Protestant New Yorkers who were well-to-do or, if
not, "belonged" through their family connections, and
who occupied positions of responsibility.

Typical specimens of this latter group were the De
Forests of Cold Spring Harbor, Long Island. An older
sister of Larry Noyes, my second and more successful
room-mate at school, had married Robert De Forest, a
lawyer, who had his hand in all sorts of railroad, bank-
ing and charitable enterprises and who was for years first
a trustee then President of the Metropolitan Museum. At
the De Forests', everything was perfect: house and
grounds, pictures, furniture and dinners. The only questions that seemed to disturb them—and that only in a
very quiet way—were the displacement of an etching or a
rearrangement of furniture. There was a soothing old
German butler, who brought us our breakfasts in bed.
The De Forests were somehow related to the New York
family of Baxters of whom Thackeray, on his visits, saw
so much, and they had a copy of the privately printed
volume of *Thackeray's Letters to an American Family.*
This attracted my attention but interested me only
mildly, for I did not know then that Thackeray had

fancied himself in love with Sally Baxter and had said that she was the original of Beatrix in *Henry Esmond*. Though I roomed with Larry Noyes through two years of school and shared an apartment in New York with him and other friends both before and after the war, he was not one of my most stimulating companions. We would swim in the waters of the clear and quiet Sound and discuss, after we went to college—I to Princeton, he to Yale—what had happened to our former school-friends. I learned from Larry the lyrics of Cole Porter's Yale smokers, in which he took the keenest delight. He belonged to the race of Middle Westerners—his father was in the chemical business in St. Paul—whose family roots are in the East and whose great idea is to come back East and keep up their connections with their Eastern relations. They develop a special kind of snobbery more self-conscious than the Eastern kind. T. S. Eliot was something of a case in point. Larry Noyes knew Scott Fitzgerald from St. Paul, and Scott sometimes came to our apartment, but Larry did not know quite how to take him, and Scott, on his side, did not much like Larry. In his memoir, *My Lost City*, he says of our apartment, without naming Larry, that "only the crisp tearing open of invitations by one man was a discordant note." Larry told me about Scott's pretty sister, whom Scott, thinking her technique with men, from his own point of view, insufficient, tried to transform into one of his own creations by teaching her to use on her dance-partners such openings as "Do you believe in God?" and "Tell me if my eyelashes tickle."

The Osborns were considerably more interesting. I knew Bill Osborn both at school and at college, and his brother Earl at Princeton, and I occasionally used to visit them in New York or at Garrison on the Hudson. Their father, William Church Osborn, served on all sorts of

commissions and boards of directors. I find that he was a
trustee of Princeton, a President of the Metropolitan
Museum, a director of the Phelps Dodge Corporation
(Mrs. Osborn had been a Dodge), a chairman of the
Democratic State Committee and a legal advisor to the
State Commission in Lunacy. His brother was Henry
Fairfield Osborn, the well-known palæontologist and
President of the Museum of Natural History. One felt
oneself here at the center of everything that was going on
in New York. I remember hearing first at the Osborn
house of Vernon and Irene Castle, as if the Osborns had
advance notice of everything. They were cultivated as
well as civic-minded. William Church was related to
Frederick Church, the Hudson River painter, and there
was one of his landscapes in the dining room. He had a
Manet and other pictures by I forget what end-of-the-
century French painters. It surprised me that he should
have read Huysmans. Mr. Osborn was almost too perfect.
One felt that he was completely confident that he always
knew how to decide and what to do in any situation,
and that he always had all the answers. This was
conveyed, however, without pomposity and with a
certain bland ironic humor. I remember it as characteristic of him that when our friend Wilton Lloyd-Smith
once told him something that he "thought might surprise
him," Mr. Osborn said, "Nothing surprises me, Wilton."
He knew about the *New Republic* when it began appearing—at the time that I was reading it eagerly—as he
knew about everything else in New York, and said, in his
decisive way, that its tone was "predominantly Hebraic,"
though only two of its six editors were Jewish. I thought
it was attractively old-fashioned of him to address Mrs.
Osborn as "my love."

   Bill and Earl Osborn had enough of their father's self-
assurance to make them different from almost anyone else

I knew at Princeton as well as different from the exceptional individualists, who were likely to be artistic or literary. Bill's reactions to everything were lively and fresh. It was great fun to go on walks and rides with him. Before we went into the war, he had the courage to take a stand against it, though, once we were in, he served and was wounded. Earl was much more subdued, slow of action and speech, but he also had reactions and opinions that were not the expected ones. The longer I knew them, however, the more it came to seem to me that their lives were in the long run directed by their parents. This appeared to me all wrong, since I found myself, in fundamental ways, so often in opposition to mine. I was annoyed when Bill explained to me one day a principle, which I suppose he had learned from his father, that one ought to know at least something about all sorts of subjects in order to be able to talk to anyone that one happened to sit next to at dinner. I thought that one ought only to inform oneself about subjects in which one was interested. It seemed to me something of an advantage to have a father with whom one disagreed and to whose principles and opinions one did not necessarily defer. But Mr. Osborn, I suppose, was the kind of man—with his calm and authoritative certainties—that there was really no way of opposing or even of arguing with.

The family of my friend Bill Brown were somewhat more unconventional. His mother was a cousin of Larry Noyes, and I first knew Bill at school, but though he afterwards went to Yale, I continued to see a good deal of him. They were the Browns of Brown Brothers, the bankers, but the current generation of Browns seemed to take little interest in the business. One of the brothers played the violin; another had some special rather curious interest that I find I have now forgotten; William Adams

Brown, the father of my friend William Adams, Jr., was a professor at Union Theological Seminary. I was thrilled when the news reached school that he and another professor were to be put on trial for heresy before the tribunal of the Presbyterian Church. I cannot imagine that any such case would now as it did then make the front pages of the New York papers. But when I later tried to read Dr. Brown's books, I was not at all thrilled by what seemed to me a rather insipid doctrine of watered-down Presbyterianism. He was an extremely likable man. He was called "Doggie" Brown at the Seminary, primarily because he taught Dogmatics but also, I imagine, from his having the appearance of a large and good-natured dog. A man who had once been a student there told me that Dr. Brown was conspicuous among the professors for arriving every day in a limousine. Dr. Brown had an excellent library and the kind of literary taste—discriminating but up-to-date—that I understood. I was surprised that he should speak with contempt of the poems of Thomas Bailey Aldrich, who had become so much an accepted figure of the literary magazine world that I assumed he would be respected by all the older people. I happened also just to have read Aldrich's poems and did not take them very seriously, but I protested that a few were not bad. "Which ones did you think were good?" he asked. It increased my respect for him to see that he was not prepared to take anything for granted, and I was further impressed when I found on his shelves Archibald Henderson's huge biography of Bernard Shaw, then and now one of my heroes. I had acquired this volume at school, and though Shaw's plays were seen and read by the older generation, I was surprised that a member of that generation, and especially a Presbyterian clergyman, should go so far as to read Archibald Henderson. Bill took it down and looked at the pictures, one of

which had the caption, "Ahenobarbus at Rehearsal."
"What does Ahenobarbus mean?" he asked. "A red-
bearded fellah," said his father. "What do I send you to
school for?" This made me feel a twinge of inadequacy,
because I had not known, either. In one of our spring
vacations from school, Dr. Brown took us to *Patience,*
which he seemed to enjoy as much as we did. The New
York productions of Gilbert and Sullivan were not always
very brilliant; but they usually had the advantage of the
unique De Wolf Hopper, who played all the comic roles
originally created by George Grossmith. When, as Bun-
thorne in *Patience,* he pretended to be fainting, he was
offered a flask of brandy by one of the heavy dragoons. At
first he waved it away, but then took it and poured a
drink into the cup of the lily he was holding, as if the
flower itself needed reviving. Then he pretended to smell
the lily and swallowed the brandy. I was delighted by
this.

The Browns simply did what they liked. They did not
at all give the impression of being built into a world of
New York social life and civic responsibility. The Doctor
and Mrs. Brown seemed to live more or less independent
lives. Mrs. Brown, who wore a wig, always struck me as
having an odd detachment from the other members of the
family. Bill Brown had his father's amiability, and his
own kind of dogginess, which was manifested in a sometimes disastrous leaping and throwing himself around. In
spite of his thick lenses, which gave him a professorial
appearance like his father's, he was the only one of my
friends who showed a strong and outspoken enthusiasm
for sex. For years he had some sort of affair with the
daughter of a Swedish psychiatrist, who was evidently
of a more exciting temperament than the conventional
débutante. He had also an enthusiastic affection, which
seemed to me quite unusual, for a sister who was still a

child. On the eve of a school vacation, he would cry out in joy at the prospect of seeing this little girl again. They were very touching together: his sister had lenses as thick as his, and neither was particularly handsome, but both were extremely sympathetic on account of their high spirits and their affection for one another. Bill, at the time of the war, went to Russia in some capacity—I suppose that his defective eyesight disqualified him from active service—and roused my envy by coming back with *Anna Karenina* in Russian. He then went to Peru for Brown Brothers and returned with tantalizing tales of the gallantries of the ladies of Lima. He ended as a professor of economics at Brown University in Providence, a rather tame destiny, it seemed to me, for a once so rambunctious person.

I continued to see the Browns when they came for awhile to live at Princeton and rented the house of Henry Van Dyke, whose admiration for Tennyson had impelled him to name his daughters after the heroines of *Idyls of the King* and to call his place Avalon. There was nothing about the Browns of this factitious romance. In Avalon, they seemed as serene and detached, as oblivious of their surroundings, as they had in their New York house. I remember here a strange outburst in my presence on the part of the little girl's English governess, who was speaking not to me but to herself: "Why can't they admit that they don't speak English? Why don't they admit it's a different language?" I was surprised that she should have had so much difficulty in understanding our American version of English; but I suppose that, not very adaptable, she had been constantly baffled and annoyed at hearing familiar objects called by unfamiliar names. It was at Princeton that I got to know John Crosby Brown, Bill's elder brother. He was gentle and rather handsome and always good for a serious conversation. He was something of an invalid then and died not many years after. It was later to depress me, looking back, to take account of how many of these friends, with excellent training and so much opportunity, seemed unable to live up to these. I had thought that we were all pretty brilliant and were headed for distinguished careers.

In looking up these New York families for the purposes of this memoir and learning facts that I did not then know, I am struck by the extent to which such families constituted a genuine "Establishment." They were likely to be intermarried, and they seem to have had more or less in their hands all the more respectable public activities. To what extent has this Establishment survived? My later life, from my Greenwich Village days, has been so alien to this kind of world, that I have had little chance to observe it. But I should say, from some of the marriages of a generation younger than mine, that it cannot be any longer so self-contained.

The New Englanders were quite different from New Yorkers. I had been in Boston only once up to sometime in the early twenties—I had gone to stay with friends in Cambridge for the Harvard-Princeton football game, and I then noticed almost nothing but the special local accent. When I inquired the way to somewhere, I was told to "Take a cair to Pairk Street." I did not find out till years later that this had been the way that *ar* had originally been pronounced. Ben Jonson explains in his English grammar that the sound of *a* in *art* is the same as that of *a* in *act*. Dickens, in *Great Expectations,* when he makes his characters speak of "the ma'shes," is indicating a pronunciation very similar to that of Boston.

But I went often to Washington, Connecticut, where I had a good many friends. One of these was Sterling Carter, who roomed next door to me at Princeton. The sons of Princeton alumni were in those days assigned to the dormitories for which their fathers' classes had contributed funds. Both Sterling's father and mine were of the class of 1885, so we were put to room in Hamilton Hall. It had happened that Sterling's father had been in the habit, during their college days, of helping mine through his mathematics, and Sterling, who was also a dab at mathematics, performed the same service for me; but even his expert guidance did not prevent my flunking Coördinate Geometry. He was one of the most amiable fellows I have ever known. He would listen to me, in the evenings, reading Bernard Shaw's plays aloud, and one night when I was kept awake by the flapping of the rope on the flagstaff of the tower of Campbell Hall, he climbed up with me and helped tie it down. His father was now the minister of the Congregational Church in Washington, a particularly handsome one, always kept in good repair by the Washingtonians, who took great pride in their distinguished town. The Carters—Sterling had three sisters, two of whom went to Vassar and one to Radcliffe—lived in an old-fashioned rather Spartan way. They had no central heating, and in winter it took some courage to tear oneself out from under the covers and wash in the bedroom washbowl. But I found in my bedroom a college text of a selection from the Greek Anthology and discovered—what I had not known—that William (Johnson) Cory's *Heraclitus* was not an original poem but a translation of a poem by Callimachus. This was later, on a visit to Italy, to suggest a poem I wrote there called *Boboli Gardens*.

I am glad to have known this Connecticut town and to have got some firsthand idea of what the best of this New England life of small communities must have been like in the past. Washington was largely dominated by a boys' school called the Gunnery and a girls' school called

Wykeham Rise. There were a conventional New England "green" and a "general store." A number of families had houses in which they spent only their summers, but they were as much imbued as the natives with the peculiar local patriotism. There were a choral society and a dramatic society, in the performances of which everyone who could participated. I sometimes went up for New Year's, when the Gunnery put on a show. I remember taking part in an operatic burlesque of the *Aeneid*. In summer, we went to a camp on Mount Tom, under the chaperonage of Mrs. Will Brinsmade, the widow of a Gunnery headmaster. The Brinsmade girls, also at Vassar, were among the attractions of these trips. We dived and swam in the lake; went on walks that involved chaste flirtations; in the evenings, played the phonograph, read poetry and concocted games. I enjoyed all this very much, but I felt that it rather lacked piquancy, and I sometimes had the impulse to shock them. When Kenneth Simpson was there, with his witty fast-talking Irish "line"—I cannot stop to explain him here—we would sometimes, in private, make common cause as sly and sophisticated New Yorkers, who did not really belong in that so blameless milieu.

My closest friends in Washington were not, however, real New Englanders, nor were they exactly New Yorkers. They belonged to the New York sub-species of old-fashioned Brooklynites and took one back to what I always thought of as an American version of Victorianism. One of my most interesting friends at the Hill School was Alfred Raymond Bellinger, with whom I was closely associated in connection with the school magazine. His grandfather, Rossiter Raymond, was a man of some note. He was primarily a mining engineer. I learn from the *Dictionary of American Biography* that he "exerted a unique influence among American engineers during the

formative years of his profession." His activities in his
own field—extremely varied—had taken him all over
the United States and Europe. It was quite usual for the
professional men of his time to have cultural interests
apart from their professions, but Dr. Raymond was well-
read and well-informed to an altogether astonishing degree. Not only did he write much on mining and translate foreign works on this subject, but he published also
children's stories, poems, a novel and a life of Peter
Cooper. (The first I heard of Herbert Hoover was when
Dr. Raymond, with pride, produced a translation from
the Latin of a sixteenth-century treatise on mineralogy by
the German scholar Georg Agricola, which had been
made by a young man of that name and his wife.) He
had the huge set of the Delphin Classics—the whole of
Latin literature (with a few unaccountable omissions) in
a hundred and forty volumes. I enormously admired
these and eventually found a set for myself. He told us
that he and his father had once stayed in a Swiss hotel at
the same time as Walter Pater but that they did not know
about him then: "We could have talked classics with
him!" There was also a complete bound set of *Punch,* and
when, after the deaths of the Raymonds, this was burned
in a fire in the Washington house, the Bellingers bought
another. I don't think they could imagine a household
that did not possess a complete set of *Punch*. Dr. Raymond was a short brisk man, full of energy and enthusiasm, with white sidewhiskers and a sparkling blue
eye. Indoors, he always wore a black skullcap. He was, to
be sure, rather vain of his accomplishments and achievements. He had been decorated in Japan with the Order of
the Rising Sun, and from time to time he would have it
brought out and shown to guests. But he was never dis-
agreeably egoistic. His manliness, frankness, good humor,
his radiant enjoyment of himself were usually irresistible

to his audience. His opinions were of interest to me as anachronistic examples of another era than that in which I felt myself to be living. He had always, in his relations with labor, been opposed to unionization, and he occasionally got threatening letters. His opinion was that low-grade "foreigners" had come to the United States and greatly improved their standard of living, and that they were therefore only being impudent in asking for higher wages. He was one of the people who voted on the bestowal on dead celebrities of the privilege of having their busts installed in the ridiculous "Hall of Fame" attached to New York University, and he was opposed to the admission of Poe—I suppose, upon moral grounds as well as for what he regarded as the insubstantiality of his work. A supporter of Poe had attempted to convert him by inducing him to read *Eureka;* but he declared that it was worthy of Marie Corelli and should provide no passport to the Hall of Fame. (I find, however, that in that year—1910—the supporters of Poe won out.) When Mark Twain's *Mysterious Stranger* was posthumously published in 1916, Dr. Raymond pooh-poohed it as something that Howells must have advised Mark Twain to suppress. "We Christians," he declared with elated confidence, "don't care about such things!" But, although in certain ways so Victorian, he was not really narrow or prudish. He was a member of Henry Ward Beecher's congregation and one of the pillars of Plymouth Church, and he loyally supported Beecher all through the latter's great scandal. He told once of having been in Utah and having had to transact some business with Brigham Young. He mimicked him and made him sound, I noted, exactly like some old farmer from upstate New York, in which region Young had spent his youth.

The Raymonds had lost their only son, who had left a great legend of promise as a worthy successor to his father. I do not think that Mrs. Raymond had ever recovered from this, though she and the Doctor were perfectly certain that they would be reunited with him in the other world. Alfred's grandmother would come downstairs for only brief appearances and wore a green eyeshade that, like Mrs. Smallweed's bonnet in Phiz's illustrations for *Bleak House,* concealed the upper part of her face. She was looked after and the household directed by the inevitable maiden aunt, like my own Aunt Laura, who had found it her destiny to fill this role. She was Dr. Raymond's sister, and he called her by the obsolete nickname of "Sukey"—the only time I had ever heard it: I had only seen it in books. On one occasion, after dinner at the Brooklyn house, when the Bellingers and I were going out to the theater, Aunt Sukey hastily came downstairs and stopped us at the door. Mrs. Raymond had understood Alfred to have said something disparaging of Wordsworth and was very much perturbed about it. Alfred had to go upstairs and reassure her before we could leave. Even Alfred's pretty, shy little sister, in her quietness and her dresses and her way of wearing her hair with a comb, seemed more like an English girl of the Lewis Carroll era than the then already old-fashioned Concord girls of Louisa M. Alcott.

In the summers, I would visit the Bellingers and Raymonds in their house called Hilltop at Washington. I became great friends with Mrs. Bellinger, who had inherited her father's cleverness and who, rather to my surprise, read more sympathetically than Alfred did such pessimistic writers as Hardy and Housman who were then among my admirations. Alfred and I, who had private jokes and exchanged epistles and verses, had an agreement that every year at Christmas each would send the other a book which the other would not otherwise be likely to read and which he well might fail to appreciate.

On one occasion, I sent him *The Brothers Karamazov*, which I had just read at college with enthusiasm. On Alfred's part, it met with incomprehension. I asked him why he seemed to be appalled by it. "Why, there's not a Christian character in the book!" This made me take account of the chasm between Alfred's Congregationalism and Dostoevsky's Slavic Christianity. Mrs. Bellinger, who liked Trollope, gave me *The Warden* and *Barchester Towers*. I read them and mildly enjoyed them, but decided it was a waste of time to read any more Trollope, and have never since then done so. At the next of our Christmas exchanges, Alfred gave me *Phineas Finn*, which is still on my shelves unread; whenever I see it there, I suffer a twinge of guilt. Mrs. Bellinger seemed birdlike and frail, but she lived to be well over ninety. When I saw her last, in New Haven, now confined to her bed and no longer able to read, she was listening to recorded novels. Alfred taught classics at Yale, and then became an authority on classical numismatics. He used to write excellent prose and verse, and I have always regretted that he did not continue. I still remember with pleasure some of his poems in the Hill *Record* and the Yale *Lit*.

I saw something, too, of New Hampshire. Adelaide Knox was now married to André Champollion, and they lived in Newport, New Hampshire, where André's mother's family, the Corbins, had a place, which included a hunting preserve that had been stocked with wild boar and buffalo. In the summers, Sandy and I sometimes went to stay with the Champollions, and these visits were so delightful that I have still a recurrent dream in which I seem to be back at Newport, and try to enjoy returning, although André and Adelaide are gone, and other people are now living there. We rode, under escort, in the hunting preserve and were warned to be careful of the buffalo. I encountered only one, which looked at us but gave us no cause for alarm. I never saw a wild boar, though I heard one plunge by through the underbrush. André used to send venison and boar-meat to my father, with whom he got on well, though my father would never admit that André was anything more than "one of the better of the idle rich." I was fascinated by André's library, which included French and German and Italian classics. There I first attacked Baudelaire, and my attention was particularly drawn—I have always had a taste for the macabre—to the poem called *Une Charogne*. I started to read it aloud, with atrocious mispronunciations; whereupon André took the book and read it to me properly. I liked him, but was slightly antagonized when he scornfully dismissed Whistler, who was then a great hero of mine, calling his painting "weak and effeminate." His own paintings of New Hampshire landscapes did not seem to me particularly interesting. He liked to imitate the local characters and sometimes told smutty stories. Though I had stubbornly resisted the evangelism of Hill, the fanaticism about sex of the formidable headmaster's wife had to some extent intimidated me. Though before we went away to school, my cousin and I had kept in a notebook a record of all the dirty jokes we heard, I was embarrassed, after a year or two at Hill, when one of the older boys attempted to entertain us with one, and now I was too shocked to laugh easily when André would come out with some such saying as, "I don't mind you fucking Sally on the sofa, but I won't have you wipe your cock on my best lace curtains!"

André at home was very much master, and was, I thought, sometimes brutal with Adelaide. I remember his tearing out of the fireplace a fire that she had just lighted and that he thought it was not cold enough to need. Her extrication from the fibres of her family

had not been without pain, and André used to mimic
mockingly her yearning for her favorite brother, whom
she still called by his childhood name. I took account of
the fact that the behavior of André was very different
from that of my own family, as I had first been made
aware in Paris, when I had been driving with him
somewhere in a cab and he had talked to me quite
frankly, as if I were an older person, of his having come
over to Europe in order to be with Adelaide. Another
incident on a visit to Newport was striking as an illustration of the lack of inhibitions of the rich. One of the
Corbins had dropped in, a rather jaunty man with a cap,
and, in the course of the conversation, sitting on the steps
of the porch, made some reference to "my wife—a dreadful woman, you know her." This shocked as well as
amused me as the story about Sally had.

I remember with particular pleasure one visit to that
part of New Hampshire. Concord was not far from
Newport, and I also had Concord friends. Edgar Woodman, an old school-friend of Sandy's, lived across from me
in Campbell Hall at Princeton, and we could shout at one
another from our windows. He was by this time more to
my taste than he probably was to Sandy's. Sandy was
now more social and smoother than ever, whereas Edgar
was laconic, non-gregarious and anything but smooth. He
was interesting to me as well as likable as the only New
Englander of his species in college. He was quite self-
sufficient, he roomed alone and he took part in no college
activities. He had something of the old Yankee country-
man, a shrewd ironic humor, which was always expressed
without laughter but with a quiet gleam from his spectacles. He cherished a steady but restrained adoration for
a somewhat older married woman. He told me about
something that had happened which moved him in a
curious way. There had been a litter of kittens which had

just glutted themselves with milk. His beloved had stepped on one of them, and the kitten had exploded on the floor. I could instinctively understand that this had given him some sexual satisfaction, but I was not quite certain why. In Concord, I stayed with the Woodmans. Edgar's father was dead, and he lived with his mother. As in many houses furnished for themselves by women in that period, one found on the tables beside the beds little lamps with crinkled pink silk shades, and this seemed to me quite incongruous with the plainness and sharpness of Swift's *Journal to Stella*, with which I read myself to sleep.

On my train journey up to New Hampshire, I had already read James Huneker's *Egoists*, which had upon me a peculiarly exhilarating effect, as Huneker was likely to do on the young people of my generation. I had never before found such a stimulating account of the excitement to be derived from the writings of Stendhal, Flaubert, Huysmans and Baudelaire, and when I got back to college, I improved my French and read every one of these authors. Edgar took me one afternoon to tea with an aunt or a cousin, an occasion which I remember as a moment of charming color: a whitewashed stable with pigeons, a house full of flowered chintz, a cheerful old lady who gave me the impression of always having been goodhumored and never having been ill. The increasing somberness of our own Red Bank house, under the shadow of my father's neurotic illness and the strain of my mother's discomfort, heightened my appreciation of what seemed to me more harmonious and less disturbing households. I think that this old lady reminded me of the amenities of my grandmother's house at Lakewood. My father cared nothing for attractive surroundings. His study—then called an "office"—had as ornaments only a deerhead and a moosehead, a great horned owl and a black and white loon, and a mediocre portrait of himself, painted at the request of some admirer, for which he had never been willing to sit for more than a few minutes. The living room, besides family pictures, had photographs of Roman ruins that my mother had brought back in 1908, and small engravings of Walter Scott, Robert Burns, Mary Queen of Scots and a bagpiper that she had later brought back from Scotland. My bedroom was ornamented with colored Remington prints and strings of picture postcards from Europe, and an enlarged kodak snapshot of the Sugar River falls at Talcottville. It was not until my father's death that my mother bought a new and more cheerful house and imbued it with something of my grandmother's bright good taste. In the old house, she had really, I think, had nothing that afforded her satisfaction with the exception of her splendid garden, which won prizes in garden contests.

Edgar Woodman had a cousin, Charley Walker, whom I knew through my Yale friends. Like Alfred Bellinger, he wrote for the Yale *Lit*, and in those days the awakening spirit of what has been called "the American Renaissance" was stimulating us in the colleges. I followed the Yale *Lit* and saw the beginnings there of Charley Walker, of the poet Phelps Putnam, of Stephen Benét and Archibald MacLeish, and I first became acquainted in the Harvard *Lit* with the names of Gilbert Seldes and John Dos Passos. I did not know the Harvard writers, but through my school-friends I did know those at Yale who belonged to my own year. The staffs of the Yale and the Nassau *Lits* occasionally paid visits back and forth and entertained one another at banquets. Charley Walker wrote both prose and poetry. I shall have more to say of him later. It is enough to note here that in his college days there was something Apollonian about him; that it was said of him that he reminded you of the lines about the poet's eye in a fine frenzy rolling. This contrasted with his parents' Concord household, which I thought had not outlived a certain New England gloominess. When Edgar and I called, we were received in an old-fashioned "parlor," which seemed to me as dark and austere as the one in Eatontown, New Jersey, of which I have already spoken. It has always seemed to me impressive as an example of the tough persistence of New England idealism and intellect and the strength of character which backs it that Charley should have pursued through fifty years his early-begun study of labor relations till he has now, in this field, an international reputation, without losing the poetic ambition which has finally realized itself in his admirable translations of Greek plays.

But another of the Walker family houses presented a special interest. The only American, so far as I know, of conspicuously superior abilities who fought with the British in our Revolution and who afterwards lived in Europe and had an impressive career there was Benjamin Thompson of Massachusetts and New Hampshire. He lived for some time in Concord and married a Walker there. He was one of the men of that period who, like Franklin, combined scientific interests with the desire to promote human welfare. He was a physicist, mathematician and engineer, and the inventor and discoverer and administrator of innumerable devices and principles and projects. He was a member of the British Royal Academy and of several German academies. He served the Elector of Bavaria as aide-de-camp and privy councillor, and in Munich he created the Englische Garten, in which there stands a monument to him. When the Elector made Thompson a count of the Holy Roman Empire, he chose the title of Rumford, the original name of Concord. After the death of his Walker wife, he married the widow of Lavoisier, but the marriage was not a success: her appetite for social life could not be adequately satisfied by this serious-minded man. He was still a New Englander in France, and seems to have led rather a lonely life. When he died, he left a bequest to Harvard, and Harvard and the ancient Academy of Arts and Sciences, which still awards a medal he established, now keep up his grave in Auteuil. I was taken by Edgar Woodman to an eighteenth-century house, where I saw portraits of Rumford and his mistresses, and a library which seemed to contain all the classics, ancient and current, that would be needed by a cultivated man of the period. I supposed that it was the library of Rumford but learn now that it belonged to Charley Walker's grandfather. In any case, it took one back to an earlier age of New England.

At the center of my memories of that summer is a very attractive cluster compounded of Huneker's fireworks, the handsome Champollion couple in their un–New England modern house, the rides through the dense forest inhabited by unfamiliar animals and a vista into the eighteenth century that unexpectedly opened up out of these.

I want to add here some account of a glamorous "phenomenon" of my school and college days who came to us from the South and could not possibly have been produced by either New York or New England. When I first went to Hill, I soon became aware that a boy named Walker Ellis from New Orleans was the most, or most showily, brilliant figure in the school. He seemed to be extraordinarily accomplished and had his adroit easy hand in everything. On consulting the school year-book, I find that he was President of his class, and a member of the Dramatic Club, the Glee Club, the Choir, the Dance

Committee and the Inter-Club Debating Team, and that he won prizes in Elocution. He, also, I think, went in for track, and he was so lithe that he could bend over backwards and rest the flat of his hands on the floor. He was the editor of the school magazine, to which I began contributing in the spring of my first year and so came into contact with his formidable charm. He was extremely goodlooking, with a scar across his mouth that only made him seem more dashing. He was always very smartly dressed, and his perfect Southern manners and worldly sophistication made him unique among us Pennsylvanians and Jerseymen, Californians and Middle Westerners. He was quite above the heavy morality and the genteel code of conduct of the Hill School, but, with his innate tact and ready instinct for playing the proper role with every kind of person, he was, until the very end, always on good terms with his schoolmates and ingratiated himself with the authorities, who accepted him on a plane of maturity. The beautiful bindings and good quality of his books and his ability in Latin class to make elegant and fluent translations commanded my envious admiration. For the purposes of our magazine, he could apparently turn out without effort graceful lyrics, agreeable short stories and descriptions of picturesque New Orleans. The boy with whom Walker roomed was also more mature than the rest of us and always remained for me something of a mystery. He was not eloquent, not particularly goodlooking, took no part in school activities, or later, at Princeton, in those of the college, and had nothing in common with Walker except his wit, more corrosive, and a cynical attitude toward school conventions. They created surreptitious scandal by singing to tunes of their own invention one of the bawdier ballads of Villon, and a more serious public one when they refused, in their Six Form year, to attend an important spring track meet at which attendance was supposed to be obligatory. For this failure in loyalty to the school, they were condemned by a Sixth Form council which had certain disciplinary powers to ostracism for the rest of the year. Nobody was supposed to speak to them. Since I, too, resented the insistence on being present to cheer at athletic events, this made them seem to me heroes and martyrs. As I remember, the ban was not to be removed even for their graduation, but I think that most of their classmates disregarded it. When Walker's parents and his sister came to school, I observed them with much interest, and it seemed to me that there was nothing to account for Walker. The father, a cotton broker, was a small man who looked rather dry.

It was only after Walker left school that I learned of his brazen duplicities. It is true that in his last year at school he plagiarized a story in the *Record* and was compelled to resign his editorship. But such was the spell he cast that I was willing to accept the excuse that he had had to fill the magazine—the story, rather nauseatingly, I thought, called *The Little Lady and the Philosopher,* ran for two instalments—and that he had not signed it with his own name, but merely as by "Pip, 'll." But he had seriously shattered a friend of mine—who could not compare with Walker for elegance—by first cultivating him and then snubbing him. And just after his graduation, he repeated in Philadelphia an oration he had delivered at school in favor of woman suffrage. When a devoted feminist in the audience congratulated him afterwards, he said to her, "Oh, I don't believe a word of it, madam." His actual ideal of womanhood was the traditional Southern lady. It was the first time I had ever encountered a type of which I was afterwards to know other specimens: the clever and charming, apparently amiable but latently insolent person who believes that he can get away with anything and up to a point succeeds.

At Princeton, Walker Ellis made himself a reputation in connection with the Triangle Club, which put on a musical show every year—he usually played female parts and liked to deliver monologues; but he did not figure much in other campus pursuits. He had an apartment on Nassau Street—independent of the student dormitories— where he lived with his usual luxury and had a circle of acolytes. My cousin Sandy and Scott Fitzgerald both more or less sat at his feet. They all belonged to the Cottage Club, which was social and convivial in a light-weight way. Though I did not by that time take Walker very seriously, I always found it rather a pleasure to meet him on the campus, smart in his bow-tie, holding himself proudly erect and walking with a kind of blithe elastic step that made his head nod slightly from side to side. In his last year, he won a prize with an essay on François Villon. This was printed in the *Nassau Lit* under my editorship—I had taken it for granted without reading it—but when I did begin to examine its precious and dated prose, I was dimly reminded of something, and I found the whole thing, word for word, after a brief preliminary passage, in John Payne's introduction to his translation of Villon. This had been published by Thomas Mosher of Maine in one of his then thought exquisite editions, which, I believe, could not be bought in book stores but had to be ordered directly from him. Walker had undoubtedly counted on no one else in Princeton's possessing this book—only five hundred copies were printed. I was annoyed, but I could not expose him. I do not know whether there may not have been in these treacheries and impostures of Walker's some element of the malice of the Southerner in putting something over in the North.

After college, Walker went to Harvard Law School, but he did not remain there long. He decided to go on the stage and came to look for a job in New York. Scott Fitzgerald's play *The Vegetable* was then being cast, and Walker applied for a part. The only thing that Scott had to offer him was the very minor role of a newsboy who made his sole appearance to shout "Wuxtry! Wuxtry! All about the big fire!" (I do not find this in the published text, but the play was revised many times.) Walker, of course, declined and complained that it would have been a little too much "to play a newsboy in Scotty Fitzgerald's play." He then applied to Somerset Maugham, who at that time was in New York, also having a play produced. Maugham was not prepared to give him a part, but offered to keep him in style—a proposal that Walker also rejected. Scott told me about this with a certain glee—he was no longer beglamored by Walker and was, in any case, always competitive with anyone who threatened to outshine him. "Think of Walker," he said, "looking for a job and getting an offer to be a harrlott!"

Walker had no success on the stage. The only time I ever saw him—in, I think, a play by Philip Barry—his stage presence seemed strangely pale. The last time I saw him off the stage was on a visit to New Orleans in the twenties, when I met him in Jackson Square. His face was now florid and bloated. I imagine that at home in New Orleans he had never seemed so enchanting, because not so exotic, as he had in the steel town of Pottstown. I next heard vaguely that he was living on the Riviera. He died sometime in the forties. I have known other New Louisianians who more or less belonged to Walker's type. They seemed gifted and delightful in youth, then, despite their agreeable conversation—and the social life of New Orleans was perhaps the most agreeable of the South—might become rather soddenly dissipated and sometimes have sordid ends. They used to spoil early down there.

Princeton

1912–1916

[In the summer of 1914, at the end of my sophomore year at college, I spent a summer in England, with four of my friends, Stanley Dell and Noel Robinson from Princeton and Larry Noyes and David Hamilton from Yale. John and Bill Brown were with us in Scotland and turned up from time to time in the course of our travels. The arrival of the ship in the mouth of the Mersey was for me a great event. We all looked to England then; it was the era of the Anglophile expatriate. "England!" I thought, in awed ecstasy. We bicycled from Edinburgh to Tintagel. We saw the Scotch and the English lakes, and in the evenings I read Wordsworth's *Prelude*. Since Larry, who was to be an architect, was much preoccupied with cathedrals, we visited a great many cathedral towns. I got rather fed up with cathedrals, which did not interest me as much as they did him. We only cheated, as a party, by taking a train through the industrial part of Wales, but I did a little cheating on my own by going off for two nights to London in order to see Shaw's *Pygmalion,* with Beerbohm Tree and Mrs. Patrick Campbell. I think that I eventually saw *Pygmalion* three times, and I practically knew it by heart. I still remember lines that do not appear in the printed text. It was the only Shaw production I ever saw in which he allowed star actors to run away with their parts. He had usually employed merely able actors and, in directing, kept them firmly in their place—that is, firmly subordinate to the author. The combats between Shaw and Tree have several times been described, and Shaw finally walked out of the theater. Both Tree and Mrs. Campbell were badly miscast: the latter was much too old and stout, and the former too lisping and vague. I have never seen a really good Higgins. But the production was none the less most amusing. I felt, when I rejoined my companions at Bideford, that I had rather disgracefully let them down, and I long felt somewhat guilty about it.

In London, we stayed at the Langham Hotel. I then began keeping a notebook, in which the first entry records a pilgrimage to Meredith's house in Surrey. He was a great admiration of mine. I asked the way of a country-man, who walked along with me to show me. He said that he had often met Meredith taking a walk by himself. He would be talking to himself—I assumed reciting his poetry: "You'd think he was a mad farmer!"]

Meredith's House

It stands at the foot of a long low hill, whose pines make a dark screen of verdure for the bright square little cottage, itself green with ivy and other creepers, which allow only the brass-knobbed door and the five six-paned windows to be seen. Each of these latter is decorated with a window-box full of red and pink geraniums, and a border of red ones almost reaches to the windows of the first floor. Two huge crescents of smooth round box surround the small lawn with more geraniums and large sweeps of gravel drive, which the house commands, but from the road these hedges are hidden by the trees and shrubs which come down on either side to square brick gateposts and a white gate. The whole place has something of Meredithian cleanness, neatness and vivid complex beauty.

The chalet, where half a dozen great novels were written, stands higher up on the hill and some distance to the right of the house—tiny and brown, but relieved by the white woodwork of windows and the flowers of pink and white geraniums.

Box Hill, Surrey

[When England, on August 4, declared war on Germany, I paid little attention to it. It annoyed us because it prevented us from going to France. There was great excitement in London of a rather frivolous kind. It must have been the same sort of enthusiasm as had been manifested over the Boer War; the great popular song of the Boer War, *Soldiers of the Queen,* was sung in the music halls. Bank Holiday was prolonged for I think two more days, and people rode on the tops of taxis. At night a crowd would congregate outside Buckingham Palace and insist that the King and Queen appear on the balcony again and again: "Mary, Mary, we're wyting!" The Americans were mainly concerned to have their travellers' checks cashed—a number of banks had closed —and get passages back to the States. After long struggles in the Atlantic Transport office, Larry and I got a cabin on the little American liner *Minnehaha.* It was later torpedoed by the Germans.

When I got back, my father was shocked that I had not visited Parliament, but pretended to take an interest in my bibliophile exploits in provincial old-book shops.]

————

Ruysdael, Steen, Teniers, de Hooch, Maes

———

The stifled heart of Strasburg stirs.

———

[In Oxford, we had found Frank MacDonald of the Princeton English Department. We saw a good deal of him in London, and Larry and I came back on the boat with him. The following is evidently an anecdote of some interview he had had, as an undergraduate, with the big shots of the Princeton faculty.]

West and Westcott
a comedy of character
Messrs West, Fine, Thompson, Westcott and Mac-
Donald.

"Do you read much?"
"No."
"Do you play cards much?"
"No."
"Do you study much?"
"No."
"Well, what do you do with yourself?"
"Oh—nothing much!"
"Have you a sense of humor?"
"No."
"Well, how would you like to take a year out of college?"
"Wouldn't like it!"
"Why not?"
"Shouldn't get back again."
"Oh, afraid of your father!"
"No." (A long pause.)

"Who are you most afraid of in the world?"

"Professor Fine." (Loud laughter.)

"Has anybody got anything to say for him?"

Mr. Westcott (hitherto silent): "He was the only man in my class who knew who wrote *Empedocles on Aetna.*"

Mr. West: "Oh, Matthew Arnold." (Heavily jocose—at his worst.) "Well, if you can come to me to-morrow morning and pass an examination on *Culture and Anarchy,* I'll let you through. Will you take me up?"

"No! I've never read *Culture and Anarchy* and I don't intend to!"

Mr. Westcott to the departing MacDonald: "All right, my boy, it isn't so bad as it seems"—

[John H. Westcott was called "Livy" on account of his devotion to that author. I had been in one of his classes and, though I did not do at all well in it, I always found his dry humor delightful. Against Andrew West, who by my time in college had become Dean of the Graduate School, I had a very strong prejudice. He had been Woodrow Wilson's chief opponent, and their critical great battle had been over the location of the Graduate School. West had won and was now ensconced in this luxurious mock-English mock-Gothic affair, located, as Wilson had not wanted it to be, aloof on a hill and at a distance from the college. Woodrow Wilson was a hero of mine, and my father—though he did not much like Wilson—did not like West either. He would tell me of West's rapacity in sitting at the deathbeds of millionaires, in order to get bequests for his projects for Princeton. And this prejudice was increased by my contacts with him. He was one of those tiresome snob humanists who put on airs about Greek and Latin and always are ramming them down people's throats. It was a feature of the Horace and Catullus course, compulsory in sophomore year, that West should appear about once a month and take all the sections together in one of the big lecture rooms. He would have himself hauled down from the Graduate School in a kind of open hack, in which one would see his great round paunch protruding above his long thin legs, as if it were a watermelon resting on his lap. He would then address the class in an arrogantly patronizing tone. He would pick out some name at random and make the student stand up and attempt to translate an ode. When he had made a fool of this student by interrupting him and holding up to ridicule the ineptitudes of his rendering, he would announce, "Now I'll give you an example of the *art* of translation." What followed would be something almost equally awkward. He would stumble, try word after word and never arrive at any very great felicity. We would all be extremely glad when he got back in his hack and departed.]

Religious Revival at Princeton, circa 1894. [Another anecdote of Frank MacDonald's.]

The unregenerate soul cornered by inspired friends: "No, I don't want to see you and I'll give you just about two weeks to get over this rot."

At this period, college was closed for two days on account of religious meetings which were held at all hours.

"There is one continual scream of laughter throughout the entire play."

"Told him what transpired between he and I."

"Yes, social prejudice stands between us like a brick-wall thirty feet high with broken glass and barbed wire on top." [This was evidently a line from some bad play.]

———

A lady at a performance of *The Pillars of Society* by the E.D.A. [Elizabethan Dramatic Association]: "Yes, it's all written and acted by the students. Ibsen is a sopho-more down there now."

———

The Roman-Catholic youth to Mr. Mac, who has just told him of someone's conversion: "Gee, Mr. MacDonald, I don't see how anybody not brought up to it could swallow it!"

———

Mrs. Jesse Lynch Williams aside to Mr. M., the only one of her guests who has not complained in detail of ailments, "After this, I feel so disgustingly healthy: there's never been anything the matter with me, you know, except babies."

———

The Abbé to Mrs. C. [Adelaide Champollion], who has been laughing: "How can you laugh at such a time, when France is fighting for her life?"

Mrs. C.: "I've given my husband to the war and you've given nothing, but now you grumble at me for cheer-fulness."

[André had enlisted in the French army, and at the time he was training in barracks, Adelaide had gone over to be near him.]

———

Sky and water of pale clear blue; for horizon, a yellow sand-strip with its row of summer houses. Across the river the dark green hills of the Highlands [the Atlantic Highlands on the Jersey coast], whose forests, mysterious and inviting from our shore, conceal only more summer houses and dusty motor roads. Behind us, the fresh green of swamp rushes. Three or four row-boats, from which men patiently sink crab-bait, hang motionless on the surface of the river. A woman from the isolated little community watches a man painting his weatherbeaten house from a ladder, evidently giving him occasional advice. A train slides along the distant sandbar, like a train in a child's picturebook. Laden with passengers to the city, a squat white steamboat shoves into view and, in passing, sends waves which splash surprisingly against the row of piles and lap at the shore where we lie. We wave and the unknown people on the steamboat wave. The crabbers gaze at them. The helpful woman steps to the side of the house for a better view. Our humble river-swan disappears; the men resume contemplation of their taut lines. The painter has his counsellor again, and on the water the lines of those unwonted waves grow fainter until the images of the boats and piles reassemble disintegrated atoms and, quivering only slightly, regain their solidity in that smooth blue mirror.

———

That state of affairs so nicely symbolized by our football clad statue, whose academic gown is slipping off. [The statue of the "Christian Athlete," given to Princeton in honor of one of the Dodges. It was so much ridiculed and so often desecrated that it was eventually removed from the campus.]

———

Crème de menthe as a restorative for one in a swoon.

———

The gentleman ran an egg-farm with great profit. He was a combination of New England shrewdness and a very artistic temperament, so that he would send in the egg-boxes favorite quotations from Plato, the Bible and other great books—"And they shall go on from strength to strength," being particularly apposite. On one occasion he read Tennyson's *Ode on the Death of the Duke of Wellington* to the hired man, who, when the gentleman, overcome by emotion, burst into tears, counselled him not to take it so hard, sir; perhaps it wasn't all true, after all.

———

Some nocturnal band whooping it up for old something or other, obviously no mere tyro freshmen, since they all insist on singing second part and thereby produce a rather weird effect.

———

Playing chemistry in the Lab.
[The system of teaching chemistry then in practice suffered from the same defects that A. N. Whitehead complains of in another field in his *Introduction to Mathematics*: the unnecessary multiplication for students who are not going in for the sciences of problems that represent principles which the student ought to understand but should not be obliged to see illustrated over and over again. I was interested in the basic conceptions, but the formulas and experiments bored me. Our laboratory work was a farce. You had to work in pairs, and I worked with Bill Mackie. When we failed, as we usually did, to

produce from the prescribed ingredients something like sulphuric acid, we simply got the sulphuric acid jar and poured some into our retort. I was always attaching the Bunsen burner to the water pipe instead of the gas pipe and getting a fountain of water in the face. Bill had alarming spasms when he would madly mix the contents of the jars at random to see what the results would be.]

———

"Oh, she's a lady! When she's drunk she can go home in a hack."

———

Τὸ γὰρ δίκαιον οἶδε καὶ τρυγῳδία.
ἐγὼ δὲ λέξω δεινὰ μὲν δίκαια δέ.

Aristophanes: motto for G. B. Shaw

———

The sky was pink at the horizon, shading into blue above, like a piece of litmus-paper dipped in acid.

———

"—the West didn't inspire me with as many poems as I had expected it would—directly, that is. I wrote quite a lot, but, oddly enough, they weren't most of them about the West at all."
[This must be John Bishop.]

———

Supplement to Blake's *Auguries of Innocence*.

Who doth disturb the harmless roach
On Hell's gridiron shall surely poach.

[This was improvised by my friend Bill Mackie, who in my early years at college was one of my favorite companions. He came from Philadelphia, was an orphan brought up by an aunt. I have never known anyone droller or more sensitive to literature. He and I and one other were, I think, the only people in our class who cared enough about reading the classics to continue with Greek and Latin beyond the early requirements. Bill and I did Tibullus together in the evenings. When I came to his room, in which he lived alone, he would hide and when I found him would say, "Instinct of self-preservation!" In the later years of college, I saw much less of him. We belonged to different clubs, and his life became increasingly convivial whereas I did not drink at all. He now lived in '79 Hall at the other end of the campus instead of just across the way in Campbell. I remember once going to his rooms when he was not there and seeing on the floor his piles of books, Greek, Latin, French and English. I felt a distinct disapproval of his greedy and purposeless miscellaneous reading. I thought there was something immoral in reading without system or aim. I had myself often yielded to this kind of temptation. Bill loved Restoration comedy and the literature of the eighteenth century. He once wrote me, in vacation, a huge epistle with long s's, dated 1775. He had just read Henry James's *A Small Boy and Others*, "parts of Charles Eliot Norton's letters, which were mightily entertaining," "large quantities of Rossetti, Swinburne, who rather bored me," and Austin Dobson, *Alice Through the Looking Glass*, *Lady Windermere's Fan*, "which I found quite tedious," "*Tristan and Iseult*, done into English by H. Belloc, which I do protest is the most moving and sad tale ever writ," *Aucassin and Nicolette*, Percy's *Reliques*, Pater's *Greek Studies* and *Appreciations* and Max Nordau's *Degeneration*. He told me further that he had just bought Boswell's *Johnson,* the *Morte d'Arthur,* the *Anatomy of Melancholy,* Shelley's poems, Pepys' Diary "and sundry other works." This letter was addressed to me as "The Honorable," and it was delivered to my father's office, since he was often given this meaningless title. He evidently did not approve of it.]

———

"—your friend gives a little cough and disappears."

———

The autumn perspective of Prospect Street, with its gray leaf-strewn pavement under the pale dull gold of the trees—all dimmed by little lines of rain.

———

Fritz Barbour: "I came back a month early this fall, with two conditions resulting directly from drunkenness, and, since college opened, I haven't touched so much as a single gill of fermented barley."

[The Barbours, who lived in Rumson, were immense and genial people. Fritz had a kind of humor which reminded me of DeWolf Hopper. It depended on a combination of formidable physique, perfect dignity and meticulous pronunciation.]

———

The brown puddles in front of Alexander Hall shine with surfaces like mahogany.

———

Miss [Ruth] Pickering to F.P.A. [Franklin P. Adams], who has taken her to lunch, upon meeting her at Cornell: "Now, Mr. Adams, by publishing that poem of mine, you've spoiled all my chances of getting the jobs

I wanted. You've no idea how far a thing like that goes."
[This poem, innocent as it would seem today, was then
considered an indiscretion.]—The whole thing was an
example of the instinctive caddishness of newspapermen
and college students, with no small touch of the meanness
and false prudery of girls.—When the "poetesses" of our
exchanges [magazines of other colleges, with which we
exchanged the *Lit*] approach love, they are virginal with
a demure dewiness, and everybody thinks that it is quite
proper; but let any undergraduate maiden—undergraduate youths, of course, can go as far as they like—express
desire howsoever frankly and, as it were, purely, and all
your young men will make asses of themselves, and all
your alumnae freeze into shocked propriety.—An elderly
lady in Princeton once confessed her nicest sensibilities
outraged by Mrs. Gerould's *Vain Oblations*. "Think of a
woman writing such a thing," she exclaimed, "And, do
you know, they say that she actually wrote it before she
was married!" (As a matter of fact, she wrote it in college,
like poor Miss Pickering.)

———

H.W.'s town girl, upon his proposing marriage, and
her deliberating upon it: "I think the town boys are
much steadier."

———

Princeton Verse [an anthology, published by the University Press]: During the final years of the last century
the attitude of college students toward girls in general
seems to have been markedly different from the present
one. This volume is full of sentimental trifles of the
Dobson-Bunner school—triolets on a kiss, rondeaux on an
"arch look." There seems to have been a delicate sort of
gallantry about the whole thing. Nowadays verse of that

kind is absolutely unknown in college. The only example of *vers de société* published lately in the *Lit* is Ham Armstrong's *Propose?*, which is harsh satire altogether characteristic of the time. "Going to dances" and "having girls down to games" couldn't have been so coarse as they are now, when Mr. V. L. Collins, Mr. J. L. Williams and Mr. Booth Tarkington went to college. How can coquettish courtliness exist at a tango tea?

——

Bill Osborn to Stanley Dell, protesting against the youth of the girls at the dances to which he is invited: "But, really you ought to go, they're just about the right age; they're a nice bunch to know. When you're older, they'll be just the right age to marry—you really ought to go."

——

McCosh lecture-room: upon the lowered yellow shade are outlined distinctly the mullioned windows and, more dimly, the all but stripped autumn branches with their few waving leaves. Another window reveals a silver morning sky behind gray trees. The lecturer, [Norman Kemp Smith] swaying from side to side and regarding us from under that solemn brow, explains, in his full deep Scotch, the closely linked chain of philosophic thought through the centuries.

——

[My most interesting professors at Princeton were Norman Kemp Smith and Christian Gauss. Both had been brought there by Woodrow Wilson, whose installation of a first-rate faculty was one of his really fine achievements. I have already written a memoir of Gauss, and I have briefly mentioned Kemp Smith at the end of

Europe Without Baedeker, but I have not fully done him justice. He was a Scot from Dundee, and, after leaving Princeton—he returned to Britain at the time of the war—held the chair of Moral Philosophy at Edinburgh. He was one of the most admirable men I have ever known and one of the most rewarding. He had written on Descartes and Kant and was a master of technical philosophy, but philosophy meant for Kemp Smith the study of everything that men had thought about themselves and their world, so that he was interested to talk about anything. He used to invite me for Sunday dinner, and afterwards we would go for a country walk. He was not a talkative man but what he said was always to the point. In his lectures he did not trust the random taking of notes, but at the close of some discussion would dictate a few formulations which he had been at pains to make clear and compact. His technique was very similar in conversation, and this made it rather difficult for the other person, for when you put a question to him or tried to introduce a topic, he would dispose of it in a very few words, and afterwards remain silent. One had then to think of something new. At the time when it was a question of whether or not to invite Billy Sunday to speak at Princeton, I asked him what he thought about it: "What Meredith said applies: 'The grossness of the disease may be gauged by the grossness of the cure.'" His wife was a great women's rights woman, and I once asked if he believed in woman suffrage: "Yes, but I don't care to hear about it." One day a little pig crossed our path on its way to its mother, who was nursing her litter, and he volunteered a remark: "Strange the univairsal attractiveness of the young! Even little pigs are dainty." It must not be thought from this that Kemp Smith was gruff or blighting. He was much liked in both Princeton and Edinburgh, and I felt I had a friend in him all my life. I always went to see him when I visited England. He surprised me on one of these visits by what I felt as a lapse of language. "You were never," he asked me, "bitten by the epistemological bug?" In his lectures at Princeton, he had made very clear the problems of epistemology and had asked at the end of one of them, "Is there anybody now who thinks that he can know the extairnal world?"

Stanley Dell has supplied me with another anecdote about Kemp Smith: "I remember him, on a Sunday visit at his house, dandling his new baby (some months old) on his knee, staring into the little vague eyes and murmuring: 'Just to think that only in such a little head can we expect to find *pure* sensations!' "]

————

It is said that the astronomy professor [Henry Russell] used to work himself into an ecstasy about the sun: "Oo, gentlemen, it's enormous!"

————

Mr. Robert de Forest wrote a genealogy of the de Forest family ($7.50, 2 vol.), but, for fear of offending the present generation, refrained from putting in the dates of their births.

Mr. de Forest: "I see scarcely anyone down here, except when I have girls down to visit me. I often have girls down." [I noted this remark because it seemed so incongruous. Henry de Forest was an elderly man of the utmost sobriety and dignity, and it seemed to me surprising that he should like young girls.]

At Cold Spring Harbour, in November, the forests on the hills were as bare and discolored as if they had been burnt out by fire. A white flock of gulls had gathered on the sand-spit and stood out sharply against a great patch of green slime.

———

Meredith was more successful, it seems to me, than any other novelist in extracting and bottling the quintessence of life—which is the real soul of the novel, without which the thing lies dead. In the case of Meredith, one's attention is not, as it is so often with Henry James and others, drawn chiefly to the beautiful symmetry of the bottle; it is absorbed by the liberal draught of his effervescent and stimulating essence.

———

There was a time when it was not allowed to teach French and German in Princeton, "because of the atheistic writings in those languages."

———

The ice-house door held a little rectangle of winter: infinitely pale sky above the pale dry brown of hills and the gray roofs and towers of the town.

———

March: The rain had stopped, but we still walked in goloshes, for the pavements were covered with melting snow and the roads were turned to mud, which looked like corrugated lead in the twilight and reflected the street-lights dully. A ramshackle delivery wagon, driven by a colored boy, turned idly from the curb and rattled off, starring the darkness with its red rear lamp.

———

A Kimball family group: my grandfather and grandmother, Walter Scott and Helen Kimball; my mother, Helen Mather Kimball, sitting between them; my uncles and aunts behind them; reading from left to right: Winfield, Laura, Paul, Adeline, Reuel.

E.W. with his mother at Red Bank, New Jersey.

My father, Edmund Wilson, in youth and in later life.

My mother, Helen M. K. Wilson, in youth and in later life.

Left: my father and mother in Karlsbad in the summer of 1908.

Center: my father and Uncle Reuel in Karlsbad.

Right: Aunt Caroline and Uncle Reuel in Karlsbad.

Adelaide Knox as a young woman.

André and Adelaide Champollion in Munich.

New York young girls are not allowed to go alone with young men to matinees in winter, because, although in the spring it is perfectly proper, since the sun sets late, it isn't to be thought of that they should come back together through the dark.

——

"Is she all right?"
"No: of course she's not all right, or I shouldn't bother about her."

——

As the Greeks so nicely phrased it, ἐκπετήσιμος [fledgling, used by Aristophanes as a metaphor for marriageable daughters].

See Frogs 89–97 for passage on minor poets: χελιδόνων μουσεῖα, the chirpy school of poetry.

——

The Treasury of Human Abnormalities.

——

Fifth Avenue from the bus-top: Just below is seen moving between those high stratified banks the double tide of motor-tops, beneath whose uniform glossiness we can guess at the derbies, silk-hats and flowered bowls of a variety of life. In the private limousines, grave successful money-makers are on their way to particular places which they must reach for particular business at particular hours; they are hardly less naïve than their dear aristocratic little girls, who are just as gravely out for the ride. You may know the little girls at a later stage in the fatuous faces of marriageable daughters, whose whole scope of life has perhaps been no more wide or stimulating or beautiful than the inside of these limousines; who, it may be, have never even enjoyed the marvellous Olympian purview obtainable from the top of this bus.— And the motor-roofs which catch the confused light with a special smoothness and shininess cover the rich Jews whose countenances have so little human meaning for us.

In the taxis are a more miscellaneous class: almost anyone, it seems, may ride in a taxi, and most of them are curiously torn by the pleasure of the exhilarating ride and the increasing pain which the thumbscrew of a taximeter administers. We may gauge the quality of the taxi-riders by their various appreciations of the artificial flowers in little glass vases before them.

———

[I used to skate with Bill Osborn on Stony Brook at night.] Behind the bridge and tower were the smoky gray of the clouds and the faded rose of the sunset, which the white ice caught in a fainter pink. When the sky grew darker, I could just make out his loose figure dancing and gliding in the dusk and hear the dim scrape of his skates. At last, when the shadows crowded close around us, we jumped on shore, gropingly put on our shoes, and left the lake to night.

———

"German short stories are terribly gloomy. A man goes out and is eaten by a bear, you know, and that sort of thing."

———

"It must be nice to live in New York, where there's a fire every day."

———

At the Graduate School [Howard C. Butler succeeded West as Dean of the Graduate School]: Butler of a Persian cat: "Ah, Miriam's an expensive luxury; aren't you, dear child? Yesterday she bit the largest pearl out of my scarf-pin, and very nearly swallowed it. I've been calling her Cleopatra ever since." Miriam went off eventually in the limousine which her owners sent for her.

———

Mr. Mac [Frank MacDonald]: "I remember when we used to hold the English Faculty Meetings in Axson's rooms (over the grocery store). Spaeth would get up and lecture for an hour on the comparative merits of *Fra Lippo Lippi* and *Andrea del Sarto;* somebody else would insist that *Sesame and Lilies* wasn't so good for the freshmen as *Unto this Last,* because "by the time they get to the end of freshman year, there's a certain maturity." We'd debate for hours about the cultural value of four or five sonnets of Keats in the curriculum, and then, all of a sudden, we'd hear a bunch of students coming down from the Inn—the Inn was open in those days—singing 'Going back to Nassau Hall,' and gosh! the futility of the whole thing, don't you know—!"

[Frank MacDonald had grown in the Princeton soil and clung to the Princeton walls like some odd but rather attractive plant. All large colleges, I think, have such characters, but MacDonald belonged to a species which could only have been indigenous to Princeton. His scholarship was non-existent, and he made no pretentions to any; his usefulness, though real, was peculiar; but he was so much a part of the Princeton scene that no one could have thought of uprooting him. He had returned to Princeton after a spell in New York, with which he was unable to cope, almost immediately after graduation, and had been ever since, first for years an instructor, then at last an assistant professor. He was in some way a protegé of his classmate Roland Morris, a rich trustee, who always seemed to be coming to his rescue and guaranteeing his permanence. MacDonald was a most entertaining man, a great raconteur and gossip—I have recorded here many of his anecdotes—and he loved to dine out in the houses of the rich Princeton families who lived outside the university and to whom he always referred to as "the good and the great." His provenance was somewhat exotic, for he had been born and spent a part of his youth in Siam, the son of a missionary, a confidant and adviser of the King, who—MacDonald was later to tell me—was an agreeable and cultivated gentleman, quite unlike the ignorant boor presented in *The King and I*, and the begetter of innumerable children. The young Crown Prince, however, he said, had so worn himself out in this exercise that he could hardly have proved a worthy successor to his father. Frank liked in his vacations to go to the East, and he was never really at home in America anywhere except at Princeton. He always remained a bachelor, and although he had many times to change his lodgings with great labor in moving his library, had for a long time his most commodious quarters in rooms above the Nassau Inn. He imagined he had been in love with a Princeton lady who had married someone else; but I never could see any evidence on Frank MacDonald's part of anything more than a social interest in women—he liked to converse with the clever ones such as Katherine Fuller Gerould, but his affections were mainly engaged in sentimental friendships with students and others. He had large blue eyes with shaggy eyebrows, a disproportionately large head with a high squarish boxlike forehead and a rubbery kind of body that drooped and sagged and bent.

I saw a good deal of Frank and usually enjoyed talking to him, though he sometimes exasperated me, but it would never have occurred to me to take his course. I believe that he was very successful in communicating an appreciation of poetry to boys who might not otherwise have been touched by it; but, aside from this love of English poetry—he knew nothing about any other kind— he had really no serious interests of a literary or intellectual sort. His library grew and grew, but it contained, besides his collection of books on Siam, which he had built up with assiduity, the complete works, lovingly assembled, of a number of minor English novelists, which seemed to constitute his favorite reading. He was ignorant of many, if not most, of the classics, for he did not really like to read anything that made upon him any demands. It did not matter in the least to him—as I discovered in the case of Stendhal—that a writer who seemed to make such demands had an impressive reputation. He might have about such a writer ideas of only the vaguest kind: he had no curiosity whatever. He bristled against the reputations of such writers as Ezra Pound who were setting new standards in the United States and giving our literature new life. He resented the cockiness of Scott Fitzgerald, who sat in one of his classes, and irritably "told him off." The habit of Frank MacDonald's that annoyed me most was his humming and swinging one foot when I was talking enthusiastically of some writer about whom he did not want to hear. But he had so much humor and charm and was so youthfully uninhibited in expressing his prejudices that—except for the serious people who could not like him because they could not take him seriously—he had a great many friends in Princeton. He had been a strong Wilson man, and when Wilson was defeated by West, I think the passing of this wind of idealism left him feeling rather stranded. He liked to meet the students as friends, to put himself to some extent on a level with them—though with occasional revindications of seniority and magisterial authority —as a first-rate teacher will rarely do; and I think he was very much gratified when he was made a member of the Ivy Club. He told me at least twice that the brilliant Greek professor William Kelly Prentice had once said to him, with his cutting arrogance: "You're the sloppiest man intellectually I've ever known," and this had apparently stung him. Kelly Prentice was in every respect the opposite of Frank MacDonald. No student would have thought for a moment that Prentice could be friendly with him, and I think few professors were. He had all the snobbery of Albany, a peculiar provincial brand, which is prepared to challenge any other snobbery. He was good-looking, elegant, slim, intellectually distinguished. His advanced courses in Greek literature, which he varied in subject from year to year in order not to bore himself, were among the best in Princeton; but he had the bad habit of insulting his students when he thought them deficient in literary taste or otherwise in some way inferior. This insolent sharpness, however, was preferable to the self-centered patronage of West. It surprised me to hear that Prentice had in his later years embraced Buchmanism. It seemed a come-down for a man so disdainful. His love of the classics was intense, and it made him, for all his acridity, something of a shining figure. But I suppose that this cultural light must have failed him in his later years. He was engaged in no great task of scholarship that would have carried him along to complete it. Frank MacDonald was in serious straits in the latter part of his life. I believe he had had to retire before the retirement age, and he always seemed behind on his rent—hence his necessity of moving into smaller apartments, always with a bigger library. But he finally made some deal with the University, which involved turning over his books to it. He had a stroke, and the last time I saw him, he was propped in a chair in his room, still above the Nassau Inn, enjoying and sharing with me the one martini that was allowed him at five o'clock, and to which he looked forward all day. He made no complaint of his helplessness but was as agreeable, though subdued, as ever.

Frank MacDonald, who was one of those people that leave college intending to write and then do not quite get around to it, hiding unfinished manuscripts for decades, did finally, late in life, actually publish a novel, a rather feeble detective story. But he also kept a day-by-day diary, which he seemed to take very seriously and which I thought would surely be of interest. When I last saw him, he said he had destroyed it—which depressed me even more than his then half-paralyzed condition, for it showed what a low valuation he put upon his work and his life. In these later years, however, he also published a book of poems that I thought had some very moving things in it. The people who compile anthologies always stick to the same accepted poets, and I feel sometimes that I could make up an excellent one entirely composed of poems that had never appeared in any other. Here are two of Frank MacDonald's:

"There's Rosemary"

Like a white flower afloat on deep
Mysterious waters of the night,
Heavy and odorous, half-asleep,
Between the stream and the moonlight:

Such, now I fancy, such thou art,
O, long-lost city of my birth,
Still the fair city of my heart,—
One perfect city of the earth!

. . . Could I from usual modes escape
And of my love my skill inform,
Out of my memories I might shape
Temples and towers, white and warm,

With roofs resplendent in the sun;
And thatch a thousand cottages,
All bamboo-built, and every one
Embowered in richly-blossomed trees;

And grow palm-gardens by the flanks
Of many-branchèd, mighty streams,—
Dark, languorous waters, by whose banks
A universe is lost in dreams;

And set a fleet of boats afloat,
Giving to each a lazy oar,—
Fill them with mellow fruit and boat
My delicate cargoes, shore to shore;

And fix a firmament of stars
In constellations new, and gay
Bedeck with planets all the bars
And tangles of the milky way;

And for Orion's belt emboss
A new design to dazzle night;
And touch the symbol of the Cross
With deeper mysteries of light;

And show the way the Buddha went,—
By more than foot-prints in the stone . . .
(Since the long way to His content,
To me, for ever is unknown . . .)

. . . Or nearer yet, of dearer days
And fonder memories far, I might
A broad-verandahed mansion raise,
And to its cordial rooms invite. . . .

Or to the lawns, beneath the shade
Of mango-branches, low with fruit,—
To many a flowery esplanade. . . .
And paradises, absolute!

There should magnolias be. The scent
Clings to my English fairy-tales,
As if from out the Orient
Came argosies of English sails . . .

(O, could I listen once again!
There is a grave upon a hill,
Mournful in sunshine or in rain . . .
No more: the magic tones are still . . .)

Go, dreams and memories, go! I fain
Would waken, waken and forget;
Here are the grey skies and the rain,
Bare trees in windy gardens set;

And straight long streets where people pass,
Traffic and chatter, till they seem
Themselves but shadows in a glass,
Or figments of another dream.

Another dream! Ay, dreaming still!
. . . Grey towers upon an autumn sky;
Dream-locked on an enchanted hill,
While yonder all the world goes by!

O, flower-like city of the past!
O, little town of towered halls!
Ye are the two where, first and last,
The day rose and the twilight falls . . .

The day rose on a sunny strand
Where joys at end were joy's increase;
The evening falls, and through the land
I hear the folding wings of peace.

The Visitor

The door is closed, yet in you come;
The clock strikes late, you do not go;
I shut my eyes, my lips are dumb,—
I have no charity to show . . .

My eyes are shut, but you I see;
My lips are dumb, with you I speak;
My heart is yours for charity . . .
Go, go, now, for my soul is weak

With watching, and I fain would sleep!
My bed is here, my prayers are said,
And must I still at midnight keep
This long communion with the dead?

Nay! Sleeping, I should dream of you;
Should see the gladness in your face;
Should old acknowledgments renew
And hold you in the old embrace . . .

Then stay, friend! there is much to say . . .
At best I can but think and rhyme
Of you, who died but yesterday
And have been dead so long a time!

———

B.H. [a faculty daughter]: "Well, I suppose we all have to come to a preceptor after all!" [Note added later]: And she did!

———

It is said that N.M. was once introduced to a girl in this remarkable fashion: "Get used to Miss —." (Variation: "Shake hands with Miss —")

———

[Conversation with Bill Mackie]
"Sir, you look very *recherché* to-day."
"Sir: I feel very *réchauffé.*"
"Life is an imposition."
"Oh, it has its points."

———

The beautiful city of Boston
The city of beans and of cod,
Where the Lowells speak only to Cabots
And the Cabots speak only to God.

The beautiful town of New Haven,
The city of Truth and of Light,
Where God speaks to Jones in the very same tones
That he uses for Hadley and Dwight.

[Having got to the age now when people like to retell
old jokes and anecdotes, I shall insert here a few more
scraps of college folklore.

When the English professor George Maclean Harper
made his new discoveries about Wordsworth and published his book *Wordsworth's French Daughter,* someone
made the following rhyme:

If only Byron could have known
About Wordsworth's French daughter,
How the feathers would have flown
Above Winander water!

Henry Van Dyke, a genteel and insipid writer very
popular with the feminine public, was the subject of
many stories. At one time, he was invited to lecture at the

Sorbonne, and the *Revue des Deux Mondes* devoted an article to his work. The courteous author of this article said that the only book of Van Dyke's which exhibited anything like "Gallic esprit" was that called *Fisherman's Luck;* but the French printer transposed the capital letters. Could this have been a made-up story? It would have happened before my time, but was told me in a most circumstantial way. Students and faculty, one by one, I was told, stole quietly over to the library to consult the *Revue des Deux Mondes,* and Lisherman, it was said, became the hero of the hour.

We heard with particular joy that when Paul Bourget, during a visit to London at the time of Van Dyke's cultural ambassadorship, had asked Henry James about him, James had answered, *"Il n'existe pas."*]

———

From Cleveland tower we saw, in the bare bright setting of a February afternoon, the strange miscellany of buildings which makes Princeton; the gray Gothic of Campbell, Little, Blair and the rest was nearly lost among the older and more obtrusive vagaries of our earliest architects, above which, none the less, Holder's slim spire redeemed the aimless peaks and clumsy protruded windows of Alexander Hall, and those classic irrelevancies, Whig and Clio, shone pleasantly beyond such examples of mere hideous planted bulk as Witherspoon and Brown. Nearer, the dingy Seminary buildings on the left and the dismal stretch of Alexander Street on the right, trailing along so far its dead unpainted houses, which might have been bits of bleached sea-wreckage left together in a chance line by some receding tide—presented the ugliest aspects, and nearest of all was the golf-course, a meadow washed and yellowed by winter. Low uninviting hills which spring had yet to touch enclosed that mélange of halls and houses, huddled or scattered, in no sort of order, fair or unsightly, with art, on the whole, in abeyance, just as our brave but uncertain career had left them: a record of our history.

———

Amenities of Club-Bicker [negotiations which, toward the end of Sophomore year, preceded the invitations to be members of the clubs]: Walker Ellis, after convincing with his matchless eloquence a band of sophomores that they should go Cottage, met B.L. on his way out and, with polished bravado, offered to introduce the other visitor to "the new Cottage section." He granted L's request and stepped out, leaving him alone with them. When he attempted to reënter, he was told that they had all gone Cap and Gown, and was asked to leave.

A Terrace member went around explaining to the sophomores that Charter imposed an initiation fee of $150 and dues of $25 extra per month, etc., etc.

———

The egregious Mercer [an evangelist: I put him in my story called *Galahad*—this is evidently a memory from my school days]: "And the old father, sitting in his office, takes his will out of his drawer, and adds a codicil to say that he disinherits his son. So Mercer was cut off from everybody: he was down in the depths.—Well, my picture appeared full-length on the front page of a New York paper, and when my father saw it, he came straight to New York and sent for me. I put on a silk-hat and a frock-coat—yes, Mercer put on a silk-hat, and walked up the steps of one of the wealthiest hotels on Fifth Avenue. My father met me in the lobby and when he saw me dressed like that, he said: 'My boy, my boy, my boy: my God, forgive me!' Is salvation real?" . . .

———

"Jim" [he worked for Walter Hall, and was brought to one of his preceptorials as a sociological exhibit]: "It began when we was settin' at home one night. I was there —I was thinkin', see, all de time, what father was thinkin': 'Here I gotta support a lotta bums 'at can't do nuttin'.' So I went away the next mornin' on the trolley." (Jim later ran away with his benefactor's fur overcoat and was never seen again.)

———

Sam Shoemaker to Bill Osborn on the subject of Wilton Lloyd-Smith's mild heterodoxy: "But I can't understand how Wilton at this age can set himself up against a wonderful speaker and mature man like Dr. Fitch!" [Dr. Fitch, orotund and pear-shaped, was a great preacher at schools and colleges.]

———

Mr. Alfred Noyes: "This Indian fellow—a Brahmin he was—said he saw an English officer strike an Indian gentleman across the face with his whip. Awful liar the fellow must have been, you know! He couldn't really have seen it." And later he told a number of stories about German outrages which he had gotten from sources it had apparently never occurred to him to doubt.

"I was talking with a publisher, when a man came into the office and said, 'Have you heard about Dick?' The publisher said, 'No,' and the other man said, 'Shot.' He just stopped a minute, you know, and drew a breath, and then went on talking business with me, as if nothing had happened. Afterwards I found out that it was his second son he had lost. The first had been shot some time before.

And, you know, his life had been wrapped up in these two chaps. He had given them the best education and provided for them well, although he was shabbily dressed himself."

[Noyes was then teaching poetry at Princeton. He was a smug middle-class Englishman of the kind that Shaw liked to caricature and that the Sitwells lived to shock. I always thought his poetry a fake. He asserts quite untruly in his book of reminiscences, *Two Worlds for Memory,* that I was one of "a small group of students" who "used to meet me once a week to discuss their own work in prose and verse." I may have gone once out of curiosity. The only time I remember discussing literature with him was when Stanley Dell and I were invited to President Hibben's and found Alfred Noyes there. I had the impression that this occasion had been specially arranged by Noyes in order to "get at" Stanley and me. Unaware that Shaw and Wells were among my favorite contemporary writers, he exhorted us to lead a crusade against them. When Bernard Shaw wrote his pamphlet *Common Sense about the War,* Noyes said he ought to be thrown into the Tower of London. An even greater provocation for the luxury of expressing a sense of outrage was given later by Joyce's *Ulysses.* Noyes tells, in *Two Worlds for Memory,* how he tried, by similar tactics to those he had tried with us at Princeton, to recruit, at "a little luncheon," a group of right-thinking influential figures for a campaign against an announced B.B.C. broadcast by someone who was said to think highly of Joyce. He later notified Lord Darling, the judge who had condemned the book, that a "sumptuously bound" copy of *Ulysses* in the library of the late Lord Chancellor was about to be sold at auction, with the result that Lord Darling immediately alerted Scotland Yard; and he announced to Hugh Walpole, a guest in his house, that it

"was time that his bag should be packed," when Walpole
—with mischievish intent, no doubt—recommended the
book to "an innocent girl," one of Noyes's daughters.]

———

Bill Osborn: "But there is a certain pleasure in the
mere expenditure of physical energy."

"He lives entirely on milk and graham crackers, it
seems,—because he has this great big family estate but
hasn't money enough to keep it up. Oh, it's not so terribly
big, but it's a vay respectable house, vay old—and he
saves all the time to keep it going. He has two bachelor—
uh—spinster sisters who live there; and he lives there
himself in ve summer, I fink."

———

Bill Mackie apostrophizing a pigeon: "Sir, I wot you
will one day be made into a pie.—He remains mum-
chance."

———

John Peale Bishop: "My sense of humor is growing so
that I am afraid I shan't be able to write any more
poetry."

———

Bill Mackie (upon being asked to describe his missing
slippers): "Sir, they had red-morocco heels four inches
high. The Birth of Venus was broidered on the toe of one
and the Rape of Helen on the other."

———

Charles Walker, upon being asked what he intends to
do upon graduating from Yale, invariably answers that he
is going into the drygoods business.

———

[Canoeing at Stony Brook]: The air was stifling: horribly dusty along the roads and heavy even on the water, which was itself almost tepid. All sharpness of color was toned from sky and lake and trees by a kind of gray haze, which changed greens and blues to soft new glaucous tints. The very sunlight, hot as it was, seemed somehow dusty and dimmed. On the shores, we saw men and sometimes women sitting on the grass. A kingfisher hovered about the bridge. In the Mill Pond, two or three men in rowboats were fishing for perch. From the lake, we heard the hoarse shouts of a coxswain exhorting his naked oarsmen in their needle of a shell, which pierced through under the bridge and disappeared.

———

—The persistent and mechanical rasping of the guineafowls.

—The sharp harsh gasps of the locomotive.

—The Clubs: monuments to the mediocrity of human taste and ideals.

—The canal was muddy and made the white clouds muddy in reflection.

—The nasal clangor of the bell in Nassau Hall, ringing for a class. [I later included this phrase in a poem, and it was questioned by Alfred Noyes on the ground that it might lead the British reader to make a crack that in America even the bells had nasal voices.]

—The First Presbyterian Church, that picturesque but inconvenient enclave.

———

"After the dance, he had a breath you could chin yourself on."

———

Mr. Preston, who had been hunted out from the guests at a party and introduced to a young girl whose "mother had known him years ago and had wanted her particularly to meet him": "Well, now you've seen me, you can go back and tell her what I'm like." [This was the second husband of Mrs. Grover Cleveland. His bad manners were legendary.]

———

F. Scott Fitzgerald: "Why, I can go up to New York on a terrible party and then come back and go into the church and *pray*—and mean every word of it, too!"

[Scott was then a practicing Catholic, and though I sometimes used to kid him about it—he was the first educated Catholic I had ever known—I now think it was perhaps unfortunate that he lost his faith as he did. In his college days, the older men who were most interested in him and whom he most respected were Father Fay and Shane Leslie. I suppose it was inevitable that in an all-Protestant college—I do not remember in my time any other Catholic students, though there may have been a few—a college which had for him, a Westerner, the prestige of an acme of Eastern smartness, he should have imitated his companions in not taking religion seriously. But this left him with nothing at all to sustain his moral standards or to steady him in self-discipline. His desire to be a great writer only intermittently spurred him to effort. He had put on record before his death that he wanted to be buried in the Catholic cemetery in Baltimore with the other members of his family, but this was denied him by the Church, to which, after breaking away from it, he had never made his resubmission.]

———

Wilton Lloyd–Smith: "But the dances at Philadelphia and Washington and Baltimore are much worse than the

New York ones.—Oh, *no, no, no*: the girls don't get drunk; but they get so *dizzy*, you know, that they can't dance any more and have to sit down. Although sometimes people can dance when they can't walk."

———

The Princeton crew race had a sort of near-festive quality. Crowds of townspeople who could hardly be described as "brightly dressed" and a few students with the girls they had invited to a recent club dance lined the banks. Canoes clustered about the judge's float. Dr. Spaeth, coaching from his official motor-boat, maintained the only very partially holiday atmosphere by roaring a message about an essay through his megaphone at "Lillian" Russell, who was some distance away, and hereby startling a number of intermediate persons who thought for a time that they were being savagely reprimanded. The finishes of the races evoked cheering of that semi-ironical kind for which Princeton seems always to be so ready. Even the rowers didn't take their proverbially overwhelming exertions as hard as usual, but recovered, after a momentary collapse of lowered heads and motionless oars, to return vigorously to the boat-house.

———

Nocturnal voices in a chanting chorus addressed to John Wyeth, who is playing Debussy and rapt in iridescent dreams when most people have gone to bed: "Cut out that goddam noise! Cut out that goddam noise!" etc.

[John Wyeth was the pure aesthete of the class of 1916. I had already known him before college—he had been one of Sandy's friends in New York, the son of a distinguished surgeon, and at Princeton we belonged to the same club, Charter. He had no "crowd" of his own. It was not merely that he was shy; he had, I think, no interest in making friends. He did have one companion, however, from whom he was almost inseparable, the late Bert Friend, who was already engaged in the studies that led later to his becoming an authority on Byzantine art. I rarely saw John save at meals, but he and I had certain things in common. We were, so far as I know, the only students then in college who had seriously read Henry James. Though I won an essay prize by a paper on James—based, however, on an incomplete knowledge of his work—I did not find him entirely satisfactory. I think there was too little "love interest"—that is sex interest—in James for a young man of my age to appreciate him. I was used to Bennett and Wells, Meredith and Thomas Hardy, and James, after these, seemed rather pale. What led me on to read him was the discovery that he was sometimes "realistically" dealing with contemporary America. It was very much in the air that our writers should write about their own country, and the passages about Albany in *The Portrait of a Lady* were a good deal more interesting to me than all the rest which takes place in Europe. It was not till I read *What Maisie Knew*—recommended in the *Smart Set* by Mencken as a "passionless masterpiece"—that I found a work of James that I could wholly admire—though it had nothing to do with the United States—and I still think the short novels of this middle period are much better than most of his longer ones, which are likely to start off invitingly but in the second volume to run into the sands. I was also rather worried by the way James's people talked. This was certainly not less artificial than the way George Meredith's talked, but the brilliance and electricity of Meredith kept me from minding this. It was John Wyeth who first explained to me, when I complained about James's conversations, that every artist establishes a convention, in his dialogue as in everything else, and that Henry James's convention was no further from actuality than that of many other writers.]

———

The distinctive Irish style: at once pugnacious and graceful.

———

Douglas Russell, introducing two little sisters to visiting friends of his: "They're my sisters—don't know 'em very well."

———

"Joe's": That long desolate room of oil-cloth and white woodwork and little tables covered with soiled tablecloths, with its dirty soda-fountain at one end and its undisguised refrigerator at the other. [It was only a step from my rooms, and I would go there late at night, after I had finished working, to eat a hot fried-egg sandwich.]

———

[Canoeing on Stony Brook]: We went past the "Sheepwash" and the railway bridge and came to where the stream was narrow and difficult, because the thickets on the bank sprawled into the water and the rank clumps of pond-lily leaves clogged our passage. However, we fended off the branches and pulled ourselves along by the heavy lily stalks, till we found wider water and banks that were the edges of forests and meadows. Among these and in the turbid stream which presented them again, crimped and reticulated and a little tarnished, we saw all the amazing details of color which even the commonest collection of living creatures displays: the bluejays and kingfishers, the full red of red-winged blackbirds and the vermilion of the cardinal bird, tiny summer yellow birds and flickering chimney swifts. They made an occasional robin seem bourgeois and ordinary. Wild pigeons, crows, song sparrows and chickadees were less striking; and the little spindled sandpipers seemed as humble as the mud which they were made so nicely to match. Also, there was the lavender of a wild-iris and even the yellow of the coarse round lily buds. Painted turtles with red-scalloped shells floated at one side, obliquely poised. And always we had blue and silver and green from sun and sky and trees and water. . . . We returned at last into the Millstone Pond by way of that wide and slightly dreary gate, where the water is always nearly black and there are always many trees whose branches are still quite bare.

—Which reminds one of the famous writer on nature who, upon stepping out one beautiful morning, remarked to a friend: "What a fine day for phrases!" [This was an invention of mine.]

————

Bill Mackie: "Come on, Mr. Mac, this is no nunnery!" [He had balked at telling some story.]

(Spring, 1914) after an exam: "My God, it's all over; I could sit down and cry like a child."

————

A balloon-monger on the curb with a bouquet of gas balloons, whose transparent globes of green and red and blue and orange bounced and rebounded together at a breath of wind.

The red and yellow ones are like monstrous currants.

————

Mr. Pomeroy [Ralph Pomeroy, the rector of the Episcopal Church] to Mr. Mac: "You don't look at life as a narrative; you look at it as a series of dramatic episodes."

———

T. K. Whipple of Charley Walker: "At Princeton, he'd be an irresistible force moving in a vacuum." [I have written about "Teek" Whipple in *Classics and Commercials*. At the time I entered college, he was a senior and the editor of the *Lit*, but he went on to the Graduate School and continued to contribute to the magazine and to take an active interest in it.]

———

If Henry James had written *The Reef*, he would have begun with the second book and allowed the episode related in the first, the very best and most characteristic thing in the novel, to transpire through the subsequent conversation of the characters.

———

Earl Osborn, [who had enlisted in the ambulance in France]: "I stahted off in a gweat fit of enthusiasm and fought it was going to be a gweat adventure; then, when I found out more about it, it didn't seem so pleasant; and ven, when I fought about it more, I wasn't vewy keen on it.—You'h going to be undeh military discipline all ve time, you know; and ve work's going to consist chiefly in running a Fawd night and day wif a load of poah fellows gwoaning in ve back. In ve füst place, you may come back a physical wreck; and ven, you may get brutalized.—Oh, I don't know—seeing so many dead men, and seeing ve human body mangled like vat . . ."

[I tried to reproduce the way that Bill and Earl Osborn talked, the reason for which I never understood. Their parents did not talk in that way. John Dos Passos, in his youth, had somewhat the same pronunciations. It has sometimes been a fashionable affectation not to pronounce *r*; but I don't know why these young men should have been influenced by this. I believe they all outgrew these habits.]

———

"It isn't the principle of the thing; it's the way it looks."

———

Bill Mackie, on being derided for his remissness in not securing a room: "Well, something usually happens for people who can't take care of themselves, I think,—don't you?—I mean, they usually come out all right. . . ."

———

At the Seabright Beach Club, on some summer mornings, the very sea seems to have become merely pretty and lazy and trivial like the summer people who come to bathe in it and lie upon its sand under parasols of red and green silk.

———

Bill Mackie (summer of 1914), on beholding a cathedral spire at Bruges (?): "Wouldn't that just make you fall down before God Almighty!" [This was reported to me by Sam Shoemaker, with whom Bill had been travelling on the Continent. Sam, who came from Baltimore, was then preparing himself to take orders in the Episcopal Church, and I predicted for him a worldly career in a smart well-to-do parish. But what happened was somewhat different. He was for years Frank Buchman's chief lieutenant in what was later called the Oxford Movement. This still left room for Sam's snobbishness, since Buchman made special efforts to acquire prestige for his group by capturing for it the socially prominent. Sam left the movement, however, when Buchman came out for Hitler. In college, he was always eager to note any signs, on the part of his friends, of an interest in religion. Hence his telling me of Bill's exclamation, which I do not believe can have indicated any great preoccupation with God. I used to take walks with Sam, and, in recurrent discussions of religion, we would do our best to find common ground, but I always felt a little afterwards that I had been wasting my time, that he did not understand my point of view but complacently accepted it as confirming his own. He had a Southern and somewhat hollow geniality, and he maintained the pretence of a capacity for gaiety by having a piano in his rooms and playing upon it occasionally the only tune he seemed to know, a song from *The Belle of New York*.]

———

Bill Mackie (spring of 1915): "I'd love to go on the loose tonight. Last night the campus was alive—really, it was wonderful—till 2 in the morning—and I had to study philosophy notes all night!"

———

[The eating clubs for juniors and seniors were all on Prospect Street, and the freshmen were not allowed to walk on it till the end of freshman year.]

The freshmen came parading down Prospect Street for the first time, hot and excited in the lurid pink of their torches. Their Roman candles popped little comets against the blue night sky of June and showered sparks upon their hands and heads; but they did not mind this: it only added a little exhilarating danger to this last prescribed adventure of freshman year. They saw the clubs all alight and the diners at the doors and on the curb, in the dress clothes of undergraduates or the fantastic soldier, sailor, artist and Arab costumes of alumni. Some of them held champagne glasses in their hands; and this touch added glamor to the paraders' impression that they were in presence of arcana more mysterious and magnificent than anything else Princeton had to offer. Some day they might have the right to visit one or another of these pleasure palaces; they wondered which it would be. And every man there, oddly enough, pictured himself a member of one of the clubs of highest repute. Friends from the clubs saluted them, and they were still prouder and more impressed with the brilliant possibilities of Princeton. Upperclassmen they knew, the very sophomores who had been a short time ago so near to them, had subjected them so unceasingly to their ridicule and criticism, took on new values as they were seen to move in this little-known and iridescent element. Ah, when they, the new sophomores should reach this culminating phase, how clever and famous and happy they would be! The friendships of freshman year, new and tentative and delightful now, would be old and unalterable and wonderful then. They would be exalted by extra-curricular honors; they would be able to stand on the curb, like these others, with dinner jackets and champagne glasses and the consciousness that their names stood for something; they would be celebrated characters like these, gifted like these with this or that talent.

The chief reason for the immense difference between life at Princeton and the Princeton attitude and life at Yale and the Yale attitude is that the latter holds off so much longer than the former that disillusioning climax which is the real turning-point in the transition from boy to man. [By this I meant the college social climax, which in Princeton is over at the end of sophomore year, but in Yale, not till the end of junior year.

Fraternities are banned at Princeton, and we are unique, so far as I know, in having only eating clubs. These clubs are remarkably uninteresting. In my time, before the new Commons was built, you could be sure of getting better meals there than if you ate at the old Commons and less expensive ones than if you ate at the Princeton restaurants. But there was little or no serious activity in connection with these eating clubs. At my club, we arranged an occasional evening when some member of the faculty was invited to dinner and we had some sort of discussion afterwards; but, aside from this, since I did not play billiards or bridge, there was nothing in the club house to occupy me except to sit, as I did sometimes in winter, in front of our big open fireplace and read the papers and magazines. The sophomores were chosen during "bicker week," but some of them were always left out, and thus unfairly humiliated. Periodical efforts have been made to eliminate the clubs altogether. Woodrow Wilson attempted to abolish them and encountered the most determined resistance. The point was that the alumni members had invested so much money in them during the period of conspicuous spending of the early nineteen-hundreds that—though Wilson wanted to convert them into university buildings—it was not really easy to abandon or dispose of the often very large and luxurious edifices that lined both sides of the street. They were vying now with one another as to which should make the most impressive show. The Cottage Club had been designed by Stanford White. Another, the Colonial Club, displayed an enormous colonial façade, which, like a Hollywood set, had almost nothing behind it. A second attempt to get rid of the clubs was made, just after I graduated, by Dick Cleveland, Grover Cleveland's son.

He set an example himself by refusing to belong to one, but his rebellion, like all others, failed. Repeated attempts have been made to arrange that no student shall be left out of the clubs; another is in progress as I write.

The situation at Yale was quite different. You were first asked to join a fraternity, and you could live in a fraternity house—we were not allowed to live in the clubs till the days when we came back as alumni. The election to the senior societies took place at the end of the junior year at the solemn ceremony of "Tap Day," when the class waited under a certain tree for the seniors to run out of the society buildings—windowless and forbidding stone tombs, illuminated only from the top—tap their men and say "Go to your room!" Mysterious rites followed, which the members were pledged not to reveal. Of these senior societies at Yale, Skull and Bones was by far the most important. It was supposed to take in only the ablest men, and they were supposed to be dedicated thus to be "leaders" in after life as well as at college. They took Bones with extreme solemnity. If the word "Bones" was spoken, they were supposed to have to leave the room, and it was said, I do not know how truly, that they could not relinquish their society pins even when they were taking a shower, at which time they had to hold them in their teeth. No Bones man, after college, was supposed to fail; his career in the larger world was intently followed by his brothers, and if he showed any signs of weakening, they arranged to prop him up.

Scott Fitzgerald once had the idea of bringing out the word "bones" in a Triangle Show, and then having two men dressed as tattered old bums get up and leave the theater. All of this side of Yale was, in general, the object of a good deal of kidding on the part of Harvard and Princeton, and the climax of the Yale song, "For God, for country and for Yale" was called the greatest anticlimax

ever written. And yet I felt a certain respect for the
importance given at Yale to intellectual achievement.
Scholarship counted as well as athletics, and the editor of
the Yale *News* and the editor of the Yale *Lit* were
ex officio tapped for Bones. At Princeton, you had no
incentive to excel in any such pursuit. ΦBK had no
prestige, was considered, in fact, rather second-rate, and I
remember that I felt John Bishop had undergone a slight
degradation when he found that he had earned this
distinction and went to a ΦBK dinner. In the years when
he and I and Whipple and Hamilton Armstrong and
Stanley Dell and Scott Fitzgerald and John Biggs were
operating the *Lit,* we actually made a profit, and yearly
"cut a melon" which afforded us $50 apiece. But this kind
of thing you did on your own incentive and under your
own steam. When you were faced with the lack of
competition that followed election to a club and found
that it involved nothing but a comfortable place to eat,
you had to keep your own fires stoked, and this was in
some ways a very good thing. The pressure of Yale competition sometimes had the result of making the poets as
well as the political and business types too eager for conspicuous success. And stimulating though I usually found
the Bones men, I became aware, later on, when I shared
an apartment with three Eli's, and saw a good many of
their friends, that unless you had fared well at Yale and
were confidently headed for some substantial achievement, you were by no means a loyal son of Yale but were
likely to look back on it with bitterness. A blistering instance of this was the speech made by Sinclair Lewis
when he attended an alumni dinner. He said that in his
years at Yale his classmates had paid no attention to him,
had simply thought him a "sad bird," as we said at Princeton. But now that he had had some success—publicity,
reputation and money—they were making a fuss about

him. The implication was that they could go to Hell. The Princetonians, on the other hand, had usually an affection for Princeton, which sometimes became quite maudlin. An uncle of mine—neither of those mentioned above— when he had already been some years out of Princeton, returned in tears to his brother's house because Princeton had lost the big game. Examples of this childish loyalty— always, accompanied by extreme conservatism in regard to old college usages and by strong opposition to "liberal" ideas—still turn up in the correspondence columns of the Princeton *Alumni Weekly,* and I am glad to see that the editor does not encourage these outbursts but comments on them sometimes rather tartly. I used to note, on my visits to New Haven, that the dissipation at Yale was practised with the same earnestness as everything else, whereas the Yale men used to make fun of us for what they considered the childish namby-pambiness of "going to the Nass for a beer." Yale was a burning religion, with, however, a good many unbelievers; Princeton a well-dressed and convivial group, to which, if one were not convivial, it was easy to remain indifferent.]

At the '85 headquarters in Thompson Hall, Father was plotting with his classmates an unveiling ceremony which was to be one of the features of their class banquet: the public removal of a wig with which one of their number had sought to counterfeit the original head of hair which they all claimed to remember with so much pleasure and as to which they professed themselves impossible to deceive.

[This was to be accomplished by a hook let down by a string from the ceiling.

My father seemed quite to be enjoying himself at this thirtieth reunion with his classmates. He did not really

have much love for Princeton. In college, he and his
brother John had edited the *Princetonian* and had led a
campaign against what they regarded as certain persecu-
tions on the part of the faculty. I have never understood
what this was all about. Though I have from my father's
library the old bound volumes of the *Princetonian*, the
references are so guarded that it is impossible to tell what
the issues were—except that the students complained that
the faculty were spying upon them. The cartoon of
one of the professors which brought the agitation to a
head does not throw any light on the matter. But it
resulted in a student's strike, and my father was arrested
by the proctor on his way to a strikers' meeting, at which
he was going to speak—he was a celebrated Whig Hall
orator. He was accused of being one of the fomentors of
rebellion, on his way to inflame the strikers; but he declared that he had meant to quell them. He was "rusti-
cated" to Kingston in the house of a minister, and an
effort was made—it was in his senior year—to debar him
from graduation. But, on account of his brilliant record,
this move was overruled by other elements in the faculty
who were friendly to him.

His attitude toward Princeton was never enthusiastic,
and I was grateful to him for tipping me off to some of
the Princeton frauds.

The President of Princeton in my time was John Grier
Hibben. He had a clear and straight gaze, and was
generally liked by the students, who toasted him in their
"Faculty Song" with,

> Here's to Hibben, we call him Jack—
> The whitest man in all the fac'.

He had been ordained in the Presbyterian Church: at
that time, every president of Princeton still had to be a

Presbyterian minister. Besides this qualification, he had risen to his position, partly, I believe, from not having committed himself in the battle between Wilson and West—Wilson had accused him of a base betrayal. He had been a friend and classmate of my Uncle John and had visited at the house of my grandparents. But my father had a low opinion of him and said that he was an unarguable refutation of the saying that it is impossible for anyone to lift himself by his bootstraps. Kemp Smith, an importation of Wilson's and now head of the Philosophy Department, of which Hibben had been formerly head and in which he still taught a course in logic, said of Hibben that, in spite of several books on the subject, "he doesn't know what philosophy is, you know." But he was, I think, by no means the worst of our mediocre American college presidents, who seem sometimes not to have any competence at all in any of the departments over which they preside.]

———

Kemp Smith: "He has an attractive ugly face like Huxley's: like a good-looking codfish with a mouth like a letter-bawx."

———

Gauss (asked about his little collie's name): "Baudelaire." [Gauss had not, however, named him. He had been left with the Gausses by the Jesse Lynch Williamses.]

"Really?"

"Yes: it's a fact."

"Will he answer to any line from the great poet?"

"Oh, he barks at those."

"You should dye his hair green."

"Yes, he ought to have that."

"But he seems to be a perfectly normal dog."

"No, he's not a normal dog: he likes to listen to French lectures."

When someone [in Dante class] translated "Never was a man fitter than he was for the guillotine." (*gelantino.* I. XXXII.60.) Baudelaire emerged from under Gauss's desk, looking rather pained.

Gauss: "He'll stand for almost anything, but that's too much.—Ain't that some anechronism? Awful—awful—hawrrible—a scan-dal!—It isn't that *I* object to your not knowing these things, gentlemen: I don't care; but I'm sorreh that you haven't the intellectual curiositeh to look them up!—It's bad intellectual form; it's awfulleh bad form; it's like going around with your face unwashed.—Ah, well! it's the University's fault, I suppose, as much as yours.—Mr. Clarkson, translet!"

———

Sandy, in Freshman year, used to be annoyed at hearing through a thin partition his next-door neighbor rehearsing his part in the Triangle Show, repeating with varying intonation and emphasis: "You know well enough what I mean; You *know* well ee-nough what I mean," etc., etc.

———

John Wyeth at Walker Ellis's Ivy Oration: "And his poor mother's here, and she's proud of him. Isn't it pathetic!"

John Wyeth and Bert Friend wanted, in the summer of 1915, to take a cottage in the château district of France and amuse themselves by playing Debussy!

———

At the fish store on the sea-shore [Jersey Coast]: The bins with their overwhelming smell of fish, which disclose great slabs of bluefish mixed with scaleless bonita mackerel, with their neat little tails and their bodies of galvanized tin, or the dark shining armor of live lobsters lying in a confusion of claws and feelers.

———

—The sudden squeal of the telephone.

———

[An English pansy that Sandy crossed with when he came back from Europe after a trip with his room-mates and who afterwards trailed them to Princeton]:
"I haven't drawn a natural breath for ten years!"

———

"Oh, she doesn't mind my making love to her in the evenings: she's tired then."—[Ebe Faber, I think, one of Sandy's room-mates. The Eberhardt Fabers were a German family, in the pencil and eraser business. Ebe Faber was a remarkably likable fellow.]

———

Sandy, after graduating from college. "I feel just as I did when I graduated from school: as if I were only going out of one educational institution into another." [He was going to medical school.]

———

The sun that steeped the undulating grain with light and barred the road with shade.

———

"The liqueur courses through my veins like a subtle fire." Bill Mackie.

———

Elinor Glyn to an American youth she had just met: "And what are you doing during the vacation to indulge your youthful passions?"

The youth, somewhat embarrassed: "I—I'm going home."

———

The mist had graded the trees from green to gray and skipped so many shades between that foreground, middle distance and background were set off against each other as if they had been three scenic silhouettes.

———

John Wyeth, lingering in Princeton after his graduation: "I'm really getting perfectly maudlin, you know. I feel as if I were sliding off a slippery precipice, over a yawning abyss—just struggling to get a foothold!"

———

Bill Osborn, years ago, explained that pigs were naturally clean and that man had perverted and degraded them by taking it for granted that they liked filth.

———

[The following was written on the occasion of a visit to the offices of my Uncle Winfield, the youngest of my mother's brothers, whose collegiate patriotism I have mentioned above. He had seemed to have no special ambition, no interest in any profession, and his older brother Reuel, with whom he lived after college, did not know what to do about him. One day he explained to a man he knew in business that he had a kid brother who did not seem to know what he wanted to do. "I know that you business men don't want college men, but could you possibly give him some kind of job?" The result of this was that Winfield started in as an officeboy in the firm of James White & Co., linen and burlap importers, in a little old building downtown with a brass plate on the façade. He never worked for anyone else, and finally became a partner. He never married and he lived all his life at the Royalton, at that time a bachelor apartment house, and at the Princeton and University Clubs. His only recreation was playing golf, at which he won a number of trophies. Though his firm imported its goods from Scotland, and he liked to entertain the Scots and to repeat their funny Scotch stories, he never left the United States. He eventually became quite well-off and, having nothing else to do with his money, put several boys through Princeton. When he died in his sleep at the Royalton, he had left most of his money to my mother, and at the present time I am partly living on it. He was the only man in the family in business and the only one who had anything much to leave.]

In Worth Street, the buildings of importers and wholesale dealers make no attempt to emulate that smartness and magnificence which give the uptown emporia a perpetual look of newness. These gray buildings least of all, perhaps, are affected by the rapid architectural changes of this most rankly growing of cities. They are the same now as they were fifty years ago; and lay no claim to anything but a venerable commercial dignity. Even the saloons wear solemn and respectable faces and seem to have been designed, with their modified swinging doors and shallow show windows of shelved bottles, to present an essentially wholesale appearance.

The traffic consists mostly of trucks and the sidewalks are blocked with the crates which are being unloaded.

Colloquial.

off him, it, etc.

horsing

whaddye mean, so and so? (obsolete)

haven't a prayer (Yale)

{ a whiz
  a dinger
  a snorer
  a dope

{ craunch down on
  crack down on

ease along (verb)

it, (accented, Western?)

bull

simple (boob)

gum [in the sense of gumming up something]

weak-wad [a weakling]

in the cruche (to come through; to blow) [to succeed
   or to fail at the crucial moment]

ride the gravy

gut [easy] course; hop a gut

potent

fellah! (as a term of address)

pass, as in "thought I'd pass"; pass out cold

shot his wad

a stuffed shirt

the champagne kind o' got to him

on the books; off the books

he's a snake!

gripe, crab (What are you crabbing about?)

a crab, etc.

I'll say!

up stage: 1919

———

Huysmans at Chartres.

[This was to have been a companionpiece to my poem *Whistler at Battersea,* published in the *Nassau Lit*]

. . . Make Charles-Marie-Georges Joris-Karl

. . . But I am not a little man.

. . . Sapristi! I am no farceur.

. . . Like obscene figures done in bronze.

. . . Just as the sun of dirty Chartres is changed to wonderful colors on passing through the stained glass windows, so is the sordid atmosphere of humanity transmuted into beauty through the jewelled panes of my prose.

. . . I must believe! I must believe!

. . . My hate becomes a kind of love—

. . . I am not one like Villiers de L'Isle Adam or Barbey D'Aurevilly upon whose mind, as on the iridescent surface of a bubble, the world is reflected small and unsteady and upside-down and obscured delicately by a shimmer of rainbow colors—as insubstantial and pretty as this.

. . . To taste the rancid side of life.

. . . If I could lose Durtal, then Joris-Karl might have a chance.

. . . God worked before I understood
Un Dilemne, À Rebours, etc.

———

[Words for color, partly out of Compton Mackenzie]:

aquamarine
azure
celeste
watchet
philamot
pomona green
elephant's breath

clinquant-vermeil
stammel
undern [not a color word.]

P.S. said that at Bustanoby's you took a table and spent the whole evening expecting something sensational to happen, but only to find that everyone else was doing the same thing. [It was a New York restaurant with a wicked reputation, where there were girls to be picked up.]

The (N.Y.) river and the sky were dull and dirty like the asphalt of the streets, and the whole city seemed to have blent in a gray uniformity.

Stew Link, on his engagement: "It kept on getting worse and worse until finally we went and did it . . . But she said I'd have to bring my wedding present wrapped up in a diploma."

Some people call on and talk to girls as if they were visiting the zoo and feeding buns to the animals. For them, "calling on girls" becomes something entirely apart from association with other human beings.

"Some girls have a stock of what may be called fake ideas—even a small stock of conversational heresies. You're surprised to find them using perfectly good ideas— and over and over again—to anybody with whom they happen to be talking.—The mere machinery of intercourse—they know nothing of the art."

Henry James is one of the greatest living writers, if we judge from the qualities of his mind, and the extent of his achievement; but, if we judge from what is to be got out of him, one of the least worth reading.

———

Walter Hall on Evans Clark: "I knew he was in love, because he got to writing these poems. He wrote a poem a day and used to come in and read them to me every night. I was surprised when he stopped writing about socialism and began writing about love. I remember that there was one poem that had only one line, I think, about a strike.—Oh, they were all about why worship, why go to a stuffy church for religion, when you can get it in your beloved's arms? Pretty tough on the poor devils who haven't got any beloved!"

———

Kemp Smith said that a professor of his acquaintance was driven out of the parish in disgrace by the congregation of the little Scotch country church in which he had been preaching, because he said in one of his sermons that the weather was almost certainly not managed by Providence but probably the result of natural conditions.

———

[Stanley Dell and I went to summer school at Columbia in 1915.] Stanley said that Franklin Giddings, [the sociologist] looks like a fat chipmunk with a chestnut in either cheek.

Giddings said that administration was a businesslike way of doing things which should never have been done.

———

Stanley: "I was getting out a passport for a lady at St. Moritz, and she said she wanted it for herself and three minors. Two of the children were right there, but I couldn't find out where the other was. Finally, after a good deal of awkwardness and beating about the bush, it turned out that it hadn't been born yet.—Later, when I was coming back on the boat, I heard some peasant woman in the third-class cabin being questioned about her passport or something. They asked her how many children she had, and she said four and one here.—And I thought how much more lovely!"—

———

New York is neither so amusing nor so American as Paris.

———

Overheard on the street! "D'ye think a fellah oughta kiss a girl, when he's not engaged to her?"
The Lady: "Aw, hell! What's kissin' anyhow?"

———

—the brisk tinkle of a music box
—a smart succession of little crystal waves
—the apartment house presented a façade heavily encrusted with ornament: plump urns and robust goddesses, cornucopias overflowing with fruit, and a profusion of flowers in ropes and wreaths.

The series of screens gave warp and woof to the trees and sky and broke them up into tapestried panels.

The imitation marble columns in the lobby of the Manhattan look as if they were made of Roquefort cheese—livid and veined with green.

The loose scaturience of the fountains in front of the Columbia Library.

———

Very few people nowadays read the New Testament: if it were commonly read, fewer people, no doubt, would profess themselves Christians.

———

The sun in the foggy sky was like a little pink wafer on an immense piece of gray blotting paper. [I had not read *The Red Badge of Courage* then.]

———

The Dark Hour
(Swift in His Last Days)

They marvel that their vileness can provoke
A flame that burns me, when they feel it not.
The sacred brand must smoulder here now hot!
To char the bearer, choked with stench and smoke.
Now would it not be something of a joke
Were I to tell them plainly on the spot
That all my wrath is nothing but a plot
To hide my own corruption with a cloak.

Mine is the cruelty I curse so loud,
And mine the vapid folly I deride;
And mine the filth I find in everyone.
Pride is my god, and so I lash the proud.
Oh, Madness, who alone can break my pride,
Come, blur my soul's black nightmare and have done!

New York. August, 1915

———

A gentleman went among the Pennsylvania Dutch distributing tracts and sacred pictures. He had a hard time arousing any interest in one farmer, until he showed

him a picture of Christ wearing the crown of thorns.
"Jesus Christ," said the man. "Look at the big Indian
chief!"

———

Overheard in the hotel lobby: a lady whose eyes are
rimmed with black and whose face is lividly white with
powder: "Oh, they went off with a party.—I didn't
go—oh, because—do you know the difference between
my sort and the hotel sort?—well, they are the hotel sort.
Some people can go with them, but I can't do it. They
make friends with you inside of a day. I never could do
it!"

———

[I went to California with my parents in the summer
of 1915.]

[San Francisco.] The blue bay, the fleckless sky and
the scarred bleached hills that turn to a golden blur when
the sun sets behind them.

[San Francisco.] We met a grim-looking lady whom
Cousin Alice knew, in the Cubist and Futurist exhibi-
tion. [Alice was one of our Kimball cousins, who lived in
California, a pretty blond spinster, whom I very much
liked. We used to go to the 1915 World's Fair together.]
"What do you think of it?" she asked, and we laughed in
reply. She regarded us a little sternly through her eye-
glasses: "Did you hear the man lecture about it?" Cousin
Alice said that she had. "And didn't it mean anything to
you then?" Cousin Alice smiled and said that it didn't.
"It didn't? Good Heavens!" said the lady. "I wonder," she
went on, "how long it will be before we can take one of

these and read it right off as easily as we do an ordinary picture now."

[Pasadena.] Irene Hunter [the sister of my classmate Allen Hunter] on life at a Western Cöed College, the University of Colorado: "Of course, a great deal of work isn't done there. One of the first things you do is get a crush on some girl; then you wait for her outside her dorm every day and go to class with her and carry her books; and after class you come and get her and walk back with her. After a time, you take French and Italian in order to sit with her during class. And out of class you spend all the time you can with her. Sometimes the girl takes courses in order to be with the man; but, of course, that's something of a sacrifice, because it isn't much trouble for a boy to take French or Italian, but it's a different matter for a girl to take calculus or mechanics or something like that."

[Pasadena.] Ash Hewitt had apparently no opinions of his own but was in the habit of getting them ready-made from his parents, so that he had Father's or Mother's authority for a final judgment on every subject—social-ism, Christianity, American greatness, Bernard Shaw, woman suffrage, etc. He called our attention very seri-ously to the fact that the spread of woman suffrage had been coincidental with the spread of Mormonism. He said that he opposed socialism, also, because father said it was impossible: the men who had the brains would always be on top. Look at the men who were on top, Carnegie and Rockefeller and Morgan; they were the men with the brains every time."But," he would usually conclude, "I come of a radical family: father always was very radical, and I was brought up to it." [He was the grandson of Abram Hewitt, an iron manufacturer, who became Mayor of New York and was something of a municipal reformer.]

———

The New England valley was below us: the broad mountain sides covered with forests, across which were blotted huge cloud-shadows, and the village at the bottom, with its sharply white and red buildings, steeped in a pool of light.—Those feathery forests . . .

———

French tragedy and Roman comedy are academic enthusiasms.

———

Kelly Prentice told us to read Gilbert Murray's *The Rise of the Greek Epic*. "It's not a text-book," he hastened to explain. "It's a gentleman's book."

———

Bill Mackie, after flunking out: "When I took that course in Shades and Shadows I had no idea I was going to suffer a total eclipse."

———

Kemp Smith: a man who thinks he can understand politics by reading a book on sociology is very much like a man who thinks that by reading psychology he can understand his sweetheart.

———

Sam Cooper telling Mr. Mac about his adventures at the [San Francisco] Exposition. He had done the Zone with the Hoola-hoola girls, together with a gentleman who professed to be their brother and consented to act as chaperon. "And, believe me, Mr. Mac, they were straight all right: you couldn't go through the Bowl of Joy with a girl without finding that out."

Mr. Pine [a former English master at Hill] at the head of the Gilman Country School. A southern aristocratic youth came to him one day in a rage and said that a coon around the place had spoken to him by his first name. Mr. Pine did not take this with all the seriousness the fellow had expected. Next term he did not come back, and after some time, Mr. Pine heard that the boy's mother had said she was afraid to send her son there, because they might even try to teach him that Abraham Lincoln was a great man. Arthur Jackson told this story when I reproached him for having remarked that he was glad the United States had been founded under a gentleman like Washington rather than under Lincoln.

The turbid autumn dusk dulled the rich colors of the trees, which paved the road with red and gold. Over the grass was a thin film of mist.

The freshmen in the first Triangle Club trials must have looked into a small audience, some of whom were eating oranges and some of whom seemed to be hiding their faces on the seats in front of them in attitudes of prayer. After three minutes, they would be cut short in the middle of the speeches they had most counted upon to produce a happy impression; the tapping of the President's pencil was the only recognition made of their presence, and it might have been mechanical, so relentless was it. They would stand agape. "That'll do; thank you."

———

Mr. Preston to Stan Dell: "You don't smoke and you don't drink—now, tell me, what vice do you practise? Every young man has some vice. What's yours?"

———

Sam [Shoemaker] told a story about a famous American scientist who was called to give expert evidence in a trial and asked who was the greatest living scientist. He replied, "I am."—They asked him afterwards why he had made that reply. "But man!" he said, "I was under oath."

———

Gauss [in a preceptorial]: "But, Mr. Osborn, does the fact that the man is alone in the woods alter the moral problem any? Would it be all right, for instance, for him to eat mushrooms until he burst? Would that be moral?"

———

Bill Osborn: "It's just been beginning to dawn on me by slow degrees that there are some things which I have both thought about more and understand better than the family!"

———

Mr. Jesse Lynch Williams: "There's just a drop of the old Falernian left." [On a walk with some companion, we had run into the Williamses picnicking in the country.]

———

The lamps streaked the water with yellow zigzags.

———

Walter Hall told about a young radical friend of his who is the son of a professor and ashamed of not being born proletarian. He has grave doubts about going to college and wrote Bernard Shaw, whose disciple he was, to ask him what to do. He told Shaw that he had emulated him in everything, even to becoming a vegetarian. Shaw wrote back a letter in which he intimated that the boy was probably making it unpleasant for everybody and doing good to nobody. The boy thereupon decided that Shaw was a traitor to his class. When the doctor prescribed glasses for him, he refused to wear them, because he said that he might need all the beauty he had when the Revolution should come on, and he wanted to be always prepared.

———

The distant shuffle of the locomotive.

———

Pedantry: The Rise (pronounced like mice) of the Drayma.

———

L.L. was compiling a translation of Aeschylus' *Agamemnon* without having ever read a word of the original. Nor had he read the text of Homer, but was willing to support the unitarian theory with great heat, on the ground that the poet's style seemed uniform in all the translations he had read. "If Pope could translate the *Iliad* without reading Greek, with the help of two translations"—

"But look at what he did to it!"

"Yes, but look what greater and better facilities I have for translating Aeschylus!"

———

Alfred said that Stan never punctuated his life properly; it was full of uncompleted episodes which ended with a dash.

———

The foreign missionary from a small town, who is so earnestly prayed for every Sunday and whose probable pain at prolonged absence from his or her home town is spoken of with so much sympathy, has no doubt found a fierce desire to escape from her situation and surroundings strangely mingled with her zeal to convert the heathen. The intention of converting the people of China or Japan to the manners and morals of a small American town sometimes seems both pathetic and ridiculous; but the truth about it is not so simple as this and not so small.

———

Bill Osborn of Mrs. Dwight Meigs [the pretty and charming wife of the son the Headmaster at Hill]: "She's the most completely ineffectual person in the place.—She's a *real* lady! She's the only one that's a real lady!"

———

"The class-baby was Jewish twins."

———

Teek [T. K. Whipple] said that *Marius the Epicurean* would be a good book if it weren't so badly written. And of the *Lacedaemon* chapter in *Plato and Platonism* that it was "a scream: they were just thugs."

———

The Greek Lyric Poetry Club in a freshman house.

The morning silver came earlier over the roof of Blair.
The ice-decked trees.
The slow curtain of snow sliding down.

———

Frank Glick bickering to Hebe Halsey: "Come Cap and Gown, and learn to know God!"

———

I told Thayer Field that he showed an indifference to beauty in not choosing the Aesthetics course rather than the Sewerage course, when he discovered that the two conflicted. He replied, "But I could have no beauty unless somebody took care of the drainage"—very properly.

———

Alfred Noyes: "They're a witty crew, those Trees. Herbert said to Viola Tree, his daughter, once when he was going away: 'If I should die, Viola, I'll have myself cremated and my ashes put into a golden urn and sent across the sea to you!'—and she said, without batting an eyelash, 'that would be a nasty jar for me, Father!'"

———

[Some Princeton lady]: "I like Mr. Hutton: his bad-breeding isn't so polished as Mr. Matthews'."

———

Bill Mackie in the St. Patrick's Day Parade was dressed in a frock coat and striped trousers, a black coat with a large alpaca collar and a slightly damaged silk hat—apparently the clothes he had bought a year ago for his brother's wedding. He presented the most subtly and ludicrously disreputable appearance I have ever seen, a little too convincingly enhanced by the marks of real debauch in his face; but he made it all right and charming when he smiled and told us that he was impersonating Rolla. [We had just read Musset's poem in one of Gauss's courses.]

———

Mr. Mac asked Bill Mackie how good Marshall was in the Aesthetics course: "Oh, he's a nice clean old man!"

———

Luke Miller: "It's a pity that the whale has swallowed up not only Jonah but all the rest of the book, too—and that's another reason why the element of the supernatural does more harm to the Bible than good—because it becomes unduly important in some people's minds—in just that fashion, don't you see?"

[One of the last convulsions of Presbyterian fundamentalism at Princeton was the dismissal of Luke Miller, who had published a book on the historical Jesus, which had been brought to the attention of the trustees. I made a point of reading this book, which could today hardly be thought by anybody to contain anything very subversive, and I defended Miller in the *Lit*. I took the second half of a course of his in Old Testament literature, but never read the first part of the Bible till I studied Hebrew years later.

When I speak of "Princeton" above, I mean the University, not the Seminary. They had then no official connection, and when I bicycled past the Seminary in spring, I used to avert my eyes from its dark and dingy-looking building, which conveyed to me a menace from the past, from my Grandmother Wilson's Sunday morning sessions and the lack of amenity of her house. In Princeton, almost everything was amenity: green campus, flowering shrubs, new buildings with Gothic fancywork, agreeable eating clubs, undergraduate elegance and gaiety. When I had to spend the winter there in 1952–53, I for the first time explored the Seminary, took a course in beginner's Hebrew and looked up my grandfather's narrow room in one of the steep-staired and tarnished old buildings. I could see from the bulletin board how, New Yorker although he was and graduated from Amherst, he had landed in his Shrewsbury church. The notices were still being posted of openings for New Jersey pastorates.]

———

Noel [Robinson] said that Stan, who was standing on the kerb, talking to some people in an automobile with his head thrust inside, looked like a rat caught in a trap.

———

Early May: The trees were freshly green and hardly filled in with leaves. There was a light film of mist in the long grass. A great glimpse of bright pink came through the delicate gray draperies of the sky. . . . The pink disappeared and the gray became dull. The pipings and chatterings of the birds in the hedges and meadows seemed a little hushed. The mist thickened in the long grass and, mounting, shut away the hills and roads beyond until it blent with the sky and became indistinguishable from it.

———

Mr. Osborn has a slight but almost perpetual irony of manner; and a slight weariness as if it made one a little tired to be always so prosperous and capable and clever and well-informed.

[Wilton Lloyd-Smith]: "—And when Bill comes back from Japan or somewhere, he simply walks in some day when they're having tea and they say 'Hello, Bill!' and he says 'Hello, Mother,' and they ask how he liked Japan and he says, 'They ought to plant a lot more grain on the sides of Fujiyama!' "

———

Jests from the Students' Theater vaudeville described by Stew Link as "six howling harlots in red tights": A man went into a hotel and said "give me a room"; they gave him a room, and in a few minutes he came runnin' downstairs with a white face. The hotel keeper says, "What's the matter?" "What's the matter?" says the fellow, "Do you know what I seen?" "What?" says the fellow at the desk. "Why, I went into the room and seen the bed-bugs draggin' the bed around the room; that's what I seen!" "Aw, hell! what didja expect, a bull-fight?"

One performer offers another a chair, "Be cheated. Oh, I mean, be 'seated.' "

———

When Earl Osborn came back from abroad, he called on Edgar Woodman, who didn't recognize him at first. After they had stared blankly at one another for a moment, Woodman suddenly remarked, "Oh! I didn't recognize you with your hat on."

"I'll take it off, then," replied Earl, laying it on the table.

———

It began to rain in spite of the late silver sunlight behind Holder Tower, and we saw the fine silver sheen playing against the gray stone and the green trees.

————

René [the son of André and Adelaide Champollion] insisted upon bringing his turtle to Seabright by boat, because he said that the railroad train "jurgled" the water all up.

————

Frank Walls spoke of the New York Public Library as being "in many ways so pathetic." Ray Cox afterwards called Walls "an emasculated Rabelais."

————

Professor William Lyon Phelps: "Ah, Mrs. Simpson [the mother of Kenneth Simpson], I suppose you know that your son is the uncrowned king of the campus?"
Mrs. Simpson: "Why uncrowned, Professor Phelps?"
Professor Phelps speechless.
It was afterwards suggested that he might have retorted, "Oh, Mrs. Simpson, there is more than one way of crowning a man at Yale, you know."

————

Bill Mackie, when he was rooming with Frank Pemberton, used to invent a pretext for getting drunk every night. He would sometimes be celebrating the Feast of St. Ursula, but Satyrs' Day was the commonest festivity.

————

Ebe Faber, asked if he were hungry: "Oh, if sufficiently cajoled, I might, be induced to inhale a prune."

He talked of "Old Ocean." "Maybe I'm not going to jump into that stuff!" [This was at Seabright.]

———

M. Moreau, at the Gausses'. He was a slight man with an entirely intellectual face. He was what the French call "*spirituel.*" He had fought and lost a kneecap; his wife had been a nurse in the hospital. The stupid cruelty of the Germans amused him; there was not a hint in anything he said that he returned their own solemn hatred. His brother was now a German prisoner and was allowed to do nothing to distract his mind during the endless and maddening waiting of captivity. And he had been forced to buy up all of some tobacco which had been stolen by the Germans—"Oh, it is too amusing!"—before he could buy the regular tobacco which was on sale at the store. But, worst of all, they wouldn't let him read.—Gauss shuddered: "Oh, that's terrible torture!"—M. Moreau himself had been in a battle where you could have crossed a river on the bodies of the dead, and the stream was dark with blood. And at one time the firing became so heavy that the living remnant of a regiment were ordered to save their lives in a wood where the wounded and dying had already been brought. In a short time, they came out again and were content to expose themselves to the fire. "But the young boys! They were the worst in the hospital. One could do nothing with them! Young boys of fifteen and sixteen. They would behave so, when the doctor was dressing their wounds—cursing and crying and shouting. One could get no sleep!"

———

Bill Jutte [he was the brother of one of the young Knoxes' wives] expounded unrepresentational art to us for a whole evening. He had studied under Sargent Kendall for a year at Yale], but, during the summer, was converted by Willard Huntington Wright's book and a clique of Cubists, Futurists, etc., so that it was impossible for him to go on learning "illustration" any more. Cézanne was "a great transitional genius"; Rembrandt a "nay-sayer." He had read a book of selections from Nietzsche, too, and considered him "the greatest mind that he knew anything about," and he had "thrown over Plato." We had rather an awful time with Platonism this summer. [I was then reading Plato with enthusiasm.] He had intended to go to the Princeton Graduate School, but was outraged when he discovered that the only course which included Nietzsche spent only one month on him and that the man who was giving it considered Schopenhauer more important. Also, H. C. Butler [of the Princeton Graduate School] had written that "since Mr. Jutte seemed to be interested not in the art of the past but in the art of the future, and since they were not clairvoyants, they did not see how they were going to be able to satisfy him!" To this Bill returned a violent letter. "It's significant that they put Art in the same department with Archæology!" But now the family stocks in Mexico had gone down, and he had only money enough to live ten weeks, so he supposed he might as well go into real estate, although it was thoroughly materialistic, because he knew that he was not big enough to be one of the pioneers in the great new movement, and that the most he could hope to do might be to join in when the thing had been developed scientifically.

———

Amy Lowell at Princeton: Mrs. Gerould offered her a cigarette. "I don't smoke cigarettes, woman! I smoke cigars!" Mrs. Gerould suggested that a cigar could easily be got. "Oh, no! Don't bother! You know I'm just like a man about tobacco: I can take it or leave it alone; it doesn't make any difference.—Let me tell you about Max Bodenheim. He's a little Jew, you know, dirty, very dirty, I met him and invited him to dinner. Well, he intimated that he wasn't exactly the kind of person one invited to dinner, but I said: 'Oh, never mind! We're all poets together. Come on.' And wouldn't you know he'd be just the kind of person to come at six when I'd invited him for seven?—Well, I'm very fond of dogs you know. Have kennels, breed them, in fact. Savage brutes they are, too. And so about dinner-time I always send a couple of servants out in the yard to protect the guests. But Max came too early and the dogs flew at him. Well, we heard all this rumpus and went out and found poor Max backed up against a tree with the dogs snapping at him. Well, when we got him inside, he was lacerated, just lacerated. We had to take off his clothes and bandage him up!" She had a large pocket in the back of her loosely-fitting skirt, and in it she carried handkerchiefs, money and, no doubt, poems. When Mr. Mac paid her—she is very rich, but refuses to read anywhere unless she is paid—she made a wry face: "Nasty bit this! I hate it!," and thrust the check into her pocket. When Mr. Mac was seeing her off, he said: "Miss Lowell, this has been great. I wish I could give you our thanks in some subtler way, but I can't say any more than that." She replied: "Why, man! I don't want it any other way; I like it just the way you give it to me."

[In London, in 1914, I had attended a reading by Rupert Brooke in Harold Munroe's Poetry Bookshop. He was a handsome young man, but extremely feminine, and his voice was almost inaudible. A woman in a back row, with a voice of the utmost distinctness and vigor, said, "Can't you read louder?" "Can't you hear me?" "Not a word!" It was only many years later that I learned from some literary memoir that the lady had been Amy Lowell.]

———

A freshman friend of Mr. Mac's found himself somewhat at a loss among his class. He had been brought up in France and sent to school at Winchester, which he hated. He demanded to be sent to an American University and, accordingly, came to Princeton, where he was greatly chagrined to find himself rooming in a freshman boarding-house with the son of an undertaker from Columbus, Ohio. He would bewail his fate bitterly to Mr. Mac: "And the worst of it is that he talks all the time about his father's ghastly trade. Now, this is the sort of thing I have to listen to." It seemed that there had been a motor accident in Columbus. Two men had been killed. "They sent for my father and wanted to have a service right away in a church near-by, so he took the corpse and fixed it up in the coffin and then started in to hold the service—but, just before, the dead man's daughter came down to have a look at the body, and when she seen it, she said, 'Why this isn't father!' And sure enough, they got the wrong corpse. Well, the service was just about to begin, but father hustled up and took out the corpse he'd got by mistake and propped it up against a tree outside the church and ran down the road and got the right corpse." It appears that the Ohio convention demands that every male corpse be buried in a dress suit. So the exchange of bodies was made particularly easy by detaching the false dress front—coat, vest, shirt, tie, all in one piece—from the wrong one and clapping it on to the right one. "Well, they hustled him right into the church, before it was time for the mourners to come around and look at him and, by the time they did come around, why, he was there all right!" The foreign-bred fellow was known to his classmates as "the Duke."

———

The great 1916 baseball victory over Yale at commencement. At the turning-point of the contest, a blue balloon was released to symbolize the fact that Yale was up in the air. Alumni disguised as Uncle Sam did wild dances on the roof of the field house. Tremendous exhilaration.

———

[One of the straight chairs in my study collapsed—not by breaking down, going to pieces, but by slowly flattening out as if it were a steamer-chair. I put it facing my Morris chair and would invite visitors to sit down in it and then watch it flattening out. I at last decided that my fun was perhaps a little ignoble and put the chair away. I thus had the double satisfaction of amusing myself at other people's expense and enjoying the virtuous assurance of behaving like a decent fellow.]

[In the spring of my last year at Princeton, I would be sitting in my Morris chair reading and suddenly have an emission—something which hitherto had only occurred in my sleep. I was naïve enough to go to a doctor, who told me not to worry. The Puritanism of the Hill School had imposed itself to this extent. It was not that I had not longed for women; but I was too shy with proper young girls who were only just learning to be improper, and I could not imagine marrying the kind of conventional girl that my friends almost invariably married as soon as they got out of college and from whom they were later on, in the twenties, likely to get divorced. I never went to dances, since I had never been able to learn to dance. I see that, in the class book of 1916, I got eight votes as "most

likely bachelor." My feminine ideal at this time was not
the kind of girl that I saw at the proms, but one of those
lively and slender brunettes, capable of serious interests,
for whom the heroes of H. G. Wells abandoned their
passive wives. When I stayed in hotels, I would dream of
amours with complaisant chambermaids, but I would not
have had the least idea how to initiate one. I was also a
non-drinker at Princeton, except for a glass of champagne
once a year at a club banquet, and my father was rather
surprised when, at the age he had stipulated, twenty-one,
I said that I did not want to smoke. I had tried it, and I
could not see anything in it. I decided that it was one of
the things that people felt they ought to do because
everybody else did them. I still regard smoking—at least,
cigarettes—as a dirty and unpleasant habit. The "sub-
limation," however, that resulted from my prolonged
period of sexual abstinence, though it left me at first inept
with women, was rewardingly compensated by an in-
tensified study of the classics which was to stand me in
good stead.

At Princeton, one evening in the days when we were
still hanging around after graduation, John Bishop, Scott
Fitzgerald, Alec McKaig and I were walking on Nassau
Street. Two girls passed us. Alec said, "They're hookers!"
I had not known we had hookers in Princeton, and, in
fact, had never heard the word before. John and Alec
went off with the girls, while Scott and I took a walk
down the hill to the lake. "That's one thing," exclaimed
Scott, "that Fitzgerald's never done!" We talked about
other matters.]

Plattsburgh
Summer of 1916

[We often became restless at Princeton in our junior year, and sometimes talked about leaving. The American four years of college, with long idle vacations, was far too much. Today one would take a job, but we never thought of anything but travelling. By the time I had graduated, I was so eager for something more active, something closer to contemporary reality, that I went to one of those Plattsburgh camps which, although the United States was not yet at war, had been set up, as part of the "preparedness" program, for training for possible eventual service. This experience I found very boring, and it completely convinced me that I could never be an officer, and that I did not want to be a soldier. The only pleasant things I remember about it were my talks with Edgar Woodman and Charley Walker, who were there at the same time; the drinking of cold milk at the end of one of our tedious and dusty hikes along the Peru road; and Anatole France's *Thaïs*, the only book I had time for reading. Emerging from college, I was entirely unable to get on with ordinary people—a condition which was later cured by two years as an enlisted man in the army—and I remember with what gratification I discovered that one of my tent-mates was a Princeton man who had once published poems in the *Lit*. One evening I ate in a restaurant with a curious character who I had found had some smattering of culture. When we sat down he said, "Let's have some beer!"; then, "Let's have some Meyerbeer!" and went to a piano and began to play. This was one of the few things that amused me at Plattsburgh.]

———

At Plattsburgh, Bradley [a tent-mate] spoke about his being accustomed to wake up early at home, because "the kids came boilin' up every morning about half-past six."

———

Pierce at Plattsburgh used to inform his squad that he had to be severe with them, because he was used to being severe. "Why, in this position where I am, if a man makes a mistake, he's sent to me and I warn him. If he makes another mistake, a word from me and out he goes."

———

At Plattsburgh, poor little Mr. Stone, capable clerk in the War Department and put in the tent with what he regarded as a lot of impossible Jews, used to come to Edgar Woodman's tent and complain sadly: "I like to come in here. There's one thing about it here. You're all real gentlemen, all real gentlemen here." The amiable yokels and small shop-keepers were kind to him, especially after this.

———

Edgar [Woodman] qualified for rapid fire: "God! when they came and told me that, I was mad enough to have bit a man in two!"

———

"Does the gun kick any harder at 800 yards than it does
at 600?"

———

[My experience on the rifle range demonstrated my
unfitness for military service. My father, at Talcottville,
had tried to teach me to shoot, but I had not wanted to
learn. I have never been at home with firearms, and I did
not want to kill birds and animals. I was so nervous on
the Plattsburgh rifle range that I don't think I ever hit the
target. The man who supervised this exercise was a little
ex-Rhodes scholar with glasses who had acquired a British
accent. When I had finished this fiasco, I was much annoyed at hearing him say in the tones of a British officer:
"Just a case of funk!"]

My father in his college club: second from the left in the back row.

The board of the *Hill School Record* in 1911: in front, reading from left to right, Henry Gray, Walker M. Ellis, W. Stanley Dell; back row, Reginald Orcutt, Robert Mc-Lean, Frank Tuttle, Sprague Coolidge, E.W.

The board of the *Nassau Literary Magazine* in 1915: in front, reading from left to right, Robert Hampton, Jr., Maurice Pate, George B. Logan, Jr., E.W., James J. Swofford, Jr.; back row, Isadore Kaufman, Hamilton Fish Armstrong, John Peale Bishop, Kirk Moore, John Temple Graves, Jr., Alexander L. McKaig, Charles Richardson, Jr.

A pyramid at Mount Tom, near Washington, Connecticut: bottom, middle and right, Arthur and Robert Jackson; second tier, right, E. Sterling Carter; top, E.W.

E.W. in uniform, still in camp at Detroit.

Roy C. Gamble in the Army.

Top left: E.W.

Top right: W. Stanley Dell, 1916.

Bottom left: William Adams Brown, Jr.

Bottom right: Charles Rumford Walker.

John Peale Bishop, about 1922.

New York
1916–1917

[I went to live in New York, after Plattsburgh, in an apartment with three of my Yale friends: Larry Noyes, David Hamilton and Morris Belknap. I had been looking for a job and had called on many newspaper offices with letters, but never found any encouragement. At last, my father went to the owner of the New York *Evening Sun*, who lived at Rumson, and persuaded him to arrange for me a reporter's job at $15 a week. My father had told me that when I got out of college—though I had up to then had all the money I wanted for theaters, travel and books —I should have to earn my own living: he would not give me a cent. He did not quite carry out this threat; but it is actually true that, with my three companions, I managed to live very well on little more than the $15 I made. We had a small apartment on West Eighth Street, in a building which no longer exists, in the block between Fifth and Sixth Avenues, and we kept a Chinese servant, who, on his days off, was replaced by another Chinese. We often had people to dinner. The Gonfarone was across the street, where we occasionally went for mild dissipation. The saloon in which John Masefield had worked was across the street to the right. That region was then badly lighted, and we could sometimes look out on shootings and fights that seemed to center about this saloon. We would take long walks downtown in the snow at night. Tom Paine's little house was still standing, and St. John's Chapel in Varick Street. David Hamilton and Morris Belknap went to the Art Students' League; Larry Noyes to an architect's office. I rose every morning at four o'clock and took a street-car to the *Evening Sun,* where I drowsed on my desk, read the papers and was occasionally sent out on some very small assignment. When I returned in the afternoon, I would go to sleep on the couch in front of our coal grate and wake up feeling very stuffy.]

Mr. Dieuaide [City Editor] of the *Evening Sun,* receiving me after an examination of Mr. Perry's letter: "Well, Mr. Wilson, I've a letter here from Mr. Perry to tell me what a fine young man ye are."

[He was a droll little man that I liked. In spite of his French name, I always thought of him as Irish.]

Dieuaide: "Well, Mr. Wilson, go up and see your friends at the Astor Hotel this morning and see if ye can't stir one o' them up to murder another."

[On one of my first assignments, I was sent to Coenties Slip to find out about I forget what petty accident. At that period, I was much too shy to be any good as a reporter, and from the people standing around, I could get no clear account of what had happened. It was the first time I was made to realize how uncertain human testimony is.

On another occasion, I was sent to report on a suicide —a girl who had killed herself in a miserable room. It seemed clear that she had been a prostitute. The policeman I found there had drawn this conclusion: "A furnished room and nothing on under her dress."

The *Evening Sun* had once been a distinguished paper, but it had ceased to be so in my time. It had only one good feature: Don Marquis. The writer of the editorials was an Irishman named Lubie. He had opaque but pugnacious blue eyes, and was always in a cold fury—in which state of mind he wrote. I was invited to try my hand at turning out something about the revolt against the clubs at Princeton. When Lubie read what I had written, he called me in and said, "You don't want to write like Dr. Johnson." I said that I should be very glad to be able to write like Dr. Johnson. I was never asked to do anything of the kind again. But it was not so much Dr. Johnson that impeded my acquiring a journalistic style as my infatuation with Flaubert. I could not write about any subject without striving for the well-modelled sentence and the impassive Flaubertian irony, so I never made anything sound exciting.]

———

St. John's Chapel: The broken panes between the ribs of the fanlights make them look like cobwebs clotted with dust.

———

The poor graceful lady who stands all day among the formidable marbles of the Pulitzer fountain.

———

There were a few motors and cabs in Central Park. For all the bleakness of the day, there was pale green grass behind the blackened bushes and the afterglow of April was yet strong enough to make the park lamps look as slight as candles.

———

Beautiful as they are, Pennell's pictures of the manufacture of munitions can never be as beautiful as his pictures of the Greek temples.

————

Princeton was a kind of prelude before the action of the opera had begun, when the leitmotifs which were to dominate the rest of the performance were quietly sounded, as if in play.

————

Stan Dell (returned from the American Ambulance): "Well, my peregrinations seem to have done surprisingly little for me. At first you're all cut up at the sight of the wounded, but you soon get used to it. Nothing gets exhausted so quickly as human sympathy."

————

The red and yellow tulips flare like flame from the grass; the bending cyclamen, as graceful as butterflies.

————

The old iron fence on the north side of Washington Square flowers into flat iron chrysanthemums.

————

The minister at Trinity Church [later Bishop Manning] said that the chief thing at the great Episcopalian Conference would be not the changes in church government and in the prayer-book and in the divorce law—important as these things were. No, it was not these matters about which we should feel most concern and pray most earnestly. It was as to whether the delegates would come to the conclusion that the Episcopal Church was the one true church. "Because if it is not—why, then, one man's guess is just as good as another's." He preached on Angels, for the reality of which he pointed out that we had, in both the Old and New Testaments, abundant evidence, and urged the congregation to imitate the conduct of the Angels.

———

[Coming back to New York from Long Island]: At first we had only the stars and the black, through which the low white fences slid along the road. Then there came a gray glow in the East, above which was set Jupiter (?), clear and solitary. In half an hour, the hills were rimmed with dim pink, and Jupiter began to fade out in a chill radiance that made the street lights paste. We passed trucks drawn slowly by ponderous horses, and when we came to towns, we saw that the saloons were illuminated. As we went over the Queensboro Bridge, the factories and main streets and gas tanks looked strange in the obscure dawn and the blue of the water struck a curiously clear note. We looked back and saw that all the sky was suddenly suffused with lucid yellow.—And before we were over the bridge, we had met the sour smells of the city. Fifth Avenue was as gray and calm as a street in an old college town.

———

One of the city managers, after waiting for a very short informal speech by Mayor Mitchel in a waiting room at City Hall: "There was as much ceremony about that there reception room as if it'd been a European court!"

———

"A valuable experience," "good experience," an American euphemism for the drudgery of money-getting.

———

"Oh, but his face lights up when he smiles!"

———

The woodchucks rolling around the fields like fat little puppies—like great rats.

———

Weehawken ferry: the broad gray of sky and river, so much alike that the horizon was scarcely visible. It would have been dismal but for the white that set it off, the foam and smoke of the tugs and ferry boats, the broken ice that lined the shores and the graceful wings of the gulls which make the meanest harbors strange and fair.

———

Merle Ganz, thrown into jail for leading a Delegation of Women from the East Side to City Hall in a demand for food and a protest against the high cost of living: "I'm used to being in jail. But there's a difference: no forcible feeding this time. It's only the honest people who never break the laws who can starve. The authorities always see to it that the wrongdoers get plenty to eat."

———

Movie ad on the East Side: "A grin and a gasp in every picture."

———

Wisehart: "Billy Sunday slouches around the house in a bathrobe, scowling, looks as if he ought to have a set of jimmies somewhere.—When the meeting was going on, you could hear the click of the money machine off in the next room, separating the coins and sorting them out like golden feces—but they didn't notice it, you know."

"Elihu Root tries to lash the administration with molasses."

[Karl Wisehart became my chief friend in the *Evening Sun* office. He was amusing and idealistic, and had serious literary ambitions.]

———

Abraham Lincoln: It is characteristic of America that it should be always clamoring about the commonness of one of its greatest gentlemen and parading the dismal and dirty background of his youth—about which the man himself did not boast and seldom spoke—as something to be proud of, instead of feeling shame for their country that human beings there could be brought so low.

———

The pansies with quaint little faces like kittens.

———

The Hackensack marshes from the train: a flat waste of dead reeds, strung across with telegraph poles and bordered by insignificant hills.

———

"F——— M——— is buttered on both sides."

———

Bill Jutte of somebody: "The soul of a Cossack in the body of a turtle!"

Ray Cox of Bill Jutte: "That Brooks Brothers Caveman!"

Bill Jutte of Ray Cox: "His mother's the kind of woman who reads about six French novels a week and thinks that the person who has the most manners is the greatest gentleman; but his father's absolutely illiterate. Oh, a Master Plumber!"

———

Seymour [at the copy desk during my lobster shift], to the copy boy, when the cat jumped on to the copy desk: "Here take her away. Handle her tenderly—dirty as hell! Spreading anthrax right and left!"

———

Houses: in the suburbs of Brooklyn, among the plain little lines of houses all exactly alike, one faded row with a pathetic pretension to the decorative: two tiny stories and a scant porch, with roof upheld by thin Corinthian columns of wood.

On Academy Street, Jersey City: A large square wooden structure divided into about six houses; a façade latticed with the iron scrolls which supply railings to a porch, a balcony above the second story and a series of little balconies under each of the windows of the third story. Fantastic starry designs in yellow and black shingles; a tiny terrace dropping to the street and protected by an iron fence; the slope decorated by plaques of dirty snow and fragments of childrens' toys; a flat roof fenced with another iron railing.

———

St. John's Chapel, Varick St.: A dead husk of the life of the old downtown; it rears its brown bulk, fine with the tone of age, decrepit but prouder and more dignified than the firmer and solider structures, the freight yards and factories, that surround it. The steps and the floor of the portico have been destroyed to make room for the new subway, and the splendid pillars rear their tarnished foliation straight from the dirt of the road. The small square panes of the arched windows have been broken. The first tiers of the spire, which diminish toward the top, have begun to lurch a little. The hands are gone from the obliterated clock-face, and the bell is silent.

Beside the door, inaccessible with its steps gone, is a sign which says: "Seats free. St. John's Chapel, Trinity Parish." Between the Central Railroad Terminal Freight Yards and the Sixth Avenue Elevated, it surveys the slums and has still enough life to challenge the encroachments of mean dwellings and the faceless graceless structures of manufacture and commerce, with a kind of desperate and decaying pride.

———

—That God who sends down His punishment upon the just and the unjust alike.

———

Dick Cleveland said that the last word was said about Princeton in war-time when someone wrote on the bulletin board in the University Store: "The old college life is all shot to hell."

———

Early May: the trees are greenish lemon with buds and the dandelions stud the grass with a constellation of little suns.

———

The silver gulls, with wings taut like bows, weave the air in soft curves and slide in spirals to the water.

———

May, 1917.
  "In case the worst may happen!"
  "It will. So why worry?"

———

The Palisades shaggy and black, crested with leafless
bristles of trees. In the Hudson, a yellow sand-spit fringed
with gulls.

———

One sat on a little concrete terrace that ended in turf
and felt as if one were occupying an orchestra seat for a
vast spectacle which had been set for members of the
[Rumson] Country Club alone. The boundaries of the
polo field striped the green, which was powdered with
dandelions, and, beyond lay the pale blue strip of river
with its further shore like a lath; the summer cottages
along it notched the gray-blue sky, which, with its dim
clouds and the flickering midges of birds that twittered
remotely, made the whole flat landscape infinitely spa-
cious and calm.

———

May: Even the most beautiful parts of Washington
were tarnished and blunted by the stagnant weather.

The Senate has all the dignity of a dentists' conference. [I do not know quite why dentistry was regarded as an inferior profession. Its status has changed
since. The senators seemed to me a shoddy lot.]

———

Alfred said that Stan was the "living aposiopesis."

———

Long Island: the sandy shadowed roads; the long white old farmhouses and the little ones whose long roofs sloped down so far that in front there is only room for one row of windows; the old lands that even the modest families have owned for centuries; the hills and fields so lightly and drily sketched in; and the little harbors, so smooth and blue and edged with silver by the sun on their tiny crystal surf, where the white boats ride at anchor and the sail-boats tilt like quills in inkwells and the children swim all day in the stinging cold water.

————

The dandelions gone to seed filled the grass with little globes of mist. The woods were clouded with dogwood: late May.

————

Jenny [our maid in Red Bank] sick at home: "I swim in holy water."

————

Sandy: "Nature is a luxury these days."

————

July 31, 1917. New York: One perspires profusely even sitting still.—The river looks pale and stagnant, and the opposite shore is like lead.

————

Karl Wisehart, after a diatribe against *Hearst's Magazine*: "I'm going to change all this!"

————

Ralph [Hinchman], when he first became engaged, bubbled over with high spirits. When Mr. and Mrs. Hinchman played double Canfield, which usually used to annoy him, he remarked: "I don't know why it is, but I don't seem to mind your playing that game tonight!"

Mrs. Hinchman told of the New England snob who broke off the feather on her hat in a drug-store, and the girl behind the counter helped her to put it back again. Afterwards, when Mrs. H. commiserated with her and remarked that it had been nice of the girl to take so much trouble, the woman replied: "Oh, well: it must have given her pleasure to help a lady, because I *am* a lady, you know!"

Colloquial

berry (jewel)
hoy, bull [nonsense]
knock-down-and-drag-out

Princeton

Well, so this is Paris!
Well, I guess we'll have to hand him the brown derby.
I guess he gets the lady's bicycle.

a jitney genius (a phrase of Don Marquis's)
jitney bus
The Jitney Philosophers or Nickel Platonism (F. P. Adams)
rook, rooked
have a heart!
"little small" (Southern)
rave about; wild about (girls' college)
told him where to get off
You could have crowned me with a brick, and I

wouldn't have noticed!

He certainly is a king

off that stuff

dungeoning (boozing with the new section at club elections)

a knockout

Extract from Bill Osborn's notes on Noyes: "Browning was fond of knock-out rhymes."

Vassar: catting, crush

lil toad-frawg (Southern)

Arthur Jackson: Ger-er (Goya). [My friend Arthur Jackson was not from Brooklyn, but his accent had in common with the Brooklyn accent that he interchanged the sounds of *oi* and *ir* or *er*. Sandy had told me of a schoolmate of his who had this accent and was compelled by the other boys to recite for their amusement: "The little boid sat on the koib and choiped and choiped and choiped and choiped."]

Cox: Queen of the baked apple school.

Princeton, 1917

nudo, absolute zero.

a good line

godawful

pulled a bone

D. W. "Her father comes around and helldevils her."

———

The New York Horse Show: The brown, white-rimmed lawn of the arena, studded with four red-coated, top-hatted grooms, roofed with red and white stripes of bunting and illuminated by hanging lamps, subdued by festoons of green vines. The twinkling legs of the ponies, the rocking canter, the mild and desultory interest of the scattered audience, the earnest ladies in top-hats and black coats, the chestnut trotters polished and moulded like fine bronze. The noiseless panorama broken only by languid and sporadic clapping or by the stalking judge's shout to "go slower, please!" The tandems that rear and entangle themselves. [I had gone to this for the paper.]

———

[Description for a story]: Fifth Avenue was full of sun when his car took its place in the north-bound strand of the double current of traffic. At his side were taxis half uncovered, as a concession to the comfort of the fare, shouldering green buses that bore a bright-hatted burden high above the roofs of the rest; private motors, flashing white stars from their polished guards and lamps; sober limousines that one felt it an impertinence to look into; strangely shaped tonneaus of red or yellow or maroon, in which young ladies no less bright-hued than they, with hats slanted as incisively as a fine draughtsman's line, wrenched at the wheel, barked with harsh horns and talked vivaciously to the hatless young men at their sides; and occasionally a victoria, outmoded but distinguished, or an old-fashioned hansom, like a black lacquer palanquin, in which a pretty girl and a straw-hatted youth or a father on vacation with children to amuse, would not even close the little doors of the apron between themselves and the spring.

———

[Morris Belknap, at the Art Students' League, studied under Kenneth Hayes-Miller and sometimes brought him to dinner. I was not then aware that he was one of the children of John Humphrey Noyes's Oneida Community, not far from Talcottville, where I afterwards got to know these families. He was not very satisfactory as an artist, though his paintings were not like anyone else's: a thin scholarly man himself, he liked to paint buxom rather blowsy women, who always looked, however, as if they were made of aluminum. But he was said to be a stimulating teacher and was certainly an interesting talker. I had first read about psychoanalysis in a magazine article by Max Eastman, and I now heard more about it from Hayes-Miller. It did not disturb me much. I had already once had a dream about going to bed with my mother, and I had noted, with interest, in *Oedipus* that Sophocles speaks of dreams of this kind. I had also had a childhood dream that I saw my father in the kitchen in his maroon dressing gown—where he liked to go to talk to the servants—sharpening a carving knife in order to kill us all, and I was glad to find that such dreams were being investigated. But when Hayes-Miller told a story about a Freudian who said to a friend, when the latter had thrown something into the waste basket: "You threw away a thought," it occurred to me that it might be uncomfortable to be subjected to this kind of observation.]

———

[Mrs. Knox, whose income was now reduced—I suppose, on account of the war—was not able to keep up her mansion and had rented a house on the river at Red Bank. André, who had been born in Paris, became in his twenties an American citizen; but when the war broke out, he returned to France and enlisted as a private. A volume of his letters to a friend was privately printed in 1915. They show that he had had many doubts as to the wisdom of his having done this.

"So far," he writes to this friend, "I have escaped being sent to the front, and frankly confess that I am getting less and less enthusiastic about the idea—I do not feel that I owe France the sacrificing of my life, and never did for that matter. The job of interpreter is the one I expected to get, and hoped for when I left America. I do not suppose that I should indulge in this treasonable talk, but my patience with the country I am trying to help out is damned nigh exhausted. I do not think that the French are ungrateful or shirkers; I have had many individual proofs of the contrary. But they are so infernally tied down by routine, by the old-fashioned way of doing everything. They are so hopelessly unprogressive in many ways that in their army life they give you the impression of being worse than they are. This is shown also in the French school life. Because the duty is an unpleasant one, to the French mind it must be made thoroughly unpleasant and cannot be relieved by any cheerful or pleasant features. Instead of drilling soldiers day after day, month after month, in the same irksome way; instead of making the men do nothing but unpleasant jobs unrelieved by any pleasures,—for God's sake, why the devil don't they give them a football twice a week and let them choose up sides and play soccer? It would develop their bodily faculties a great deal more and be infinitely better for their 'morale.' The English have long ago found out these things and so have we Americans. I never realized until lately how foreign, to my way of life, was the French point of view. Perhaps in a few weeks I may get the job I am hoping for; but in the meantime I feel poorly rewarded for the sacrifice I have made. . . .

"Personally I have lost all interest in the accursed struggle except to hope that it ends soon. Every man in every army engaged in this war I bet feels the same by now.—First and most important, a prompt ending, with a whole skin. Secondly and far less to the point, the terms of peace."

He was sent to the front in March and was killed at Bois-le-Prêtre in April. Adelaide had gone over to be near him in his training camp at Sens, and she was now, under a terrible emotional strain, back living again with her family. I hated to see the twitching movements, which her dignity could not control, during the cocktail conversations that went on very much as before. She later came to live in New York, and I invited her to dinner with us. She demurred: "You don't want an old crow like me!" She was thinking of her black widow's dress, so incongruous with her youth and high spirit. But she came to dinner, and, as usual, my admiration made me clumsy. When she was leaving and I went downstairs with her, we talked of my father's condition, and I said something that implied disapproval of his lack of consideration for my mother. It was, ineptly and indirectly, a kind of tribute to Adelaide, for whose suffering I felt such solicitude.]

The Army
1917–1919

[When war was declared, I did not know what to do. I did not want to be drafted, but unless I enlisted, I should be. Most of my friends were training to be officers. They did this as a matter of course; but I knew I could never be an officer and had little or no enthusiasm for the war. The most painful moments of my life have been due to indecision. I usually know exactly what I want to do, and it has been only when I could not make up my mind that I have really gone to pieces. But David Hamilton wrote me from Detroit that he was enlisting in a hospital unit and suggested that I might come out there and do the same. Base Hospital 36 went into camp on the fairgrounds in September, but we were not sent to France till November. These weeks were incredibly boring. I was to remain in the army almost two years—I enlisted in August, 1917, and was not mustered out till July, 1919.]

———

Blanchard's laughter was like the silly incessant yapping of a pup.

State Fair, Detroit: The rockets bloomed against the

black in monstrous flowers that would float for a moment and then fade.

The aeroplane was seen high up under the blue dome, like a fly on a ceiling.

Along the Mile Road, when we came from Grosse Pointe in the morning, the straw-cocks streaked the yellow meadows to the west and when we returned in the late afternoon the shadows lay toward the east.

I asked Sergeant Baker in the recreation tent what day of the month it was. He was brooding morosely with head in his hands—presumably upon his long weeks of work as director of the latrine-cleaning. "I don't know," he answered, and then after a long silence: "I don't know how long I been dead."

———

[At the fairgrounds, I had a good deal of time on my hands, so wrote a good deal of verse. I feel apologetic toward the reader for including a few of my juvenile poems, but they are part of the record, too. My broodings were expressed in verse.]

September, 1917

I

A second autumn since that sharpest day
When all the Princeton bells had ceased to sound,
And, as I looked, before I turned away,
The sunny street was like a sudden wound
And empty night hung heavy o'er the ground
Where first, beside a far forgotten shrine,
The gods of Hellas and of France I found,
And read of Dante, made through love divine;

Where first I came to know what high place might be
    mine.

II

And now September makes the autumns four
Since in the London streets I wandered late
And saw the silly mob go mad for war,
And, knowing not what powers wrote its fate,
Learned only to contemn alike its hate
And gross desires that beer and shouting fed.
Ironic lesson! I had but to wait
Four autumns ere its voice struck Princeton dead;
And I were glad of that old grief in this dull dread.

III

Meanwhile I watched the faces, merry and kind,
That talked and laughed with me and took their flight
And, laughing, left the bitter life behind
Where there is neither learning, art nor light;
And the bright walls of friends shut from my sight
The streets of wretched towns, forever mean,
(For all the sun can never make them bright
And all the rain can never make them clean,)
Till sometimes friendly walls seemed but a flimsy screen.

IV

Ah! you with whom I used to jest and sing,
Adrift in a boat beneath the stardecked sky,
I sat among you, sad and wondering
That ever song should cease or laughter die,
And, standing on your hilltop, clear and high,
(Now the last day our freest youth fulfils;
Nor did we mark how swift the summers fly),
See the last sunset strewn along the hills
In broken gold and rose its splendid breaking spills.

V

Gold we have spent and roses that are dead!
Ah, pardon me! most merry and most kind,
Beneath whose roof I soothed a troubled head,
And do not think me hard or think me blind,
Because, upon your hills, I could not find,
Among your loves and ways of life, my own,
But searched afar with eager restless mind.
Your laughter dies but still I search alone
For that great oldest thing that I have ever known.

VI

How should your love be mine? how should your mirth
Be mine, whose ship, from bitter tempest come,
Dropped anchor for a day at your dear perth;
But there was one from oldest years wherefrom
I heard brave words when all the world was dumb,
Whose face I saw when all men's else were shade,
And swore to live without the rule of thumb
That binds the mob and makes the mean afraid,
Knowing I should be strong with truth's unshattered
    blade.

VII

—Brave words to hear but broken words and few;
And I may never see his face again,
For he who, through his eyes, made all roads new—
A splendid thing the very autumn rain!—
Takes now a road whose end makes black my brain;
And I, detesting that which I have been,
My service unperformed, my skill made vain,
Go silent with the foolish and obscene.
Patience! my heart, and forge your sword and keep it
    clean.

[I knew even then that this was much too grandilo-
quent and that it sometimes fell into banality, and I never
attempted to publish it.]

———

The Trains

[I composed the first version of the following while
on sentry duty at night in Detroit.]

I heard the trains in Michigan
    Go wailing through the autumn night;
Their swift diminished ringing ran
    And faded fast in eager flight.

I heard the news their shouting told
    And oldest romance knew again,
Whose voice disturbed my dreams of old:
    Strange cities and the work of men:

"From Jersey City to the Sault
    Our wake is scotched in smoke and spark,
And dowdy people hurry through,
Like gods with something great to do—
    By fields in all-effacing dark
    By bridges rattling in the dark,
      By bridges in the dark!"

I thought of stations where, entombed
    In frigid sheds or marble halls,
I paced, reflected and consumed
    Books never bought at station stalls;

Kind trains that were to carry me,
    Rocking above the brick-red town—
So fine to look below and see,
    So grimly mean—and set me down

Where skies are bleak and hills are bare
    And molten slag makes red the night;
I found them rich nor was that flare
    The only fire that lent them light;

(Yet, grimy trains! I should do ill,
    In playing your apologist,
To hold less dear, remembering still,
The evening lights of Lambertville,
    The Delaware in morning mist,

The air with April orchards sweet,
    That wore their bridal dress so soon,
The hamlets where we stopped to eat
And found a railing for our feet
    And watched the oafs pitch quoits at noon.

Ah, smooth red roads that had no ends!
    The morning fades; the spring is past;
No more I follow you with friends,
    With friends to meet me at the last!)

—Swift trains along the Hudson's shore,
    Which left the city's faceless walls
For prouder cliffs and hills that score
    The thunder of the goblin balls—

A spirit rugged and austere,
    Yet fresher than the times can fade,
Which stands behind and stands so near
    That vast and empty world of trade;

Trains middle-class across the marsh,
    The oily gloom of Newark Bay,
Passing Elizabeth the harsh
    And Perth Amboy the less than gay,

New Brunswick, whom her river shames—
    The changeless list that Princeton crowns—

So many noble ancient names!
  So many sordid modern towns!—

Till finials prick above the trees
  From Gothic roofs in gentle fogs,
Where even iron Cyclopes
  Shuffle and pant as tame as dogs;

Trains men may overtake on foot,
  That clank and jerk, stop short, start on,
Yet, comfortless and filled with soot,
  Still stagger through to Washington—

That Washington whose candid peace
  No smoke could stain or whistle break,
But only children's ecstasies
  Of laughter on a little lake—

Where, sleeping in the summer wood
  Or chambers open to the stars,
My mind was calm and ceased to brood
  The sting and ache of its own scars.

Yet distant engines hooted still:
  "You shall not buy repose so cheap!
You must return for good or ill!
We were not fashioned through your will,
  But who are you that you should sleep?
  You needs must fashion ere you sleep,
    Must fashion ere you sleep!"

———

Princeton, April, 1917

There runs the high gray line of tower and tree,
  Which like a sharp-drawn shadow now appears,
Screened by the mist that comes so quietly,
  As if spring's happy rain were turned to tears.

There flies a flag no bigger than a midge;
    Below my train the placid lake is dun,
Where no bare oarsmen pierce below the bridge
    And no white-hatted paddlers take the sun.

Ah, might I come to Princeton now as then,
    A year ago, on some clear April day!—
(Now April makes the meadows green again,
    Before the trees have felt the touch of May)—

And smell the little courtyard dashed with bloom;
    And, winning sight to know my brothers blind,
Wear out the night with Plato in my room
    To meet the morning with a crystal mind;

And ride again along the dripping lane
    And feel the silver sharpness of the stars—
When, mocking life and unannealed by pain,
    We hardly heard the crash of distant wars.

All order acquiesced in our desires;
    All history was acted for our sport.
Surely the moon was set to light our spires;
    Surely the stars were shut in Holder Court.

Ah, Princeton, is your purpose all forgot?
    Is all your mirth and learning left behind?
I listen for your voice and hear it not;
    I search the streets for things I cannot find.

"Nay, even should you find me still more sad—
    Empty and lonely, passionless and dumb—
And should the men come back to Princeton clad
    In grimmer garb, or should they never come,

"Because my dreams are still the living ones,—
    The very dreams of empire not so large,—
Because my bells are clearer than the guns;
    Because my books are braver than the charge,

"When all the hate and foolishness of men
  Is spent, the stars that seem to glide so high
Shall never stray from Holder Court again
  Nor can the broken music ever die;

"And men who have not known the cloud shall come
  To waken laughter through the soundless street,
Where now you stand, a stranger in your home,
  Unwelcomed by the men you never meet."

[On rereading these poems, I am somewhat touched
and yet a little surprised at my lyrical attachment to
Princeton. I can hardly imagine that any young man
could feel anything of the kind nowadays for Princeton or
for any other such institution. All this was a part of the
world which, with the war, almost ceased to exist. On
revisiting Princeton after the war, as I often did in order
to see the Gausses, I had no sentimental emotions. By the
time I read Fitzgerald's *This Side of Paradise,* his picture
of Princeton life had seemed to me more or less prepos-
terous. I told him later that he had never really been to
Princeton, that he had always been drunk or deluded,
and had lived in a personal fantasy. He had made little
attempt to learn anything, as far as his courses were
concerned, and he had no idea whatever as to how the
University worked. Yet these poems and notes show that
to some extent I had shared his infatuation.]

———

The tuning up of the big horns sounded like the
trumpetings of the elephant house.

Bloomfield Hills: the reds and greens and yellows of
the woods were faded like the colors of a tapestry. The
marshes were rank with pitcher-plant gaping up with red-
veined mouths and more rarely gentians flecked the grass,
like little tongues of blue flame.

[Our unit was taken by train from Detroit to New York, from which we sailed. On the train, I read Joyce's *Dubliners* and H. L. Mencken's *Book of Prejudices*.]

Near Scranton, the midnight countryside of November was cold and bleak, with a sharp bright moon that showed the fields in a dry light and found reverberated reflection in the thicket-lined streams. Now and then there was a small town of houses, black and blank, in which an occasional pale yellow window, ghostly in these cold small hours, only made those other darkened houses of men more lifeless and inhuman.

––––––––––

[We crossed in a wretched old boat, and I, having a name that began with W, was assigned to a steerage which had been condemned: it was stinking and suffocating. I first became aware of the grievances that enlisted men feel against officers when I learned that there were empty first-class cabins in which we were not allowed to sleep. David Hamilton offered to share his bunk with me, and we slept head to feet, sardinewise. But there already were, I think, six men in this cabin, and the air was extremely bad. When it was possible, I slept on deck on one of the iron benches and was wakened very early when a sailor turned a hose on to clean the deck. The food appeared to be vile the only time I visited the dining room. A horrible smell of fish made me realize I could never face it. Those of us who had enough money lived entirely on chocolate and oranges bought at the ship's canteen. It was the roughest voyage I have ever made. The ship would swing back and forth, and the deck, first on one side, then on the other, seemed almost perpendicular to the sea. It was impossible to use the companionways. But I had only two qualms of sea-sickness, one on that only occasion when I had stuck my nose into the dining room, and once, though I managed to control it, when, at the worst of our rocking progress, I was reading in the smoking room. I spent a good deal of time in this smoking room, where, in spite of the stifling fumes and the loud talk of the men of another unit, I managed to get through those comedies of Shakespeare that I did not already know. I had here my first experience of how maddeningly monotonous the profanity and obscenity of the army can be. There was one rather curious thing that they liked to chant in chorus, with a refrain, "Where-upon they all laughed. All except the Lady Alice. *She—was—a—sour—old—bitch!*" I was later to discover that this had been taken from Mark Twain's *1601*.

In England, we had to wait a few days in what was called a rest camp at Southampton, where we slept in water-flooded tents. I there learned for the first time from a newspaper of the Bolshevik Revolution in Russia. I found in a Southampton bookshop Chesterton's *History of England* and Henry James's posthumous *The Sense of the Past,* and read them during the rest of our journey.]

[David and I, at Southampton, had a conversation with a British soldier, by whose language I was fasci-nated.]

Duffy, speaking of the little Birmingham pattern-maker: "Why, the likes of him has to put in a requisition to speak to the likes of me. I'm one of the few! French's Contemptibles, that's what I am!—We've fought a lot. How to treat mosquito bites. There's two kinds of mos-quitoes: the ordinary kind that buzzes and bites, you know. But then there's the cooties [cooties was the word for lice, and they could hardly have been classed with mosquitoes]; they have boots on and they don't bite, they kick. And them is poisonous. And you have to be treated for it. And how to treat a man with sunstroke and how to treat a man in a fit. Why, you gives the sunstroke stimulants but you don't give the fit no stimulants. You know, a man falls in a fit and he's rolling on the ground, and you see a lot of chaps gather around him and get on top of him, and if the fit don't kill him, they will, you know. But they teach us all about how to hold him down and don't give him no stimulants.—Well, I'm one of those, I know all that.—The Kayser he was standin' on a hill, lookin' down on the battle, and he says: 'Curse them! the British bulldogs! they know not when they're beaten!' And we know why he always has his hand in his coat, too. Don't you know, whenever he has his picture taken, he always sticks his hand in his coat. Well, do you know what that's for? To scratch hisself! The same ones.—I'm not going back to England, not much, though it ought to be better to live in than it ever was before.—Why, because the people'll wake up and find how they've been kidded. Why, in peace times, didn't somebody get up in the Houses of Parliament and say that a British workman ought to be able to live on one pound and eighteen bob a week and support himself and support a wife and kid? No, I'm not going back to England! I'm going to a White Man's Country!—Why, Africa!—where a nigger can't walk on the sidewalk with a white man. They keeps 'em in chains. And what's more, you can see all the lords— Lord Milner and Lord Curzon!—Oh, yes! the Yankees are goin' in! We'll stand by you! Never let it be said that we lef' you!—Oh, but it's terrible when you think of it! Fightin' in the air and fightin' under the water and fightin' under the ground. I tell you, won't it be a great day for the British army when they can come up out of those ditches and have a look 'round!—I suppose they'll send me to Rouon. Oh, there's an odd lot of officers there. Some of them's never fired an angry round. 'Do it like this: In! Out! In! Out!' Still, it's quite all right, if they can get it. It's quite all right!"

————

[The Channel boat was held up for at least a day by rumors of submarines. The British soldiers sang lugubrious songs. We slept on our packs on the decks and floors.]

————

An English soldier on the boat: "I down't give a fuck if the bowt gows dahn, it doesn't belong to me!"

————

[I described our box-car journey from Le Havre to Vittel in a story I wrote in the army. The case of this dying boy was real, and so were most of the incidents. I attempted, after the Armistice, to send the story to a magazine, but was reprimanded by the officer who was acting as censor and considered it somehow subversive. It was eventually printed in the *Liberator* and afterwards included in *The Undertaker's Garland,* a book that John Bishop and I published after the War.]

The Death of a Soldier

Henry had a magnificent thrill at the Havre rest camp. The dirty chicken-wire bunks of the French barracks were the first authentic sign he had seen of the squalor of the war. Everything in America had been adequate and new, but here the grasp had slipped; the war was gaining on them. The filthiness of these old sheds, where for three years soldiers had been coming and going, gave him a ghastly sinking of the heart, to which lurid rumours added. It seemed that things were very desperate, and they were going straight to the front; it seemed that they were going to be brigaded with the French. These wholly unfounded statements, born of the excitement of the moment, had at once been accepted as well-established fact and everybody was telling everybody else about them with a grimness not devoid of gusto.

But when he went out of doors, he was exhilarated by the November sunshine, which brought out the reds and blues and khakis of the passing uniforms and lent splendor even to the barracks. He watched the strange crowd with wonder. The English officers stalked along in glittering smartness; they did not regard the rest of the world and hardly spoke to each other. The French *poilus* seemed tired and untidy and ridiculously small. Here and there one saw an American officer, very solemn and a little self-conscious of the freshness of his uniform. He would have thought it all rather gay if he had not been in the Army and felt always the oppression of being handled like a thing without will. They could do absolutely anything they liked with him; he had felt that in the barracks as he had never felt it before. They could tell him to go to more horrible places than barracks and he would have to go and stay there. And he was dismayed to find how much the edge was taken off his enjoyment by the iron unshakable sense that he was not his own master. Still, he felt keen pride at being there. This was the World War! These were the things you saw pictures of in the American Sunday papers!—And how much he had grown up since he first went to camp in June!

He had enlisted at eighteen, on his graduation from High School. "The young men and women who go out into the world this spring," the Superintendent had said in his Commencement address, "have a glorious opportunity such as no other class has been offered. It has fallen to their lot—it becomes their inestimable privilege—to vindicate before the world the honor of our free

America! Nothing grieves me more at this moment than the fact that I am not young enough to bear arms myself, and I envy you young men with all my heart for the Great Adventure that is before you." The Minister had said in church: "Take up the sword for Christ! The German Antichrist—the Ambassador of Hell—has ravished France and Belgium and, unless we smite it first, will hold bleeding in its talons the country that we love and that we must needs defend. The Hun must be made to pay with his own blood that which he has ruthlessly spilled! He must suffer the pains and privations which he has been inflicting on the innocent! We are fighting not only for Democracy but for *Christianity!* 'Vengeance is mine!' saith the Lord!" And Henry, walking alone in scented dusks of June, had decided that even his uncle's real estate business in New Bedford was far too flat a way to begin the world.

The first weeks of his training had disappointed him a little. After the sober piety of his home, the life of the barracks shocked him. Not even when he went to High School had he heard such language as this; but, since this was the language of the Army, he would of course have to learn it, and he had soon got the hang of a vocabulary which clashed with his innocent eyes. In a month he had learned all the other things, too, that are fundamental for a soldier: the habit of not making plans and surrendering the direction of his life; the right formula in morose complaining when he was given anything to do; how to produce the impression of working when he was not working, but, when he did work, how to work harmoniously with anybody; self-repression in the presence of officers and the acceptance of a lower valuation of himself as a private in the Army than as a student in a New England High School and the son of a respectable farmer; ability to enjoy and get on with any sort of man and inability to consider any woman except in one simple relation.

Now, he felt, he was really almost a man. He had discovered with excitement that the taboos of home need not be binding. You could curse like a baggage-man if you wanted to, without its doing any harm; and the men who swore and drank most he found the most amusing of all: they seemed to have more fun in them, more imagination than the others, and they had had more adventures. As long as he had been encamped near home, to be sure, he had left the whores alone, but when he should get to France—well, everybody knew what France was! And you didn't take much risk because the Government would disinfect you afterwards. In the States he hadn't been able to drink except furtively and it was with a thrill of adventure and freedom that he went into the English Y. M. C. A. and had beer among the absurd voices of the English soldiers. If only he could get rid of that damn cold that he had caught on the ship and from sleeping on the ground at Southampton, he would be pretty well satisfied, he thought. . . .

That night he was horribly tired and had a sore throat and a headache and he tried to get to sleep early in the barracks; but there were a lot of people drunk who kept yelling and singing till midnight. And after they had subsided, everybody began to cough; it was like the barking and roaring of a menagerie. "Sounds like a goddam TB ward!" said somebody. Then all the lights were suddenly turned on and raucous voices shouted: "All out!" It was an artillery company that was leaving at four in the morning. They swore sullen oaths like heavy blows. Then some one began to sing an endless obscene song, which afforded them some relief by allowing them to join in the chorus. When they had finally gone and the lights were out again, the November fog leaked in through the paneless windows and felt for his legs through the blankets with chill fingers. He was thankful for the chicken-wire, anyway, he told himself, because, even though it was dirty and no warmer than sleeping on the wind, it was luxurious after the wet ground he had had in England. And at the rest camp he had met men who had told him about sleeping in stables on dung-heaps. Well, that was what he'd soon be doing, too! He wondered where he would be at this time next week. . . .

The next day, it was their turn to leave at four in the morning. He could hardly go to sleep for thinking how he would have to jump up quickly and get into his pack; he kept waking up and thinking the Sergeant had called and when the Sergeant did call, it found him nervously awake. He tore himself out of his blankets, buttoned his breeches hurriedly and put on his blouse and coat, then spread out the blankets on the muddy floor where the men had been spitting all night. He struggled into his pack, fumbling in desperate haste—you were always afraid the command would come before you were ready—and, holding his rifle and leaning against the wall, fell into a sort of doze. His throat was so sore that when he swallowed it seemed to have a sharp knife in it.

"All out! Fall in!" bawled the Sergeant.

They stumbled out into the night and presently found themselves in formation. An officer appeared and made them stand at attention, then disappeared and left them there. After they had stood at attention for fifteen min-utes, the Sergeant gave them "At ease."—"What the hell does he care?" said somebody. "He sleeps warm, with comforters and everything. I seen their billets yesterday." At the end of an hour, the officer reappeared and gave them the command to march.

When they had left the camp, they found themselves confronted with a blank darkness thickened by the fog.

Only here and there, as they proceeded, was the road illumined by a ghastly greenish light from a feeble street-lamp with a blackened top.

At last, they arrived at a railroad track, where a pygmy unlighted train was puffing under its breath. When they had stood there half an hour, they were ordered to get into the box-cars. The Captain, made a little self-conscious by knowing that the command would be a shock, delivered it with extra harshness. They clambered up in deadly silence. Then someone had the courage to begin cursing: "Just like a lotta goddam cows!" he muttered, and the car was filled with bitter growls.

They found by falling over them that there were four benches in the car, two at each end and parallel with the sides, leaving a clear space in the middle from one side-door to the other. They threw down their packs in a heap in this central space and ranged themselves on the benches, which proved to be so narrow that they could neither sit nor lie on them without a constant effort of bracing. Everybody felt angry and ill, and they began to quarrel among themselves. Some one had made out and explained the sign on the outside: *"Hommes 40 Chevaux (en long) 8."* It was the final wound to self-respect, the last indignity of the Army, which, although the fact was plain enough, had never before confessed that it put American soldiers on a level with animals! A universal complaint arose. "Aw, this ain't nothin'!" said a voice. "Wait till yuh get to the trenches. Then you'll wish you could set down in a box-car, what *I* mean!"

The train waited there till dawn, shifting backward and forward now and then, with much bumping and creaking. Everybody cursed the French railroads: "Hell, they ain't got no real railroads in this goddam country!" Then they seemed to be starting and got as far as a station, but only to back up again and wait for another hour. At last the train seemed to pull itself together and set out half-heartedly, as if willing at any moment to abandon the struggle. France revealed itself as a gray and desolate country, where everything was either marsh or mud. The towns were all miserable-looking and exactly alike: dull red roofs and yellow walls, with washed-out streets between. The country consisted mostly of barren fields and dismal woods, inhabited by unfamiliar birds, and there were endless lines of poplar skeletons in whose fishbone-like branches the mistletoe clumps were lodged like enormous nests. And everything was wet, saturated with fog and rain. The men themselves were wet. It had been at least a week since they had been really dry. So this was Europe!

As the morning wore on, they began to get hungry, but the supplies were in the last car and they had not been provided with emergency rations. When the train would falter to a stop in the midst of some rain-soaked wilderness, the whole company would yell for food—"When do we EAT?"—but no food ever came.

"Say, you're sick, aincha?" said a man next to Henry. "You better lay down."

"There ain't any place," he answered; the central space was already full.

"Why didun yuh go to Sick-Call at Hayver?"

"I did, but he only gave me a CC pill."

"Goddam ol' horse-doctor! These here Army doctors dono nothin'. Here, you better take the corner seat so's you can lay up against the wall."

Henry changed places with him and was very grateful for the corner. He tried to relax as much as he could without slipping off the seat. He shut his eyes and tried to forget the acute oppression of his headache and the inescapable cold in his legs. The jouncing of the train was like crockery broken on his head; the oaths and coarse words, senselessly, endlessly repeated, like something less than human speech, pounded dully against his brain like the regular blows of a hammer. He took refuge infinitely far inside him, putting himself back home.

The images were diminished in size and concentrated in intensity, like something sharply focussed through a telescope; the wood-fire in the sitting-room gave him sharp satisfaction; the pitcher of water in the dining-room was too delicious to be believed—he felt that he could drink it with eager greed. He put himself in bed on a Sunday morning under warm blankets and a "goose-chase" quilt; the gay patches of the quilt gave a feeling of familiar security; he could remember that when he was little he had thought of them as alive. The square-paned window was up, and he could see the great smooth contours of the hill-side gleaming with snow, the horizon as clear and bare as the room in which he had slept. In a minute or two his mother would come and call him curtly; then he would have to get up and dress right away, because no extra allowances were made for Sunday morning breakfast. He would dread setting his bare feet on the cold uncarpeted floor and would lie staring at the flowered wash-stand set and the signing of the Declaration in a splotched print above it. But oh! how warm it was with your feet and legs in bed! . . . Presently he fell asleep, but only to jerk himself into wakefulness when he began to lose his purchase on the seat.

They stopped at a red-tile-roofed station late in the afternoon and everybody was allowed to get out. Having had no food for twenty-four hours, they fell upon the buffet and cleaned it up. Everybody got wine, which, tart and clear, brought deliciously to the bewildered men their first real taste of the country. Everybody was laughing and joking; a faint sun had appeared. One of the young lieutenants offered to supply anybody who needed it with money to buy wine and had dispensed a great quantity of francs when the Commanding Officer, a conscientious Regular Army man, who was zealous to forestall "unsoldierly conduct," put a brusque stop to the charity by ordering that no more wine should be bought.

The Americans succeeded in conveying to two pinched and pale French soldiers, who were standing with their collars up, that they wanted to hear them sing the *Marseillaise*. But the Frenchmen, after a line or two, broke down and could not remember the rest.

When the train jolted on again, morale had enormously risen. With the wine aboard, it now became possible to enjoy the thing as a lark. If the French built toy railroads that "didn't go no faster'n a horse an' buggy," was that any reason why they should forget that they were the American Expeditionary Force, come over to kill the Kaiser? Everybody fell over Henry, who had taken the time when the car was empty to construct a bed of packs; but the wine made him feel better and he minded things less.

"Shut that goddam door! It's cold!"

"Aw, get away from it if yuh don't like it. We wanta see the world! 'Join the Army and See the World!' Christ, I could see more than this on the old Pontiac trolley-line!"

"Jesus Christ! I can't say much for this wine. Jest like a lotta goddam sour grape-juice!"

"Why, Christ, didunja get any brandy? They had brandy there, too. . . . Why, you —— bastard! of course they had brandy! Don't try to tell me they didun have no brandy! Didun Dicky get some?"

"Why Chur-rist! If I'da known that, I woulduna bought all this here goddam red ink! It ain't no good to drink!"

"Why, I find it very stimulating," chirped a professional male nurse of the Sanitary Detachment, a bland bald-headed man with the voice and manners of a shop-girl. He had had two bottles of his own wine and as much as he could get of other people's and was now softly singing *My Old Kentucky Home* over and over to himself.

"Say, look here! I can't supply the whole goddam company with brandy!" said the man who had some.

"Who's askin' yuh tuh sply the whole goddam compny with brandy? I only ast yuh fer a drop!" demanded one of the messmen, who was getting more and more quarrel-some.

"Now, I'm all set," said the man who had just got the brandy. "All I want's a woman."

"It's too goddam bad we coulduna had some wild women along. That's what I come to France for."

"One good old night in the Arcade, eh?" suggested a middle-aged man, who claimed to be a lawyer in civil-life.

"I wouldun give a good goddam fer the Arcade!" shouted the messman so loudly that he could be heard above the hideous rattle of the cars and the uproar of everybody talking at once. ("Sitdown, you big bastard!" "Lay down and go to sleep!")

"I tell you," continued the lawyer, "in the good old days when I was at Law School we used to set out on the front stoop and hail 'em in from the street. We used to ask 'em just to come in for a minute, but it was very seldom they ever got out again that night, what I mean!"

"Say, this guy's sick," said a man near Henry. "Why doncha move over and lettum lay out?"

"What did you say?" inquired the nurse.

"Aw, Jesus Christ! how many times do yuh want me to say it? Get over and let this guy lay down!"

"I can't move over any further. There's no more room.

He oughtn't to lay right next to the open door, anyway! I think it's perfectly terrible! The idea of letting a poor boy lay around like this when he's sick!"

"Well, that night," continued the lawyer with unflagging zest, (Henry could not escape that persistent voice; the others could be forgotten as dull amorphous sounds, but this one was so near and distinct that he could not fail to hear it), "we had so much to start with that Jack he just passes out before dinner's over and Flo says she's going out to look afterum. And that left me and Genevieve all alone. By and by *she* gets pale and pitches forward on the table and breaks a couple of glasses and I had just about time to get her to the couch when, Jesus Christ! I loses my own lunch right in the cracked-ice pail. I didn't come to till about six the next morning, and then I looks over at Genevieve and she was just the colour of a bum oyster. 'Well, Genevieve,' I says, 'I guess we don't want to do anything now, do we?' And she rolls her eyes over at me and says: 'No! I guess we don't!' "

Twilight had erased the faded countryside and the damp autumn air had grown sharp. The train kept slowing up and stopping as if it had lost its way. The open sides of the car brought the country all too close to them; they might almost as well have been down among those wet thickets and those cold little streams. The sightseers were finally prevailed upon to close the doors. But Henry did not feel the cold so much now and was no longer conscious of the delay; the only things he wanted were water and to be able to breathe more easily. He had emptied his own canteen and then had disliked to ask for too much from his neighbors', but now he had reached a point where thirst had overcome reluctance and he was willing to take all they would give him. His head thumped like a dynamo with a hot ponderous throbbing.

His breath came terribly hard and had begun to make a hoarse rasping sound. . . .

There was a dazzling light in his face; he turned his head to avoid it. Then somebody was shaking him out of his stupor. Distant voices: "What's the matter with yuh? —What's the matter with him?" "I think he's got a fever, sir. If there was an extra place in one of the regular cars—" "What's the matter with yuh? Cantcha hear I'm talkin' to yuh?"

"Got a cold," murmured Henry.

"Let me see your tongue. Say 'Ah.' Bowels all right?"

"If there was room in one of the regular cars, sir—" the Sergeant suggested again.

"Well, there isn't!" the Lieutenant cut him short. A former physician at Police Headquarters, he had learned that "all two-thirds of 'em need is a good swift kick."

He shook the messman, who was the nearest human item in the confused mound of packs and human bodies and commanded him to get up. Some of the men prodded him and helped him, swearing, to his feet while others undid a blanket-roll and made a sort of bed on the floor.

"Just keep him warm," said the Lieutenant, when he had finished scolding the messman for disrespect. "I'll give him something when we get there." He jumped down, and the train started.

"Aw, I bet there's lotsa room up there," said somebody. "They've got all the room they want, with plush seats and everything!"

"It's different with a well guy, but when a guy's sick like that, why, Jesus Christ! they might show a little consideration."

And the Sergeant added: "He's just as kind and gentle as a crocodile, that bird is!"

"I never heard of such a thing!" complained the nurse,

who had not said a word when the doctor was there and who had more room now that Henry was moved. "I've had professional experience, but they won't listen to me."

"Now, where am I gonta lay?" roared the messman. "Sweet Jesus! Do yuh think I'm gonta stand up all night?"

"You can lay along the roof," suggested somebody.

"Well, d'ye know what you can do?" bawled the other and told him what he could do.

"Shut up, Striker, and go to sleep! Cantcha see the guy's sick?"

"Well, Jesus Christ! he don't hafta be sick, does he?"

"Well, he's sick!"

"Well, he don't hafta be sick, does he?"

"Yes!"

"Well, he's outa luck!"

"Now, look here, fellows!" began a young man, seizing upon the opportunity to indulge a taste for eloquence. "There's a man sick in this car and we ought to try to make it comfortable for him, just like what we'd do if it was ourselves that was sick. My opinion is that if we haven't got enough consideration to give him a place to lay down in we don't deserve to bear the name of American soldiers—"

"Aw, what the hell yuh talkin' about?" bellowed Striker. "He's got a place to lay down in, ain't he? If a man's sick I'll get up and give him a place to lay down in, but what I can't stand is this here goddam High School stuff!"

"Shut up, yuh big bastard!" "Shut up, both of yuh!" "Speech! Speech!" "Give us a recitation, Shorty!"—And Shorty, already on his feet, gave them *Barbara Frietchie, The Face Upon the Barroom Floor, The Cremation of Sam M'Gee,* a series of ribald limericks and finally *Crossing the Bar,* described as "the dying words of Lord

Tennyson." Then they all became hilarious and sang *Where do we go from here?* and *The Bastard King of England.* And when the singing was over and drowsiness had made them quiet, the enthusiastic lawyer, who had never halted his narrative, was heard proceeding to a climax: "But finally I decided that I'd had enough of that and I thought I'd get me a nice girl to go with all the time. So I did—a waitress in Schwartz's she was—and I went with her regular, going kinda easy at first—I thought she was all right, see?—and then, goddam it! what did she do but hand me the prettiest little package I ever had in my life!"

The train stopped at a large station and nearly every one got out to warm himself by walking up and down and drinking the coffee and cognac which some genial chirping French soldiers were ladling out from a pail.

"We've got a sick man in our car, sir," said the Sergeant to a mild little Lieutenant of the Medical Corps, who had asked him how they were making out.

"Let me see him," suggested the Lieutenant.

"He's pretty sick, I'm afraid," he said when he had examined Henry. "He oughtn't to be here at all. I wonder if we couldn't put him in one of those ambulances and have him sent to a hospital."

"I'll see what I can do."

He found his Commanding Officer scowling at the smiling and unconscious French soldiers who were dispensing bitter coffee to the eager Americans. The Major had tasted the cognac and was standing stiffly with the cup in his hand, mute with moral indignation.

In civilian life, this Lieutenant was a bacteriologist, who pursued his work with a high enthusiasm, scientific and humanitarian, and he therefore rarely felt at home in the company of doctors; he was a gentleman, besides, and had never got used to military manners. When the Major eyed him in silence, he began to sound apologetic, and the Major was not impressed. "They've all got colds," he said and threw out the tainted coffee in his cup with a gesture of contempt. "Lieutenant Forbes has seen him. That's all that can be done."

"It's pneumonia, I'm quite sure."

"Well, we ought to be in tomorrow. He can be attended to then. I shouldn't like to let a man go like this unless it was absolutely necessary. I should like to arrive there with every man, if possible."

"But would you mind looking at him yourself?" He began to feel helpless; the Major thought him unmilitary.

Just then the train tooted and began to back a little. "Well, it's too late now," said the Major. "We must get aboard. I'll see about it at the next stop."

They reached the next stop at about three in the morning, and the Major was persuaded to look at Henry and send him off in an ambulance; there was a Base Hospital not far away.

"Now please be sure to drive very slowly, won't you?" begged the Lieutenant of the ambulance driver; (he had never been able to give a command properly.) "It may make a great deal of difference, you know, because he's got pneumonia and the jolting might make him worse."

"Yes, sir," promised the driver; but as soon as he got beyond the town he began winding up the smooth straight road like a spool of tape. It had been announced that the train of wounded he had been waiting for would not arrive till morning, and his mind was full of the plump charms of a certain café *patronne*, whose husband had just left for the front. The rush of the car drowned out Henry's no less harsh and mechanical breathing. . . .

There was a little piece of cotton in his throat; he thought if he could only get that out he would be all right. He coughed and coughed and coughed but he couldn't dislodge it. He remarked on this fact to the Sergeant and later to his sister, who, it seemed, were both there. Then he found that he was being horribly shaken up. "This is the damnedest straw-ride I was ever on," he said. "I don't call this no fun. Straw-ride without any straw!" . . . But the train was slowing down; they would have to get out and march; it was eight miles to the camp. He must be able to put his hand on his pack and rifle in an instant. He supposed that he'd be able to get into his pack all right, though he didn't feel very well. That first moment when you heaved it up and wrenched it on to your shoulders was agonizingly hard, but after that no doubt he would find that he could get around. They would all fall in and right-dress, jostling each other in the dark. . . . Ah, the train was going to stop. He reached for his rifle. Where the hell was it? "Are you going to stop here, Sergeant?" . . . Evidently not. The train was going faster again. They ought to get there in no time at this rate! . . . "We used to sit out on the front stoop," he said, "and hail 'em in from the street. And I bet very few of 'em ever got out, either!" . . . Then it seemed that he was in bed and it was harder than ever to breathe. Still, it was evidently morning and they would have to leave the barracks any minute. Could it be that he had overslept? "Is it time to go yet, Sergeant?" He got out of bed to see. "Here! what do you want?" exclaimed someone in a severe voice of alarm. "I want my shoes," said Henry. "Where's my gun?—" . . . "All right. We'll get them for you. Now, you just lie still and keep covered up." Somebody tucked him in. "Have you got a glass of water, please?" he inquired weakly. . . . Then things became more and more obscure. He was aware of the presence of a man, evidently his father. . . . No: it was the Sergeant at last, summoning him to go. He made a wild effort to get out of bed, but they held him down, and he collapsed on his back exhausted, panting faster than ever. . . .

The doctor and nurse were watching him at noon. His breath had become as rapid as the ticking of a small clock; his lids were already half-closed over his eyes, his unshaved cheeks dirtily livid and his gaping lips sticky and discolored in a gruesome inhuman mask; his head was strained desperately back, as if some enemy had him by the throat. The panting became fainter; the clock was running down. His lungs were full—he was drowning. Then he had caught breath and struggled on again till he could get no further. Three times they saw him strain to the surface, only to go down. Henry was nothing but a thread of breath forcing its way through thickening channels. Then he was nothing. . . .

"He put up a pretty good fight there at the last," remarked the doctor, noting the death in a register. "If this keeps up we'll have to have a special floor for pneumonia. I should suggest the second floor." He smiled. "Then we'll have nothing but indigestion up here. Give 'em something to do downstairs. But seriously, they ought to isolate these cases. It begins to look like an infection."

"I should think so," said the nurse. "And when you consider that the Army's hardly over here yet—"

"Now, be sure all his personal belongings get to the right place. They've been making a fuss about that lately."

The orderly assembled in a khaki handkerchief all the things in the pockets of the uniform. There were a pipe, a crushed bag of tobacco, photographs of Henry's mother and sister, half-a-dozen obscene post-cards bought from a man who had been to Paris and a little brown leather pocket-book stained dark with sweat.

———

We saw the evening darken lightly the pale buffs and greens of the sad French countryside: the Marne and the narrow canals lay like mirrors of jade reflecting dimly the high poplars that fringed them, spectral and losing their vague topmost fingers in the twilight.

———

Bill Brown: "And she sang me little Scandinavian cradle-songs at the piano! Now, after that . . .!" [A memory, going back to the already distant past of Bill Brown and his Swedish girlfriend. Having as yet no girl of my own, I must have enjoyed vicariously the experiences of my friends.]

———

Holland's bon mot for the military system: "You go to hell, Jack: I'm all right!" [The Mess Sergeant, a veteran of the Boer War. I thought he had invented this.]

[We were stationed at Vittel in the Vosges, a summer resort to which, in time of peace, people came to take the waters. The hotels there were now turned into hospitals. We at first had French army rations—for breakfast, black butterless wedges of bread and black coffee with a shot of cognac—and were put to sleep in the Vittel casino, in a large room with clouds and classical beings painted on the ceiling. We were all packed into this room and slept upon army cots. In the morning, most of the men woke up with erections and would at once begin kidding each other, either accusing their neighbors of masturbating under the covers or attributing to them homosexual practices. I occasionally encountered in the army real cases of homosexuality—an ill-favored effeminate elderly man attached to a good-looking and masculine young one—but I soon realized that all this homosexual talk was simply due to the lack of women, that it had no deeper

significance than the attempts of male dogs on their own
sex—a simple blind stirring of animal appetite. This was
confirmed by the army saying, "anything with a hole in
it!"]

———

[I was set, before the wounded came in, to various
menial tasks: carrying firewood, keeping up the stove in
the office of the x-ray operator and acting as a dentist's
assistant. This dentist, the Sergeant Baker I had quoted
at the Detroit fairground, was a crude not unlikable man
with a certain gift of speech; but I found myself in the
somewhat embarrassing position of being pressed into
service to interpret for him in his dealings with a pretty
little woman patient upon whom he had designs.]

Baker: "Now be sure to get it small enough [some gar-
ment he wanted me to buy for her]—Olga's no bigger'n a
pint o' piss, yuh know. . . . We had a whole shit-house
full o' fun with those girls. . . . Yuh don't know the
language and yuh can't trick 'em and you can't get 'em by
anything less'n assault. . . . Why wouldn't I marry her?
I just live for three things. . . .

"I was in Galveston when the troops came back from
Vera Cruz. There was rows of oleanders—pink and
white—on each side of the street—a regular Southern
town, yuh know. It had just been raining and those old
oleanders were sparkling like diamonds. And the sun
came out. And the street was made of bright red bricks.
And the bands were playing *The Stars and Stripes
Forever*. That's the sort o' stuff that takes your speech,
yuh know!"

———

Leo Rabbette said that in the army we are like magnets
whose molecules have been disordered by striking and

which will no longer draw. [He was one of the friends that I made in the unit. He had spent some time in East Aurora, New York, sitting at the feet of Elbert Hubbard, and he loved to declaim Swinburne:

"Out of the golden remote wild west where the sea with-
     out shore is,
Full of the sunset, and sad, if at all, with the fulness of
     joy" . . .

He thought of himself as a happy Bohemian, who could never be crushed by the Army.]

———

[More lament for the world left behind.]

I heard them say: "Our arms become us well.
     We find, for lives too purposeless before,
A kind of comfort in the bursting shell,
     A kind of peace in war."

But all the long-won things I thought so strong
     Were gone, like children's bubbles tossed too much,
Or like a full-blown flower, kept too long,
     That scatters at a touch.

The gentle faces watched our fire no more;
     The merry words flashed not in thought's fine strife;
And, when they smiled or spoke again, they bore
     The brand of the dead life.

For, while we watched the fire, a shadow came
     Between us and the room, and while we spoke,
A voice we hardly knew called every name,
     Yet could not spoil our joke.

And all familiar things were terrible;
     And all our lives were black with death and doubt;

The spots we loved were poisoned by a spell;
    And the old sun went out.

———

"Death is nothing terrible after all. It may mean something more wonderful than life. It cannot possibly mean anything worse to the good soldier." Alan Seeger. True! but he couldn't have meant what I thought of at first.

———

The Assistant Cook: "I say just let me cook for the Germans and I'll clean 'em up in no time!"

———

[I was convinced that American Puritanism was a barrier against sex and responsible for my own privation.]

One thing I know that saves me much remorse
    And hate for what my world has feared as sin:
    Whatever gods and manners we may win
Through our long labor and our crooked course,

Forgetting long, we have affronted her
    Who came all clean in sunlight from the sea
    And him who, Psyche's lover anciently,
Becomes her false and furtive harasser.

For these pay grievous toll to walk our roads
    Or, spurned, are like those sisters, known of yore,
    Whose poor enchanted mouths might nevermore
Speak gracious words but only vomit toads.

[Enough of this poetry—though I wrote a lot more. Some of the better pieces I published in my *Night Thoughts*.]

———

Sergeant Kenny: "It's funny when you come to think about it: these people over here seem to have everything pretty nice in a way and yet they don't get out and hustle to make money an awful lot either. . . . And yet what else is there to do after all? I figure that a man can have the things he wants after he's made the money to buy 'em, but he has to get out and hustle to make a success in business. . . . What else is there to do, after all?"

———

[Roy Gamble was another of my army friends. He was a painter who began as a follower of Whistler but had later had a certain success doing portraits of the Detroit rich. He was a sensitive and intelligent but very shrewd and canny fellow. The language in which he talked about art amused me very much.]

Roy Gamble, describing his arrival in Paris, after he had crossed the ocean alone, his intended companion having deserted him at the dock [he had come to study painting]: "Y'see, now, I'd figured that Paris would be just like New York, only more so—better—I mean, bigger—just like Fifth Avenue, only all like that—and I didn't know how to take it at first. And I didn't like it much either, see, because I thought that all the French were trying to do the Americans—charge 'em too much, see. I didn't know a soul in Paris, and all I did for the first week or so was ride around on buses—(and I saw some pretty good effects, too, then). I lived on those buses."

Roy Gamble: "Da Vinci used to take the Mona Lisa around with him, you know, in a trunk. That was about all he had. And he'd go around to these towns and make the acquaintance of the artists. And then they'd bring out their pictures and he'd look at 'em, see? look at everything they had. And then, after they were all done, he'd bring

out the Mona Lisa—wouldn't say a word, see? but just
bring it out and let 'em see it—and, Jesus Christ! those
birds would take to the hills!"—Of Memling and the
Flemish religious painters: "Those birds'd bring tears to
your eyes! No fucking on the side!" Of Rodin: "Yes,
Rodin's all right at that. But you just feel his big stiff
prick sticking up in his pants all the time!"

[Roy Gamble talking]: After General Pershing had
made Shurley and McGraw stand at attention [they were
our top medical officers]: " 'Stand at attention there when
I talk to you!!!'—Old Black-Jack Pershing!—Where does
he git that stuff?—That's what makes von Hindenburg
what he is!—But poor old Terrible Ted [McGraw, who
was a kindly and nervous man]—that's kinda hard! He's
sorta on the hummer—he's got ague, that bird!"

———

George Discher, the barber, is the son of a Prussian
shepherd who fled from Europe on a sailing-boat when an
overseer flogged his sister. He came to America, where
George was born. A year or so before America entered the
war, he spoke to George from his deathbed as follows:
" 'Babe!'—he always called me Babe—'Babe,' he said, 'in
six months America'll go into the war, and when she
does, I want you to go over there and help send those sons
of bitches to Hell!' "

———

[When the wounded began to be sent to us as a result
of the first engagements in which the Americans took
part, we carried them on stretchers from the train to the
hospital. The first lot that I remember were victims of
mustard gas. This attacks every part of the body that is

moist, particularly the throat and the genitals. Their penises were spongy and raw and swollen to enormous size, and bandaging them and unbandaging them was extremely painful. There was one doctor, known for his sadism—he liked to kick the enlisted men—who would rip the bandages off.

We had also syphilitic and shell-shocked cases. I saw one young man die of syphilis. He seemed unconscious and could not talk: he could only make a clicking sound. Of one of the shell-shock cases I wrote afterwards this account in a story I contributed to the *Liberator*]:

I remember a curious patient who came to the hospital in France. He had a small undeveloped head left naked by close cropping, and his screwed-up features were as fixed as a face carved out of a peach-stone. One felt that he was densely immured in some impregnable stronghold of stupidity or dazed by some great transplantation. He seemed the last of human creatures, something far less responsive than a dog. When he spoke, it was in some barbarous and scarcely intelligible dialect; one was always surprised to find that he could answer questions at all.

But he had a nervous system, it appeared; in fact, it was for that he was there. In spite of his strange distraction, he would start and tremble like a rabbit if anyone spoke suddenly to him or came upon him from behind, as he wandered about the halls with unassuageable restlessness. One night the orderly thought he heard him coughing and brought him some medicine in a glass. He stood by the side of the man's bed and put his hand on his shoulder to rouse him. But the patient woke up with a shriek that was like a green gash in the dark and dashed the glass across the room with a wild panic-stricken gesture. "Vat's de matter?" he gibbered and crouched, racked with trembling, in the bed.

It appeared, when the doctors cross-examined him, that

he had bayonetted a young German and had not been able to forget it.

———

[I was usually on night duty and would sit reading and listening for a bell or a call. One of the hospitals in the Parc, in summer, was surrounded by nightingales, which I had never heard sing before. I had read Keats at home, but I had not been especially struck by the *Ode to a Nightingale*. But I now came across it in an anthology. It seemed one of the greatest poems I had ever read, and I committed it to memory. But later on the real nightingales came to seem ill-timed and out of place when the soldiers all around me were dying of the flu epidemic that killed so many at the end of the war.]

[I still made no real progress with women. There was a pretty village girl who came to mass in the church across from my window. But I shouldn't have known how to approach her, and anyway she looked like a decent girl.

My admiration, however, became concentrated on a girl named Ninette Fabre, the daughter of the proprietor of a favorite café. It was partly her presence there that made this café a favorite, for Ninette was extremely beautiful. With her black hair, her green eyes under delicately pencilled black eyebrows and her perfect oval face, she seemed the survival of a type that one sees in nineteenth-century French engravings. She was tubercular, and her burning cheeks set off by her pale skin made her seem poetically romantic. She wrote poetry in the manner of Lamartine and was seriously studying English. She was very strictly guarded by her parents. Her bearded father was bad-tempered and would immediately have thrown out of his place any soldier who attempted liberties with her. I remember him standing over the stove and

swearing at it, *"Merde alors!"* Ninette said that he had
formed his habits from his earlier years in Indo-China,
when he had ruled the natives *"à coups de cravache."* I
went to the café very often. She and I exchanged English
and French, and she told me that I had *"un affreux
accent de midi,"* when, in reading French poetry, I
pronounced the mute final *e*'s. I missed her when they
went in the summer to Cannes, where her father had
another café. Ninette so appealed to some of our doctors
that they took her into a hospital to treat her, and she
became the object of a kind of homage.]

———

Across the pale fields of March, cut by a little stream,
whose line of pollard willows only we could see in the
middle distance, and lodged at the foot of a smooth steep
hill, cut out in squares like a quilt and with its flat top
bristling with pines, we saw the low red roofs and old
yellowed walls of a village, distinguished by a church
tower in the middle and set off with a few wisps of
poplar, where it dwindled on either side. The thin road
flung in free curves across the fields seemed to belong to it
and make it no less a sheltered and private thing, sunk so
firmly in its nest and toned so long by the weather that,
beside it, the very country-side looked new.

———

A French soldier on permission whom we [Roy
Gamble and I] picked up on the way back from Mirecourt. [This was the time of the French mutiny]: *"Morts!
morts! morts! des hommes qu'on n'a pas vus—qui ne vous
ont pas fait mal! Mais quoi faire? . . . Les soldats français sont mauvais avec leurs chefs. Et les anglais, à peu
près la même chose. . . . Il y a tant de misères. Il n'y a*

pas de vin, on mange du boeuf qu'on dirait du singe. Beaucoup n'ont pas de capotes. Et les soldats fusillent leurs chefs qui ne vont pas à l'avant de l'attaque mais restent aux tranchées. On se débarrasse de celui-là, on a un autre. Ah, ce n'est pas de l'amusement, ça! mais tant pis! . . . Et toujours bomm! bomm! bomm! les canons. J'en ai mal à tête! Bomm! bomm! bomm! on n'entend que ça! Deux millions d'hommes morts! Mais quoi faire? Et tuer des hommes qu'on n'a jamais vus!—ce n'est pas drôle, ça. . . . Les soldats s'embêtent. Et c'est tout en Belgique(?).   Toujours   bomm—bomm—bomm!   les canons! Ici, c'est gai, on ne l'entend pas, mais là-bas—!" I asked him why he didn't salute a sous-lieutenant whom we passed. *"A la ville, mais pas ici. Il a les galons mais il est bonhomme comme moi—pourquoi? . . . Je suis marié. J'ai deux gosses à Haréville. J'ai dix jours de permission. C'est gai d'abord, mais à partir—!"*

————

The wide low-railed bridge of Mirecourt spanned the whole valley of the river, whose smooth blue length cut the level green meadows straight across. On one side, it sent out a little canal into the city, whose walls, over-hanging it close, blackened its waters with their shade and stretched up along the slope with a crowd of dulled red roofs and gables, dominated by the plain tower of the old church that set the air throbbing with the urgent melodious pounding of its bells. On the other side, the main stream lay between a network of grassy backyards and the meadow bounded by a low stone wall yellowed by the last light of the sun. A little further it turned and was lost, save for the light line of poplars that just marked its course with the crooked threads of their stems and the yellowing mist of their branches. On the smooth low meadow, a little boy in white and a little girl in red were playing with a tiny black dog and bloomed out against the green like the flowers in Botticelli's forest.

———

An English soldier: "The situation is fucking serious!"

———

John Andersen told me that in the Danish countryside where he was born, it was always said of any boy who read a lot that he ought to be a minister. One farmer warned him: "You ought to be careful about reading so much—I knew a man once who read all the time and he got to be a Baptist!" On one occasion, his father went to a "wise woman" to have a boil removed. She directed him to eat a certain bitter herb on the nights of three successive new moons. He said that every man used to have his own wooden spoon, which he would wipe off after dinner on his coat. They never drank water but always beer, even as children. His grandmother believed in trolls.

[John Andersen was one of my closest friends in the unit. He had had some laboratory experience and he worked as a kind of assistant in the bacteriological laboratory and, when not working, endlessly read. He had already mastered English and German and now learned enough French to read. We had many outings together and talked about everything under the sun. He had been educated in Denmark in one of the popular schools established by Bishop Grundtvig. I find the note at a later stage: "John Andersen has sometimes the fine and sober smile of Erasmus." His equanimity was always perfect, and not quite devoid of a certain smugness which is often characteristic of the Danes and inherent in the cadences of their voices. When I called at the laboratory to take him for a walk, he would be likely to make some such matter-of-fact remark as, "Just wait till I burn up this leg."

After the war, he came to New York, and I tried to find him a job congenial with his intellectual interests. But in this—though seconded by Christian Gauss—I repeatedly and discouragingly failed. I had never realized before how impossible it is for anyone with no academic qualifications to find employment even in a bookstore, even as a librarian. No one could have been less helpful than Alvin Johnson, then on the *New Republic*. He was himself a self-made Dane, and one of the smuggest people I have ever known. When I told him about John Andersen and asked whether I could bring him to his office, he remarked, with no relevance to anything I had said, "I hope he doesn't have the Danish sentimentality." When I brought John around, Johnson brushed him off in a cool and perfunctory manner which left him bitter and angry. The best John could do in New York—on the strength of his non-professional hospital experience—was a job in a medical school looking after the corpses that were kept in a tank for dissection. In the course of this—his hands were constantly wet and were cracked by the cold water —he contracted a dreadful infection which made it almost impossible for him to use them but which he bore with his usual stoicism. Eventually he went West and became a farmer in Alberta, and he seems to have been quite happy. His farm was self-supporting, and he was able to lay enough by occasionally to come East or revisit Denmark. In these years, he wrote book after book— novels and idea books—and sent David Hamilton and me the manuscripts. We found them extremely boring in a way that his conversation was not. His Grundtvigian education had left him unaware of certain things: the requirements of literary art, the fact that certain subjects had already been dealt with in a way that he could not improve on. But he did get one book published, under the pen-name of John Andersen Udmark, "the story," as the publishers say, "of man's conquest of his universe," with the title *The Ground We Have Covered,* which, much to his satisfaction, got him a story and photograph in *Time.* I did not see him for years, but he did once come to visit me on Cape Cod. Everybody who met him then was impressed, as I had been years ago, by his dignity, his independence and his impassive humor and charm. A few years ago, a favorite niece who kept house for him wrote me that he was dead.]

————

A Tommy: "Ow, the Germans don't always kill their prisoners, and we do it just as much as they do. I've often seen a couple o' chaps bringin' back a wounded prisoner and they get tired of leadin' 'im and one of 'em says: 'Aw, fuck 'im, Jock! let's do 'im in!,' and they shoot 'im and leave 'im there."

————

[Roy Gamble was the painter of the unit: he painted all the signs and whatever else had to be painted, and he secured for himself a small room in the basement of one of the hospitals, where he was able to work and to live by himself. In this room, David, Leo Rabbette, John Andersen and I were often congregated at night to laugh about the doings of the unit and to discuss the problems of the world. We were joined by the Mess Sergeant, Cornelius Holland, with whom we were on very friendly terms. He was a big mischievous reddish-haired Irishman, who had served in the Boer War and actually liked soldiering. He told me—quite correctly—that I had "the brains for a sky-pilot but not the arse for a soldier." He was a nephew, I think it was, of the Gaelic scholar, Dr. Douglas Hyde, and a man of some education. He lent me a life of John Redmond, which, although I was all for Irish independence, I found excessively dull. (This and John Morley's autobiography, which I also read at this time, convinced me that parliamentary politics was a national English game like cricket, in which a foreigner could feel little interest.) Holland had a kind of stooge, his right hand man in the mess, a simple-minded Pole named Mroch, and with the cruel Irish humor, he was always playing jokes on him and baiting him: "He calls-umself a Pole! Who was Kosciuszko?" They shared a room in this basement, and Holland would rig up devices to make Mroch's bed collapse just after he was settled in it. But he had rescued Mroch from the brig, into which he had been thrown for drunkenness, and acted as his protector, and Mroch was devoted to him. Mroch often joined us in the company of Holland, and when he saw that Holland was having him on, he would protest in a kind of simpleton's voice, "Holland, I know you like a book!"

In order to get away from the mess, we would go for dinner to the Hôtel de Ville, where we ate at a big table with the family of a French business man who had had to leave Petrograd as the result of the Revolution. We all had terrible colds and would come in with deep satisfaction from the misty and chilling night. We would first go into the kitchen, where the cooking was done in heavy brass receptacles on a wide flat stove that took up all one side of the room. The soup would be heating in an immense brass pot and would be served piping hot. (When forty-six years later, I revisited Vittel, I found the Hôtel de Ville still run by the same family and the same brass pots hanging to the walls of the kitchen.) But this hotel was put later off bounds when the husband of the *patronne* came back from the front and found his wife in bed with an American sergeant, and we had to resort to another restaurant. The then uniformly high quality of the French cuisine, which extended to every provincial town, was exemplified by both these restaurants. We were very often given horse-meat, but the soup and the French frieds, the dandelion salad and the wine seemed to us invariably excellent. We took turns giving birthday dinners, and the joke among us was that Roy Gamble, who in his early life had had to learn to be very thrifty, would somehow, when his own birthday came around, get out of giving a dinner. But, though evidently reluctant, he did not fail us.]

———

Holland, in reply to John's pointing out that, in view of the St. Louis race riots, it would appear that the people of any race were capable of atrocious cruelty: "Yes, I know—and right there in Tipperary there was a family tried to burn an old woman; they said she had the devil in her! They had her there with her arse-hole over the fire to drive him out. And they had the old woman herself convinced. She thought she did have the devil in her!"

———

Roy Gamble's school friend, who had been brought up in the lower part of Detroit, always used to double up his fists at once when anyone playfully seized him by the arm or clapped him on the shoulder.

———

Leo Rabbette wrote to the editor of *The Stars and Stripes* that he had had "a year of virile pen-pushing under Elbert Hubbard at East Aurora."

Leo called on John Andersen in the laboratory to get some urine specimens, but, remaining for half an hour to spout Swinburne and Wilde, he nearly went off without them.

———

Roy Gamble: "That was why I introduced Leo to Ford [not Henry, Sheridan Ford, a Detroit wit and intellectual]. I'd heard him tell about how he was Hubbard's coat-carrier down there at East Aurora and how they used to go out on those walks, you know, trailing along in a line behind him [Hubbard]—and I thought I'd get him to meet Ford. Ford's the direct opposite of Hubbard, see. Ford throws everything behind-um. Everytime he gets up in the morning, he makes a fresh start, see! While Hubbard builds up—he lives on what he's built up."

———

Human bodies in the twentieth century were so unsightly that it was considered indecent to expose them, and sexual relations had become so sordid that as topics of conversation they were regarded as low. In America, the word *beautiful,* which, among the Greeks and the French, had covered all good taste, loveliness and nobility, became so outlawed and seldom heard that it made people self-conscious to use it. This was the greatest age of America's industrial prosperity.

———

[I picked up this note in the street]: "CHERE LELENE JE TEMBRASSE TOUT FORT ES TU CONTENTE DAVOIR LA PHOTO DE JEAN HENRI EST REVENU NOUS AVONS BIEN JOUE."

———

The hounds in the movie streamed down the hill like globules of quicksilver.

———

The poppies and bachelors'-buttons dotted the grain with plain bright colors like the balls of a rocket.

———

As we climbed the long hill that leads to Langres [John Andersen and I on a bicycle holiday], we saw above us the black ramparts and the gray roofs of the ancient town. Set in the wall was a squat round tower, from which jutted a row of gargoyles and on top of which was perched what I at first took to be another gargoyle, but what, as I came closer, defined itself as a human figure. It was an American soldier who sat with elbow on knee and chin in hand, gazing off at the immense expanse of hills, fields and towns and the great statue of the Virgin raised high on its rounded mound; and the sharp black outline of his campaign hat and bent limbs cut itself all the clearer for the stone beasts, with jaws blunted and faces disfigured by age, which hung in stiffness below him.

Behind the statue of Diderot [who was born in Langres] was a café in an old building. The reddish roof sloped down, sagging a little, to nearly the breadth of the façade itself. Below it, a row of white blinds were thrown wide against the gray wall, opening on a narrow ledge railed with iron scrollery, where "Café du Balcon" curled itself in gilt. Below this, fell a faded pink awning, which shaded the single-stemmed nickle-rimmed tables on the street and the little pine trees set in square green boxes. (The reddish shingled roof, bearing chimneys that looked as if they had been broken off at the top and three tiny lurching gables just large enough for four-paned windows—)

In those ancient backyards of gray narrow houses, the rough gables bristled with chimneys like blunted spikes, and hedges and columns of box half concealed them with their deep green.

The statue of the Virgin had been erected after the Franco-Prussian War in gratitude by the people of Langres for having been spared by the Germans. In the close cobbled square was a statue of Diderot with the volumes of the encyclopædia under his arm and on the base the names of Voltaire, Rousseau, Condorcet, Helvétius, d'Holbach, Grimm and D'Alembert.

We bought mirabelles, which were then in season, at a fruitstore near the statue and ate them from a bag in the street. Afterwards, we went into a little cathedral and rested from the hot sun in the cool gray twilight interior, high and vague above the worn stone floor.

———

[We heard the guns from Verdun, but I never saw the front till after the war.

On the days when we got leave to go out of Vittel, we bicycled or walked to the neighboring towns: Domrémy, Mirecourt, Contrexéville, Épinal. John Andersen and I were once able to get away to spend a night at Nancy. These expeditions, in contrast to our ordinary routine, were incredibly exciting and delightful. If it were merely a question of some country village, we would go to the village inn and drink the solitary bottle of champagne which these inns seemed invariably to keep on hand.

We encountered on one occasion something extremely odd. We had been told by members of the unit of their having made the acquaintance of the owner of an old château on the edge of the great dark woodland that begins in that part of the Vosges and is really a continuation, on the other side of the Rhine, of the German Black Forest. They told us that we ought to visit it: they had been very cordially received. David Hamilton and I found our way there through wastes of snow scrawled with bare bristling thickets. As at last we approached the château, which was called St. Baslemont, and looked up at its sharp peaked tower rising above us on its steep hill,

with the snow-covered sweep below it that was bounded
by the limitless forest—it must have been unassailable
from that direction—we felt ourselves back in the Middle
Ages. When we had climbed to the top of the hill, we
found a stone well, ancient and primitive, a farmhouse
sunk in mud and manure, and the old dark château shut
in from the road by a stone wall that masked the courtyard. We went in through a grilled gate and saw a
strange Mongoloid-looking servant who crossed the courtyard and did not notice us. We were received at the front
door by a hospitable little gentleman, who was dapperly
dressed in brown and who spoke English with a London
accent. We had been told of a châtelaine, and I suspected
that this host was a woman: she reminded me of Vesta
Tilley, the impersonator of English Johnnies, once a
favorite of the music halls. She presented us to a little
woman, mildly pretty and very retiring. They were having a Christmas party for the children of the tiny village.
There were presents. The local abbé was there. We had
cakes and drank cassis, the insipid blackberry wine. The
jolly host or hostess presided with her hands in her
pockets. The whole thing was rather mystifying. When
we inquired in Vittel, we were told that the châtelaine
was the daughter of the famous actress Ève Lavallière,
who had become religious and abandoned the stage. A
woman in a shop said to us, with a dry smile, *"Elle n'est
pas commes les autres."* She chose to dress as a man, and I
assumed that she was simply a Lesbian, and that the other
woman was her girlfriend. I was told that they had wild
parties and threw the champagne bottles into the oubli-
ette.

The sequel to this first visit to St. Baslemont did not
occur till forty-six years later, but I shall tell about it here,
for otherwise the reader would lose the connection. In the
winter of 1963, I revisited the Vosges with my wife,

driving by car to the places I had known during the war. I inquired in Vittel about Mlle Lavallière and was told— no doubt due to the confusion of sex that made them think I meant the actress—that Mlle Lavallière was dead. But we drove out to St. Baslemont. The approach now seemed even more forbidding than it had when I had gone there by foot. We at first tried to climb by a wrong narrow road and then found it difficult to turn around without falling off the road into a steep hillside orchard that hung below it. But when we parked beside the wall of the old château, which made it seem so sealed-up and secret, and walked around to the front, we found it in a state of ruin before which I stood aghast. The roof had fallen in. The grilled gate was padlocked and rusted. The courtyard was full of chickens, and a huge hare was looking out at us from a window on the first floor. A farmer, whose squalid place seemed always to have been part of the property, came out to see what was going on. I asked whether the château hadn't burned. *"Non: il s'est écroulé de lui-même."* I said that it was a pity. He agreed. No one lived there now? *"Si: la propriétaire,"* who had bought it from Mlle Lavallière. She lived in a corner tower, the only part still intact. I looked at this corner and thought it seemed unsuitable for anything except an owl. But Mlle Lavallière was dead? This time I was under- stood. No: she was still alive—she lived on the village street, the last house from there on the left. We went down the hill trying several houses and awakening curios- ity. These *bicoques* were also in the Middle Ages, and when we found the one we were looking for, I was surprised by its turning out—though the door and some of the windows had been painted white—just as low and mean as the others, and partly dilapidated. I knocked on the door: *"Entrez."* A little old man, with white straight hair and a squarish rather wooden face, had been writing at a wide crude work-table. I was not sure that I had the right person and asked whether she were Mlle Lavallière: *"Je suis le fils de Mlle Lavallière."* I explained that she wouldn't remember me but that I had come to the château years before. She answered that this was possible. She had got up and, instead of briskly bouncing as she had when she was so much younger, she stood with her hands in her pockets and shifting from one foot to the other. She was dressed in men's jeans and comfortable no doubt wool-lined slippers. "But you are Mlle Lavallière." *"Je suis le fils de Mlle Lavallière—Jean Lavallière."* I then tried to bring her back to the past by saying to her in English that she used to speak very good English. "I have forgotten . . . ," she answered in English, shrugging slightly and a little more feminine. I asked her if I could bring in my wife for a moment. *"Pourquoi faire? Je travaille."* And I saw that in the little room there was not really much place for guests. I was embarrassed and I simply said that it was sad to see the château like that. Yes: she had sold it a number of years ago. We shook hands. As I was leaving, she said strangely, and I did not know what to answer: *"Je suis un pauvre type."* This experience somewhat shook me. I felt that I had really had no right to intrude and put her to the boring embarrassment of explaining the situation to a stranger, and had been rightly, though politely, *mis à la porte.* That sinister old château, once the scene of outrageous revels; that queer being—I supposed, in her seventies—writing alone in her wretched cell. Was she emulating thus her mother, who had become a Franciscan nun?

It was not till I returned to Paris that, from inquiry and from a (not very reliable) book called *I'm Going to Maxim's* by an Englishman, H. J. Greenwell, I more or less found out the story.

Ève Lavallière was the child of actors. On the road, her father shot her mother, and then shot himself. She and her brother ran into the streets, where the brother disappeared. Ève was picked up by the police and sent to school in a convent, from which she ran away at seventeen. She came to Paris and went on the stage, and had a tremendous success. She married Fernand Samuel, the director of the Théâtre des Variétés. I note, in Jules Renard's journal, that he once said to her, "*Vous avez un visage qui me plaît pour sa franchise. Vous devez avoir des qualités morales, vous;*" and that, "*une pauvre petite femme très émue,*" she several times took his hand: "*Oh, que je suis contente! De tous les amis de Guitry, je me disais que vous étiez le seul à me mépriser, et j'en souffrais. Je pensais que vous n'auriez jamais de sympathie pour moi, et voilà ce que vous me dites. Oh! que je suis contente!*" She and Samuel had one daughter Jeanne; then were soon divorced. Jeanne left home and went to live with a man who smuggled dope, and when he was caught, she was sent to jail, too. But almost as soon as she got out, her father died and left her his fortune. She was some sort of hermaphrodite and at the age of eighteen had an operation performed that made her predominantly masculine. She had herself registered as male and legally married the little woman that I met at St. Baslemont. At one time, I believe, she ran a bar in Paris. Her mother was now living with a German baron, an attaché at the Paris Embassy; but when war came, he went back to Germany and was killed in the very first weeks. At first, after his death, Ève Lavallière wandered around Montmartre incognito, giving cakes to the children of men at the front and performing other kindnesses for their mothers. Then she became converted and abandoned the stage; but she did not enter a convent. She went to live in a cottage in the village of Thuillières near the Château de St. Baslemont, in which she had once lived with Samuel, to which Robert de Flers had come to read the comedies he had written for the Variétés and at which their friend Jules Massenet had visited and had written *Thaïs*. She did not die till 1929, so she must have been living at Thuillières at the time I first met Jeanne-Jean, who had inherited the château from her father. Her mother is said to have been buried in a coarse linen gown and her grave to have been marked by a plain wooden cross. I had no doubt, when I learned all this, that the child was now following her mother's path. I hope that she was writing this story.]

———

Occasionally, in the smell of summer rain or of savoury cooking on a late afternoon, I have almost recognized the odors of home—but only to be baffled, after a moment, by realizing a hopeless strangeness.

———

"Me and Father have always been just like chums together. Why, once I had dinner with him at a restaurant and, after dinner, he lit a cigar and said: 'I wish we could find a good piece of tail now!'—I'm going to live in the Philippines after the war—oh, that's the place to live! You can keep a woman there for seven dollars a week!"

———

"The Captain seen him pissin' in the camp and kicked him in the balls, and afterwards, when he talked to him about it, he said, 'What you done to me is somethin' I wouldn't take from my own father!' But afterwards the Captain tried to make it up with him and invited him in and offered him a cigar."

———

Miss Douglas [a nurse from Charleston, South Carolina] said that in a miner's house to which she had been sent to nurse, they washed the new-born baby in a basin which the next day was used to make bread and sent the midwife to sleep in the same room with the husband and children. They were Austrians.

Miss Douglas said that she could sympathize with the soldiers sent back from the hospital to the front, because when she had first gone to the training school as a girl of seventeen, forced by the post-bellum poverty of her family to earn her own living, she had been terribly frightened by the idea of working and of her relation to the doctors and by the stories she had been told of the horrors of the operating-room.

[I thought she was a very sympathetic woman. I found her again at Chaumont. She had been *du gratin* of Charleston and a member of the St. Cecilia Society, which she discreetly let me know.]

The poplars stood like soldiers halted at attention on the road.

The moonlight lay along the floor like broken bars of silver.

One of the German prisoners was a boy of about eighteen, slight and blond and very well-bred. They asked him if they could have his hat and, after a moment of abashed hesitation, he smiled nicely and replied: "Then I shouldn't have one!" They assured him that, if they took it, he would get another when he reached the hospital;

but he finally succeeded in keeping it through sheer force of good manners.

———

One patient had three-quarters of the surface of his body burned and his lungs partially destroyed. His face was purple. At intervals during the night, he would whistle hoarsely and, when I came to him, he would ask: "Are you ready to move yet, Sergeant?" He thought he was still on the march. In the morning he died.

———

I heard a story that one soldier from the South got a letter from his father in which the old man said that he hated to have the boy away so long, "But the damn Yanks have got to be licked!"

———

[Sometime in 1918, I was transferred to the Intelligence Service at our General Headquarters in Chaumont and given the rank of sergeant. This was not due to merit on my part or special favor on the part of my superiors, but entirely to my own efforts in getting my father to pull wires in Washington.

At the hospital, just before I left, I had been given a farewell dinner by the mess crew—of which I was quite proud. There were some very good men in the unit outside my own special group of friends, but in general they belonged to the lower grades of what is called the white-collar class, a kind of person that I did not like. They were great intriguers for position and takers of advantage of one another. And the same was true of the officers, who included some first-rate doctors but also a number of others for whom the uniform had been a step up and who sometimes abused their acquired rank. The mess crew I got on with much better. They were likely to be old soldiers and sailors with whom one dealt, with no regard for social lines or petty ambitions, on a comradely human basis. Some were cockneys who spoke with the cockney glottal stop in such words as *little* and *bottle*—a feature which I had thought confined to the Scotch. One ex-sailor died of syphilis. There was nothing at all bad about him; but he seemed to me to represent the lowest type of working human unit. He was swarthy and seemed foreign, but it was as if he had no nationality. In the unit, I was always called "Woodrow" or "Ed."

At Chaumont, I translated uninteresting documents, prepared a memorandum on Poland from the meager materials in the GHQ library and, working in what was called the "Department of Exterior Fronts"—a name which got a good deal of kidding—moved pins with differently colored heads on a wall map intended to keep us informed of the operations of Allied Troops in Russia and other regions outside the main theater of war. I had a great deal more liberty here, and life was very much more varied. I ran into people I knew from the *Evening Sun* or Yale and Princeton, and I made some new and interesting friends—especially a man named Eugene Arthur Hecker, a descendant of the Friedrich Hecker of Baden, who was one of the leaders of the German Revolution of 1848 and, after its failure, emigrated to America. My friend, a Latin teacher from St. Louis, was the author of a book on the teaching of Latin and a history of women's rights. He was a learned and witty man, with quite unconventional opinions. Hecker and Heber Blankenhorn, former assistant city editor of the *Evening Sun,* constituted by themselves the department for propaganda in Germany. There was also a Belgian radical, who taught me the *Inter-*

national and an Anarchist anthem with the following words:

> Debout, mon frère de misère!
> Debout, mon frère de misère!
> Pour écraser la bourgeoisi-e
> Il faut de l'énergi-e!
> Il faut, il faut de l'énergi-e!

My duties as sergeant were confined to signing passes, which I issued to everybody who wanted one.]

———

At Chaumont, near a little village center which had still a feudal look and the little river whose smoothness only the ducks and rushes broke, was a small château which Louis XIV had built for Mme du Maintenon. One saw it from a low stone wall which shut its grounds from the street; and the low gracious windows of the first floor and the little oval ones under the red roof looked out from behind the thick shrubs and trees of the lawn with the charm of a sovereign simplicity.

———

Brenicke said that he knew a man who had spent several months on the border learning all the verses to *The Bastard King of England.*

———

George Wood [a reporter for the *Evening Sun,* whom I got to know much better in Chaumont than I ever had done in the office] called English drapers' clerks "the than whomest of human mice" and said that Rockefeller had the soul of a spider. He told of his first interview with

[Charles Evans] Hughes, then just become Governor of New York: "We waited for him and then he came in—and he hadn't had a business suit on in years, you know—and he'd evidently just bought one ready-made—and he suddenly appeared looking *middle-class as hell*. And then, all of a sudden, he remembered that he ought to smile—and he smiled,—Oh, my God!—it was terrible. And he said: 'Hello, fellows!' And then he said: 'Won't you come up to the roof-garden?' And I didn't want to go; I was afraid he might say, 'Oh, hell! what's the use?' and jump off the roof or something."

———

Hecker remarked that [James W.] Gerard [our former ambassador to Germany] couldn't speak German. "Why, hell!" said George [Wood], "He don't talk English. He talks politics!"

———

Hecker said that when the streets of St. Louis had long been dark, because the Mayor was getting graft out of the lighting system and a committee of citizens went to him to demand an explanation, he answered: "Well, you've still got de moon, ain't it?" But the next time they went with a rope and the town got some light.

———

Hecker, describing [Aristophanes'] *The Knights*: "They get hold of this sausage-seller and say, 'Why, dammit, you'll have to be President of the Republic! Can you write?' And he said: 'No, but I can read.' And they said, 'Well, that's against you!' "

I said: "George, do you think Hecker used to say 'dammit' in civil life?"

Hecker: "Oh, yes! I've always sworn. As soon as I got a good look at the world, I began."

———

Christ was a radical when he was living: it is only since he has been sitting at the right hand of God that he has become a conservative.

———

Aunt Laura told me that Grandfather [Kimball] insisted on reading novels in his later years, because he said he had spent all the first part of his life reading history. It seems to me that his desire was a natural one; he must have craved the comfort of comparatively cheerful stories.

———

I told Hecker that the gods had it in for him because he had too much on them. We discussed sexual questions for some time. He resisted my view till I adduced *Tristan and Isolde* as the classical example of a laudable adultery. Then he said, "Oh, yes, of course, they ought to do it. I approve of it. Do anything in my power to assist them." He remarked later: "You better write a treatise: *Pro Adulterio Dissertatio*. Be sure to write it in Latin." As we parted for the evening, he said: "Well, we'll meet in hell presently."

———

Brossard said that he would be a Bolshevik himself if he didn't have a bank-account. [He was a Swiss who had become an American citizen.]

[The subject of the following description was a major who was the head of my department. Since it was impossible for me to talk back to him, I produced this rather venomous portrait.]:

In his pleasant gift of drollery, the effervescence was seen of something not unlike intelligence. It was only when he tried to argue or explain that one saw how little used to thought he was. Not altogether unsusceptible to ideas, he appropriated the more winsome aspects of any that were in the air and allowed them to hang twinkling in his mind until some newcomer displaced them. He was incapable of the effort of examining them for himself; but if he heard a refutation that appealed to him, he would accept as much of it as he could remember without difficulty.

He had been born in fortunate circumstances and was accustomed to country clubs and managed to pass for wide-awake and intelligent without ever harboring a doubt that might have discredited the foundations of the world he knew. His education at Yale had made equilibrium easier; at that robust school, where the battle is to the strong and so much boldness of thought is encouraged without its ever being subversive, the esteem in which his powers had been held had confirmed their limitations. At forty, he felt that, after all, his class were the rightful masters. His case was that the common man was neither able nor intelligent, that he was incapable of those fine sensibilities which might have made his lot disagreeable. Without guidance from above, he could do nothing to good purpose. Not that he himself was not as progressive as anyone; and he was honestly kindly—kindly to a fault. It was difficult for him to refuse a request, whether he could fulfil it or not, and it gave him a real pleasure to do someone a favor. But, after all, did not the superior man have the right to control in industry or in the army? And he naturally expected nearly everything to be done for him by others. Spoiled, amiable and a little absurd, without bringing any real intellectual application to the things with which he had to deal, he maintained the right to permanence of the society which had enabled him to preserve his self-esteem without disillusion.

———

George Wood told me about meeting some eminent politician or other at Atlantic City. This man and his family were climbing and had begun to put on a little side. A friend of George's, who was taking him to dinner with these people, admonished him to be sure to dress and behave correctly. The affair was very heavy and solemn until George, who had gained self-confidence from the liquor, made some awful break and then stopped aghast for fear he had offended the company. On the contrary, the host slapped him violently on the back and exclaimed: "Why, Jesus Christ! you're human! I thought I had to play up to you!" After this, the party went much better, and, when the meal was over, George and his host withdrew and got drunk together in enthusiastic fellowship.

———

Robert Jackson said that Pete Widener's parents had educated him in France to try to make a gentleman of him, but that he had only lost all the virility of the butcher strain without getting rid of any of the coarseness. [Robert Jackson was an old friend from Princeton and Washington. Learning that he was somewhere in the neighborhood, I looked him up when I was stationed at Chaumont. It can be seen that our conversation reverted to a pre-war tone.]

———

[The Armistice was declared on November 11, 1918. George Wood and I took a walk in the streets. It was damp November weather; a few of our soldiers were drunk; the French soldiers set off a few squibs. George said, "Well, b'gosh, we beat Purdue!"]

———

A Regular Colonel called his staff together and began: "Now that we have finished with this war, it is time to begin to think about the next." A Harvard man was heard to titter.

Another Regular Army man had said, in March, when the Germans had nearly reached Paris: "Well, if the Germans win and we're defeated, that'll prove they're the superior race."

———

I found that one of the library helpers was a Polish Jew and another was a Russian. The first said that he had helped the Jews in a Polish pogrom, where he had seen a Cossack nail a woman and her child, one on top of the other, to a board, and showed me the sabre scars on his hands; the second said with terrible passion that the Russians were a lot of "tam fools," they had ruined his life; if he could go back and do anything to help the Government help them, he'd be glad to, but he wished the Allies would go in and kill them every one. He had been a Social Democrat in the Revolution of 1905; at that time, all the streets had been barricaded and when his sister died, they could not get her body through the city (Moscow, I think) to the cemetery. That, he said, was what discouraged him; after that, he had come to America. Bossard, who, though Swiss, is, it seems, a baron—I hadn't known they had titles in Switzerland—by the right of a title given one of his ancestors for military prowess some five centuries ago by the French king, listened to all this. He confessed to me that he was proud to have made his own success in America. If he had stayed in Switzerland, he would simply have been put into some job and would probably never have worked at all.

————

Hecker said that, before he served in the Army, he didn't care whether he lived or died; but, since he had gone through the barrage, he had the will to live. In the midst of that hail of terror and destruction, he wondered for the first time whether it did all actually go for making the world safe for democracy. And now, he said, he was anxious to live and didn't want to die—especially for humanity: that wasn't worth dying for.

Hecker: "When a man can't explain something to you clearly, one of two things is true: either he doesn't understand it himself or it isn't to his interest that you should understand it."

————

[A little before Christmas, I was sent to Trèves (Trier), in the Army of Occupation on the mistaken assumption that I spoke German. The poem—written on the spot—and the story—written later—that follow are products of this experience. In Trier, I ran into George Perkins, Jr., a friend from Hill and Princeton, who had been assigned as ADDC to a little town on the Moselle. His duties were almost non-existent, and he lived with the Burgomaster's family, with whom he was on very friendly terms. He had to kill a good deal of time and would lie in bed reading French novels. His young wife

had just died in the flu epidemic, and I think he was
rather desolate. I often went out to see him, sometimes
spending the night and walking back early in the morning in order to be checked in at the barracks. This story
combines my own with George's experience, but it is
mainly based on things that actually happened.]

Trèves, December, 1918

Trevis Metropolis, urbs amoenissima,
Quae Bacchum recolis, Baccho gratissima,
Da tuis incolis vina fortissima
Per dulcor.

Old Verse

I

I think your ancient laughter all has died,
    Most pleasant Trèves, whom Bacchus once made gay:
    The smooth Moselle all wintry slips away
Between the naked hills that wall her side,
With purple dimmed and blackened and with grass
    All faded by the frost; a sharp rain beats
    And, dull in black, the people through the streets
Speak scarce to greet each other as they pass—
Bewilderment and wrath and blasting grief
    On faces that must once have smiled to see
    The globes and tinsel for the Christmas tree
And kept for the angels' message some belief.
These have not seemed in wonder to behold
    The gleaming leopards of the god leap through
    The leaves; and none knows now to raise anew
That tongue that matched the harvest with its gold.
    Men lift no hymns to greet a young god. Nay!
    The Gorgon here has turned all faces gray.

II

And yet with yellow wine and clinking rims
   We almost laughed the Gorgon's stare away
   Last night when we made little Bäbchen play
Der Lindenbaum, some Sousa and some hymns,
The Beautiful Blue Danube,—(ah, how wan!
   How far Vienna's swaying violins!
   Gone now with sweetest voices in the din,
With Schubert, Heine and de Musset, gone!)—
Though one of us had marched among the men
   Who reached the Marne four summers past and one
   Had bent reluctant patience to a gun,
That they might never reach the Marne again . . .
Without that song, all life had not sufficed;
   Without that hour, we had been poor and mean,
   Whose ignorant hands, still cruel and unclean,
Have rent ourselves till Bacchus now nor Christ
   Can scarce find balm for our extreme distress—
   Nor Music that forgets all bitterness.

Lieutenant Franklin

Said the Captain loudly: "This is something new!
Eating with enlisted men!"

They had sat down in the only places left, at a table
where some soldiers were lunching.

"Here, boy!" cried the Major to a waiter. *"Twa deenay,
toot sweet!* Now hurry it right along. We've got to leave
here by half past one."

"When are we supposed to get to Trèves?" asked the
young Second Lieutenant.

"Well, if we start on time," replied the Major, "we
ought to get there by quarter to ten—supposing we don't

have any blow-outs—which we unquestionably will—the
road's pretty rotten still. They ought to have put a few
Americans on it and they'd have a decent road by now.
But that isn't the frog idea: never do a thing right in the
first place if you can take a long time and do it rotten!
They thought it was a brilliant stroke of economy to put
the Chinamen to work on the roads. The Chinamen are
the only people in the world that have less sense than the
frogs. They just have a lot of fun blowing themselves up
with old hand grenades. . . . Sure: every time they find
one, they take the pin out—with their marvellous Ori-
ental cunning. . . . Sure: the whole road from Nancy to
Metz is sprayed with 'em."

The Captain repeated his reprimand: "I suppose that
since the Armistice," he said, "the enlisted men are eating
with the officers!"

"I beg your pardon, sir," said one of the privates, "but
we were here before you!"

"You better be careful!" blurted the Captain, turning
red with surprise. He was a short man with a bristling
blond mustache and a smartly belted uniform, who ad-
ministered a filing cabinet at GHQ with much severity
and dash. He looked to the Major, his ranking officer, to
take up the case against the soldier; but the Major, with
his square-tipped mechanic's fingers laid out like tools
before him on the table, only fixed the harassed and
evasive waiter with his searching gold-rimmed goggles,
behind which his black eyes themselves had the aspect of
a second pair of lenses: a double surveyor's theodolite
turning on the axis of his neck.

"Say," he shouted, "come over here, you!—Now what
about those three lunches? We've got to leave here by
half past one!"

"*Il faut attendre cinq minutes,*" said the waiter. "*La
viande n'est pas prête.*"

"*Sank minoot* nothing!" said the Major. "We've got to have it right away!—Tell him we've got to have it right away or we'll go somewhere else."

"*Il dit*," the young Lieutenant interpreted, "*que nous ne pouvons pas attendre. Nous voulons le déjeuner tout de suite.*"

"*Ah,*" replied the waiter with a shrug which mingled weariness with malice. "*On ne peut pas toujours avoir tout ce qu'on veut en ce monde!*" He disappeared with his toppling plates.

"What did he say?" demanded the Major.

"There's no excuse for this insolence!" declared the Captain. "If I were you, I'd complain to the mayor. Morale has been going to pieces ever since the Armistice, and it's high time to jack it up." He glared at the privates, who were leaving.

"Did he try to get fresh?" asked the Major.

"Well, more philosophical, I should say," hesitated Lieutenant Franklin. "That's the wonderful thing about the French: they always manage to remain philosophical, no matter how desperate the situation is."

"If they were a little less philosophical," said the Major, "we might get a little more service."

Lunch over, they went out into the street and stood a moment in the Place Stanislas, while the Major, looking out for the motor car, raked the square with his lenses.

All about them, in chaste beauty of proportion and elegance at once formal and gracious, rose the façades of the eighteenth century. Wide, many-windowed, gray-yellow, they were crowned with rows of torches and panoplies in stone; and they cherished on the *rez de chaussée* the bright cafés that sprinkled tables along the pavement. The lines of Nancy, in the cold December sun, showed as fine and dry as a Callot engraving.

Lieutenant Franklin watched the pretty women hurrying by in their brisk serious way, their clear northern complexions bitten red.

The khaki car drew up and they got in.

"We might make it by half past nine," said the Major, looking at his watch.

"What do you do up there, Major?" Lieutenant Franklin asked.

"Censor's office," replied the Major.

"That's what I'm supposed to do. But the joke is I don't know much German. I'm being sent up by mistake. The colonel's away and that damn field clerk down there who's just been made personnel officer got me mixed up with a Lieutenant Frankel. I couldn't convince him he was wrong—he thought I didn't want to go.—I'm afraid I won't be much good in the censor's office: I hardly know German at all. What I'm supposed to know is French."

"That's all right," the Major assured him. "I don't know anything. I'm an engineer."

In the Place de la Carrière, as they honked dictatorially through it, the fallen leaves of the linden trees were yellow in the straight alleys and the rows of brass-knobbed houses met winter with the sober loveliness which does not fade in a pale light. Some of the little hotels about the station had been damaged or gutted by bombs; but in that city which had been molded to harmony as if by the touch of a single hand, their scars showed as lightly as chippings.

"How do the Germans treat you?" inquired Lieutenant Franklin.

"Fine," replied the Major.

"The Hun," explained Captain Scudder, "is the most servile goddam beast in the world. When he's on top, he's a dirty brute; but when he's licked, he's like a whipped cur. They think they can get let off easy by making up to the Americans. It's a deliberate policy, inspired from Berlin."

"Do you think so?" asked Lieutenant Franklin.

"Why, of course," asserted Captain Scudder, "they're just the same old double-faced bunch. They haven't turned into angels overnight!"

At Pont-à-Mousson, the houses and shops of the square had been battered about like giant children's blocks which an adult giant had knocked over in passing.

The M.P. ran through their orders, stamped the paper and handed it back.

"Pretty quick," noted Major Liggett.

The stout arch of the old stone bridge lay sunk in the river-bed; from the banks stuck out truncated fragments. They crossed on an improvised suspension.

Beyond the river, landscape ceased: crooked trenches cracked a blasted wilderness. It was as if, by dint of titanic effort, the reproductive faculties of nature had at last been conclusively extirpated—as if the earth had been finally divested, not merely of vegetation, but even of color and form. Blackened shattered stumps of trees seemed as strange to the saps of life as the systems of scrawling barbed wire. At the side of the road, so many times wrecked that it now seemed beyond reconstruction, ragged fringes of camouflage screens were dangling in miserable fatuity. Here and there neat quiltings of graves were pricked out with wooden crosses.

"Well," remarked Lieutenant Franklin, "it certainly seems funny to be going across here as easily as this!"

For him, the front was a barrier against which four years of life and ammunition had been hurled without effect. He found himself passing it with a kind of awe, as if a wizard's circle had been wiped away and the ogrelike race it had guarded had been suddenly deprived of their power.

"This the first time you've been through?" asked the Major.

"Yes," said Lieutenant Franklin, "the first time."

"Europe's masterpiece!" said the Major.

At Metz, they had wakened from a sketchy dream and were back in America again. It was as if their eyes, long unsatisfied by the light tints and unemphasized forms of the French, were at last being fed to the full with solid shapes and thick colors. Amid what seemed now huge masonry of office-buildings and markets, the old French houses survived like fossil ferns in a rock.

Among the German additions to the cathedral, the Emperor William II still figured in the rôle of the prophet Daniel; but on the esplanade a statue of William I had been precipitated from its pedestal and lay rigid and uncanny in the street, still bestriding its horse.

"The French did that the night of the Armistice," explained Captain Scudder, laughing. "They raised hell with the German inhabitants."

It was with excitement and satisfaction that Lieutenant Franklin saw for himself that the wrong of Alsace-Lorraine had been righted. Aroused by the pleas of his college president, he had left college for an officers' training camp—had spent eight months in the Middle West and six in the artillery school at Langres, and had finally, two days before the Armistice, found the range on an invisible Belgian town.

They stopped at the station for refreshment. On one of the platforms, the French Red Cross was giving out war bread and sugarless coffee to a line of thin dull-faced women. The officers stepped in ahead of the line and received each a cup and a wedge of bread.

"They're foolish to feed 'em," said Captain Scudder. "They've got plenty hidden away in their houses."

Major Liggett, his dynamo stimulated by the coffee, beamed impersonally above the heads of the others. At the sight of the lumpish red station with its exact complicated trainyard, he had something of the feeling of reassurance of being back in Jersey City or New Haven.

"Well," he declared, "it's certainly a comfort to see a regular train again!"

Lieutenant Franklin assented.

"But now that the frogs have taken them over, needless to say, they won't work anymore."

"I guess the French can't help the bad service," Lieutenant Franklin defended them. "The railroads have been disorganized by the war."

"War nothing!" said Major Liggett. "It's the inborn inherent incapacity of the frogs for doing anything right. A ride on a French railroad train is something I never hope to forget! In the first place, the train is late. Then it turns out there aren't any seats. You have to stand up in that little narrow alleyway that runs along beside the compartments. After about an hour and a half, during which the engineer can't decide whether he wants to make the journey or not, the train finally hitches out of the station. Then he gets scared by the bad weather or something and goes back in again and waits another half hour. Finally he gets it out and coaxes it along for about fifteen miles till it dies on-um in the middle of some swamp. Every once in a while it gives a nervous twitch and a door that some frog moron has left open gets jerked back and the glass broken. Oh, la la! Somebody must be hurt!—But that't the only way you ever get any air. That's another thing about the frogs: they hate fresh air—water and fresh air. They're afraid it'll give them some disease to breathe a little raw unworked air.—Last time I went down to Paris, I was lucky and got next to a window and I swore I was going to get a little fresh air if I had to fight the whole compartment. There were two frog women sitting next to me and of course they tried to get me to close the window as soon as I opened it. But *pas compree!* Couldn't understand a word of French. Then they tried to convey the idea by blowing their noses loudly and pulling up their collars around their ears. But I was sound asleep by that time—didn't know a thing about it!"

"Still," Lieutenant Franklin reminded him, "the French have a lot of endurance."

"—And you keep your ticket for a souvenir," said the Major, throwing away his cigarette. "Nobody ever takes it up!"

On the admirable motor-road out of the city, an old woman with black clothes and a gray face shook her fist and shouted something abusive after the passing car of the conquerors.

"Did you see that?" demanded Captain Scudder, turning round to the back seat. "They don't consider themselves beaten! And they never will till we go through to Berlin!"

The mounting shadow of the short day closed over them in the Luxemburg forests, dark already with their dense pines. Lieutenant Franklin thought them romantic, like the woods in German fairy-tales and ballads.

Then the countryside was flooded with darkness, and with the darkness they all fell silent—while the presence of Germany, enormous and mute, seemed to thicken about them in the night.

At last, smooth boulevards slipped about them and lamps checked off a metropolitan embankment: houses, churches, dark Nuremberg gables, business streets in long solid blocks.

"Well-kept-up, isn't it?" commented Lieutenant Franklin.

"Sure," said the Major, "this is a regular country."

"Yes," agreed Lieutenant Franklin. "They certainly are darn efficient. How do you find them in other ways?"

"They're all right in every way, so far as I'm concerned," said the Major.

"I'm afraid you'll have to sleep in barracks tonight." Captain Scudder turned around to Lieutenant Franklin. "We didn't know you were coming this morning, but we'll fix you up with a billet tomorrow. I think you'll find yourself pretty comfortable. My quarters are really top-hole: the whole of a second floor. That's one compensation for living in Boche-land: you get the best of everything!—Drive to the barracks," he ordered the driver.

It was queer: there were no people to be seen. The streets were entirely empty, the houses all dark. Lieutenant Franklin, still haunted by the legend of that terrible race they had vanquished, felt a new vibration of excitement.

The car passed over a wide cobbled court, illumined only by the rays from the headlights, and stopped at an iron grille. The grille was forbidding—it looked feudal; an American soldier was on guard.

Major Liggett examined his watch by the murky light of the gate lantern.

"Ten-twenty," he checked up. "Not so bad."

"Just go in," Captain Scudder directed Lieutenant Franklin, "and show your orders to the Sergeant-Major. Make him fix you up. We'll get you billeted properly tomorrow."

They exchanged brief military good-nights.

"Go down the hall," said the guard, "and take the second turn to the left—and go upstairs and it's right down the hall."

Lieutenant Franklin entered the gate: it was darker inside than outside. He found himself making his way through a whole college of dark stairs and deserted corridors, vast resounding stone-paved courts and doors with harsh heraldic devices. At last, brought to a halt by the blankness of a landing, he detected a distant glimmer —a door-crack: he groped, lighting matches, to the end of a long gallery, pushed back a great door and went in.

He found himself standing in an enormous room which had evidently once been intended for some august dignitary or function. Tall gilt mirrors, beneath the high ceiling, seemed to open out spaciousness beyond spaciousness; and there was ornate furniture of heroic proportions, upholstered in red plush. In an arm-chair, feet on a table, leggings off and coat unbuttoned, sat a wide-mouthed American non-com reading the *Saturday Evening Post*.

The Sergeant got up, without buttoning his coat or, so far as Lieutenant Franklin could see, making much pretense of standing at attention. Yes: he believed it was true, as the Captain had said, that discipline was relaxing since the Armistice. But what of it? He smiled at the Sergeant as he told him of his wanderings in the building. Then he followed the clump of his shoes through more staircases, courts and corridors.

They finally entered a dark room, where the Sergeant turned on an electric-light bulb and revealed a kind of large bare cell containing eight iron beds.

"It used to be a barracks," he explained. "Then they turned it into a hospital, and now they've cleaned it out for the American troops."

"No Germans left here, of course?" inquired Lieutenant Franklin, not without something like awe.

"Only German bed-bugs," said the Sergeant.

He left, swinging-to a heavy door.

Lieutenant Franklin, alone, contemplated the raw beds with their lumpy straw-filled ticks. In the corner was a pile of rusty bed-pans. He went to the window and gazed at the foggy imprisoned court.

Tragic gloom abruptly engulfed him. Within, the room was cold and stale. Outside, the accumulated tedium of a century of pounded drill-grounds seemed to hang in the dreary air. And that empty gigantic shell, beside which the barracks of France looked as flimsy as match-box wood—the abandoned armor of the Empire which irreverent pygmies now came to explore. So they had finally hamstrung the giant! reflected Lieutenant Franklin: that was an occasion for triumph and pride. But in this great lifeless carcase, once the breeder of armies, which had pumped the blood of generations, sustaining first the rigors of the regiment, then the long down-grade against death, now evacuated even by the wounded and given up to the vermin and rust—alone in the silence, he could feel only the burden of some crushing and definitive futility. This silence was the silence of the death to which all those men had gone out, the death in which their cries and commands, their groans and howls of laughter, were extinguished; this blank was their annihilation. All the discipline, the energy, the labor, all the hammering of human beings into soldiers only in order to have their old training-school turned over to a young American who was hardly a soldier at all!

So much the better!—He took off his cap and began to unbutton his coat.—He represented the democracy of the new world which was scrapping all this outworn paraphernalia! It was to teach them to throw it away—it was to teach their democratic lesson to the pompous brutality of Prussia!—Yes: now that they had the giant at their mercy, they would spare him, they would tell him to go in peace, with their nonchalant American decency!

The Lieutenant got out a French novel and prepared to read himself to sleep.

II

When the Lieutenant, two days later, went into a tobacco store for cigarettes, it seemed to him that the storekeeper and a customer had suddenly stopped talking.

The nice-looking girl at the counter, abandoning another customer who was engaged in selecting a pipe, came forward with a little anxious air, but the Lieutenant gestured her back. The man who had been handling the pipes hastily picked one out; the other customer took leave in a low voice.

Lieutenant Franklin noted uncomfortably that the newspaper racks were nearly empty.

He bought his cigarettes, thanked the girl with a smile and left the shop blushing. The rôle of victor among the vanquished embarrassed Lieutenant Franklin. He found himself self-conscious in those streets, hushed so strangely as by imposition of a heavy alien hand. All in mourning, like droves of damned souls condemned in an afterlife to go on with business and shopping, they moved past as if they could not see him—their faces dulled and withered by grief or fixed immovably in glares of indignation or aghast in agonizing bewilderment at the breaking-up of their world. And he knew that it was his presence that made them silent; from all sides, their covert scrutiny could almost be felt as a pricking. Once when he had suddenly turned his head, a woman had looked away quickly.

The young man would have been glad to relieve this constraint—to deprecate the military formalities—to make them understand that the United States had no quarrel with the German people. He could see that they had once been nice middle-class citizens; and he wished he could make them feel the sympathy which warmed him at the sight of their Christmas preparations—gold and silver Christmas tree ornaments, children's fairy-books with goblins on the covers, the few poor half-finished half-hearted toys which were all that was to be had in the shops.

He drifted on toward the censor's office. In the windows of the picture shops, he noticed, the popular subject was the Return of the Soldier: sturdy young fellows, with rifles and belts, striding back into cozy homes, embracing their young wives with tears. Here and there, the processions of bourgeois black were threaded by the gray-green of an officer, who, deprived of his arms and insignia, was wandering carelessly at large. These officers, unlike the civilians, had the air of being relieved.

In the office, he found Captain Scudder talking emphatically to Major Bradley behind the latter's large desk. He picked up the Paris *Herald,* received in Trèves eight days late, and read with excitement that President Wilson had just been welcomed in Paris with an ovation perhaps unexampled in history. To the thunderous salutes of six-inch guns, the loud hum of airplanes, the martial trumpets, the Garde Républicaine playing *The Star-Spangled Banner* and the roaring of a crowd which at the Porte Dauphine had required thirty-six thousand soldiers to restrain it—half buried in a storm of flowers, the President of the United States, accompanied by the ladies of his party and Clemenceau and Poincaré, had driven to the Palais Murat. There he had been received by Prince Murat, his host, who had been standing in the doorway to greet him.

Lieutenant Franklin's heart was lifted with pride at the realization that a man of his nation could command such honor abroad—to be fêted by a whole foreign people and received by a foreign prince!

Then Major Liggett stalked in, and the officers sat down to a conference.

"Let's see," began Major Bradley. "Anything to report on the meetings, Major Liggett? . . . Anything to report on the theaters, Lieutenant? . . ."

They had been sent on their missions with interpreters. Neither had been aware of anything exceptional.

"Well," the Major went on, "there's an objectionable

editorial in the *Volksblatt* this morning"—the newspapers were Captain Scudder's field—"I've sent for the editor to come around." An officer in the regular army, Major Bradley had inevitably gravitated to a dominant position on the staff and now discharged the function of chief censor.

"What's the matter with the *Volksblatt?*" asked Major Liggett.

"More snarling at the French and English," Captain Scudder explained snarlingly. He took up the paper and read:

" 'It is without question somewhat difficult for the German people to believe in the sincerity of the liberal policies of President Wilson. We have in France and England too often seen demonstrated the dishonesty of this liberalism, which has clearly appeared only a masquerade for a conscienceless political opportunism. Herbert Asquith, before the War the chief leader of the English Liberal Party, did not hesitate, when British imperialism had forced Germany to fight England, to justify the policy of the British imperialist, formerly his opponents, with every hypocritical sophistry.' 'Hypocritical sophistry!' Does that look as if they knew they were licked?"

The orderly appeared from the next room and announced "a German outside."

"Bring him in," said Major Bradley.

The editor of the *Trierische Volksblatt* was a bespectacled pale-eyed man who carried an umbrella in one hand and a flat black hat in the other. He saluted the Major respectfully and came to a stiff stand. Major Bradley ignored the salute, not from arrogance but because he had been taught that no true salute can take place when the parties are without hats.

"Your editorial this morning," pronounced the Major,

in the competent German of West Point, "is in violation
of the order that no unfavorable criticism of the policies
or the governments of the Entente shall be permitted in
occupied territory. You were notified of this when the
occupation began."

He showed the man the blue-pencilled paper.

The editor of the *Volksblatt* took it nervously and
examined it with his pale eyes through his pale nickel-
rimmed spectacles.

He tried to explain: "This is not a criticism. It is a
justification of President Wilson. It is a plea for the
Germans to have faith in him." He read aloud what
followed. Though the liberals had so often sold out, they
were to hope that President Wilson would not betray
them.

"You criticize a member of the British government,"
Major Bradley unrelentingly pointed out.

"Asquith is not now a member of the government," the
editor of the *Volksblatt* protested.

The Major paused, his square bespectacled face stoi-
cally masking a check.

"In the next paragraph," the editor pressed on, "I
criticize also the German Social-Democrats—"

Lieutenant Franklin tried to help him out: "It's an
editorial in favor of Wilson. They want to explain that
he's not an imperialist—"

He halted as a motor-cycle messenger popped in and
jauntily saluted the Major.

"Oh, yes," said Major Bradley. "Are you leaving right
away?"

"Yes, sir,"—the messenger was snappy.

"I've got to write a letter to GHQ," the Major explained to the others. "They want to know how many
officers to send up. If I get it off this trip, they'll be able

to start in the morning."—"*Setzen Sie da eine minute,*" he directed the editor of the *Volksblatt.*

He wrote out his letter with precision.

After a silence, Lieutenant Franklin inquired of Captain Scudder: "Does the order apply to former members of governments?"

"That's only a quibble," said Captain Scudder. "The insolence is there as plain as day.—I certainly don't think we ought to let this get by, sir!"—he addressed himself to Major Bradley, who was folding up his letter. "It's one of the dirtiest attacks on England I've seen!"

"Asquith's a member of the English government, isn't he?" asked the Major, giving the letter to the motor-cycle sergeant, who snappily saluted and popped out.

"He isn't any more," said Lieutenant Franklin.

"He's one of their most important public men," insisted Captain Scudder.

"He *has* been a member of the government, hasn't he?"—the Major stuck to the order.

"Certainly!" said Captain Scudder.

"Mightn't it be a mistake," suggested Lieutenant Franklin, "to censor the papers too severely just when they're beginning to have confidence in us? Don't you think it's important they should realize that the President really intends to give them a square deal? If the *Volksblatt*'s adopting a friendly policy, perhaps it might be just as well to let it alone."

"So far as I can see," said Major Liggett, who had hitherto simply sat staring in his detached all-comprehensive way, "the chief objection to suppressing the *Volksblatt* is that, if we do, there won't be any papers left. We've already put the others out of business and if we hang this one up, too, we won't know a damn thing that's happening."

"That can't be taken into consideration," the Major

declared severely. "If the order is violated, the paper must be punished."

He summoned the editor back.

"You have printed an attack, have you not, on a member of the British government?" he demanded.

"No, Herr Major: Herr Asquith is no longer a member of the government."

"But he *has* been a member of the government, hasn't he?"

"Asquith was Prime Minister up until not long ago," said Captain Scudder, "and was one of the chief dictators of British policy."

"You have printed an attack on British policy." Major Bradley delivered his verdict. "The *Volksblatt* will be suspended for ten days. I don't want to suspend your paper, but you had notice of the conditions of occupation. Don't let it happen again."

"Lieutenant Franklin," Major Bradley called him back as the committee were leaving the room. "When these new officers get here tomorrow, I can relieve you in this office: I've insisted that they shall all speak German. You can go out as A.D.D.C.: they need one down the river. I'll talk to Colonel McCarthy and have your orders made out."

"Yes, sir," said Lieutenant Franklin.

III

The Lieutenant, stationed down the Moselle as "Assistant District Defense Commander," killed time every day or so by walking into the city. He had found that his principal duty—that of disarming the inhabitants—had already been efficiently attended to by the Burgomaster of the little town. The latter, before he arrived, had had all the weapons collected and put away in a room in the town hall, to which he gave Lieutenant Franklin the key, so that there was nothing left for the Lieutenant to do except post a guard at the door. His other duty—billeting new troops—he was never called upon to discharge, as no new troops ever arrived. And the afternoons opened like pits into which he had a horror of falling.

Night would come rapidly down as he walked back along the Moselle. The hills that walled his path with their frost-blackened trees and naked vineyards, would lose their purple in darkness. The bleak river, breaking the cold, would flee away like fluid iron. From the factories—or from the hills?—there would emerge a sort of stunned race of Nibelungs, who seemed, some to be returning like automata from regular daily work, some simply loitering in suburban roads or under iron bridges, as, if, work having suddenly stopped, they no longer knew what to do.

Coming home late one afternoon thus—he had been billeted in the Burgomaster's own house—he was surprised to find Captain Scudder.

"Well, old chap," the Captain greeted him, "how goes it? I've just been out for a little hike and I thought I'd look in and see how you were. How are you getting along out here?"

"All right," replied Lieutenant Franklin, "but it gets to be pretty monotonous. Nothing to do except eat."

"What do you do?" asked the Captain. "Have a mess just for one?"

"Oh, no," said Lieutenant Franklin. "I eat with the family here."

"You don't have to, you know," said the Captain. "You could have them bring you your mess in your room—or make them serve you first."

A lady appeared in the sitting-room door but, seeing the Captain, did not enter.

"Oh, I beg your pardon," she apologized in French. "I didn't know you had a visitor!"

"This is Madame Hoffer," said Lieutenant Franklin, rising and coming to meet her. *"Je vous présente le capitaine Scudder."*

Madame Hoffer bowed; the Captain rose, as if perfunctorily.

"What became of you?" asked the Lieutenant. "I looked for you everywhere. I went to all the *Konditorei* in the square."

"Oh, it's not a *Konditorei*," she said smilingly. "It's a little restaurant. You thought it was a *Konditorei* on account of the cakes!—Well, you shall have some *Baumkuchen*, after all! We brought some back with us for you." She held up the paper bag and smiled: her amiable eyes and easy manners carried off the dowdy taste of her dress and the dullness of her mealy complexion.

She nodded to the Captain and withdrew.

"Not French, is she?" asked the Captain, who had been watching the dialogue with attention.

"Oh, no," said the Lieutenant, "but she usually talks French because I don't know much German and she doesn't know much English. They all talk French here—the whole family: she's the Burgomaster's daughter. They're quite interesting. They give me German lessons in the evening."

"Look here, old chap," advised Captain Scudder, "I wouldn't get too much mixed up with these people, if I were you. Remember you can never trust a German: that's been proved a thousand times!"

"Oh, they're all right," said the Lieutenant. "Really very nice, in fact."

"I wouldn't let them get too pally. Just keep your distance!"

"Well, after all—" demurred the Lieutenant: he felt

more and more hostile to Captain Scudder, "I mean, the war's over now—"

"Don't be too sure of that," cautioned the Captain. "Remember this is only an armistice!"

They talked about the German food and wine, but as the Captain got up to go, he returned to his former subject. "Just let me give you a tip," he said, lowering his voice and holding the front door half open so that the outer cold came into the hall and blasted its already feeble warmth. "Better be careful with the natives! The French have been complaining lately about the American troops getting too friendly with the Germans. I have it direct from GHQ that the C.-in-C.'s taking the matter up. You'll hear something about it very soon!"

"Well," the Lieutenant cut him short, "let's not worry till we hear something definite."

"All right, old chap: I'm simply telling you."

"Thanks a lot for coming out."

"Not a bit: good to see you again!"

"Don't miss the path: the third street to your left."

"Right-o!" He saluted. "Good-night."

Lieutenant Franklin closed the hall door and pushed out the overpowering blackness.

They sat at first only five at dinner; Lieutenant Franklin felt the empty place. There were Frau Hoffer and her youngish husband, a schoolmaster, with cropped bristling head and a black shiny alpaca coat; the Burgomaster, whose white upturned mustaches still followed the fashion set by the Kaiser; and an American sergeant, all in one chunkish piece, who had been assigned Lieutenant Franklin as interpreter on the strength of fifty or sixty words of German handed down from Michigan grandparents and lopped in the transit of most of their inflections. Frau Hoffer found the Sergeant amusing and always spoke of him as "Monsieur Schwab."

"Well," announced the Lieutenant triumphantly, "I see that Clemenceau has come out for a League of Nations."

"That will be a League of Nations for the Entente and not for anybody else," said the schoolmaster, "if it's Clemenceau who is organizing it. The Entente is already a League of Nations. No doubt, it's that he means."

"But America," protested Lieutenant Franklin, "will insist upon a league for the whole of Europe!—"

The Burgomaster's second daughter appeared and took her place at the table. She was a small but sturdy girl of twenty-two, whom the rest of the family called Bäbchen —red cheeks, dark serious eyes and a straight profile almost American.

"It was so stupid of me to miss you today!" said Lieutenant Franklin eagerly. "I'd been counting on it. I'm so terribly sorry!"

"We were sorry, too," she smiled. "However, we brought you some cake."

"That was very nice of you: I don't deserve it." And he returned to the international situation with an ardor stimulated by her presence. "That's precisely the reason," he insisted, "that the President has come to Europe. He isn't merely working for the Entente: he's working for justice for everybody!"

The schoolmaster shrugged his shoulders: "I don't think it's possible to have justice in Europe. The nation who wins will never consent to it."

The old woman who waited on the table told the Burgomaster there was someone to see him, and he excused himself and went away.

The liveliness which had revived with the oil-lamps of dinner declined when the *Baumkuchen* had been finished. The conversation suddenly lapsed; all stared blankly into their plates. The terrible ennui of evening was upon them.

"*Encore une soirée!*" said Frau Hoffer, with a sigh. "*Je veux dire—encore un soir!*"

"That's just what we need—a soirée!" Lieutenant Franklin rose to the idea: the visit of Captain Scudder had made him particularly genial. "Why not have a party tonight?"

"Go to the Sans-Souci?"—Frau Hoffer glanced toward her husband. "Do you have to work tonight?"

The Burgomaster returned. "There is an affair," he said, "that it's impossible for me to arrange. Two French soldiers, coming from Trèves, have driven off old Hermann's cow.—Old Hermann," he explained to Lieutenant Franklin, "depends for his living on the milk from his cow.—*Voici le règne de la justice qui commence!*"

"What a shame!" said Lieutenant Franklin. "But I suppose the Americans can't do anything about it." Not knowing what else to say, he returned, after a pause, to the party. "Do come with us!" he pressed Herr Hoffer. "We'll have some wine at the Sans-Souci."

"Very well," the schoolmaster consented, lighting a cigarette—a little like a Frenchman, thought Lieutenant Franklin. "I shall go badly prepared to my class tomorrow."

They were cheerful as they put on their things. The Burgomaster stayed behind.

Outside, the river-mist obscured everything: only a fur of ammonia vapor revealed the manure pile.

They found the Sans-Souci a clean bright room, orange-lighted with oil-lamps and heated by a glowing stove. The old lady and her daughter who ran it were delighted to be receiving a party in winter. They brought yellow cake and clear yellow wine, which, on the red and white checkered cloth, looked more cheerful to Lieutenant Franklin than anything he had seen yet in Germany.

"Here's to peace!" he proposed, beaming, as they clinked their goblet rims.

"To Justice!" suggested Herr Hoffer.

"To Peace with Justice!"—the Lieutenant took him up. "How marvellous Moselle wine is!"

"We should have some music," said Frau Hoffer. "Play us a waltz, Bäbchen."

"Oh, yes: do!" urged Lieutenant Franklin. *"The Blue Danube Waltz!"*

"I'm afraid I can't remember it all," said Bäbchen. But she took her place on the piano-stool and, sitting straight-backed as if at drill, went through it with military precision.

Lieutenant Franklin, dancing with Frau Hoffer, wondered at the vigor in Bäbchen's small arms.—They were strong people, fine women! The arrival a few days ago of Bäbchen had greatly improved Lieutenant Franklin's state of mind. Before that, the French novels to which he had become addicted, had been exciting him and making him uneasy. He would lie under the feather-bed in his room and dope himself with them for hours. It was partly on that account that the afternoons were distressing: he would break away and walk into Trèves and find himself eying the girls in the streets and wondering whether any were prostitutes. He disapproved of prostitution, and since Bäbchen's return his emotions had risen quickly to a higher plane. She was not like a French *jeune fille* and not like a French married woman, as one read about them in the novels—she was something much more like an American girl. She had been married a very short time: her husband had been killed in Galicia.

When the dance was done, he ordered another bottle. Bäbchen started another Strauss waltz.

"Come!" Frau Hoffer invited the Sergeant, who had

been waiting like a good dog. "Don't you want to dance, Monsieur Schwab?"

The Lieutenant filled Herr Hoffer's glass and sat down at the table across from him. They smiled frankly at one another. Any lingering military self-consciousness which had hitherto inhibited Lieutenant Franklin had been wholly dissolved by the wine. The whole thing—Americans and Germans, officers and enlisted men—was irregular, to be sure, from the point of view of Captain Scudder; but to hell with Captain Scudder!

"What did you think of the French?" he asked Herr Hoffer.

The schoolmaster had been captured in the first battle of the Marne and had spent the whole of the war in a French prison-camp.

Herr Hoffer shrugged his shoulders—yes, Lieutenant Franklin thought again, almost exactly like a Frenchman: he had evidently learned all that in France. "They treated me well enough," he answered. "When they found I was an educated man, they set me to doing clerical work and they allowed me to have books to read."

Through the long unrolling rhythms of music that wove the room with their sweet wreaths, the Lieutenant saw in Herr Hoffer's face the tarnish of those four years of prison. Like the blotting out of four years of life! And then to come back, at last, to these evenings, so heavy with impotence, so desolated with ruin, to take up teaching the undernourished children in the now dismal village school!

"—I read almost the whole of French literature."

"How did you like it?"

"Remarkable for polish and form—but superficial in thought and feeling."

"Come, Karl!" said Frau Hoffer, returning with the

Sergeant. "You haven't forgotten how to dance, have you?"

Sergeant Schwab sat down beside Lieutenant Franklin. Bäbchen began unexpectedly to bang out *The Stars and Stripes Forever*.

"Well, well!" the Lieutenant hailed it. "An old friend! Do they play that much in Germany?"

"It used to be a great favorite."—Frau Hoffer danced off with her husband.

"I heard the band play that in Galveston," said Sergeant Schwab, taking a drink of wine, "the day the troops came back from Vera Cruz.—That was one of the swellest things I ever saw in my life. There was big rows of oleanders—pink and white—on both sides of the street, and it was paved with red bricks—a regular Southern town, yuh know. There'd just been a shower of rain and then all of a sudden the sun came out and shone on the red bricks and those old oleanders were sparkling like diamonds! And the bands were playing *The Stars and Stripes Forever!*"

"That must have been great!" said Lieutenant Franklin.

"That's the kind of thing that takes your speech!"

"Still," observed Lieutenant Franklin, after giving it a moment's reflection, "I suppose that the Germans were being thrilled by their marches just as much when they were getting ready to raise hell with the French!"

He ordered another bottle and made Bäbchen join them at the table. They received her with cheers and clapping; the Lieutenant proposed her health. Then Frau Hoffer took her place at the piano and began playing tunes from *Das Dreimäderlhaus*, the great German popular operetta of the wartime, with a score put together from Schubert's music.

"*Dreimäderlhaus* is wonderful, isn't it!" said Lieutenant

Franklin to Bäbchen. "I went to see it three times in Trèves!"

"It is the true story of Schubert's life, you know," Bäbchen explained seriously, charmingly. "He was in love with a lady who did not love him. He wrote his most beautiful songs for her."

Sweet and deep he drew it from her eyes, the romantic longing of the music. How much he would like to kiss her! Those merry young fellows in *Dreimäderlhaus* with the Konzertmeister's daughters!—so free and gay, in blue brass-buttoned coats, in the fresh Viennese spring . . . drinking under the lilac trellis, drinking to the lindens and their loves!—But it wouldn't, he thought, be correct to—besides, she mightn't like him enough.

But he came out with a bold proposal: "Won't you let me take you to the theater in Trèves some night?"

"Thank you: I should like to very much.—If it is possible." She smiled.

Possible? Why shouldn't it be possible? Who were the Scudders to bully him?

"It's not very amusing here," she went on. "We don't have much music now. In Dresden, they have good music in all the cafés. We used to go to the opera every week."

"Dresden must be a marvellous city!" exclaimed Lieutenant Franklin.

"Yes: it is a fine city. I like Dresden very very much.—We used to go out very early Sunday morning—my husband and I, with our friends—and have breakfast in the Grosser Garten. We would have breakfast on the shores of the Carola-See—a beautiful little lake. We'd feed the swans with the crumbs. They have beautiful swans in the Grosser Garten. I liked Dresden very much."

He saw her sent back to her provincial sewing—that old threadbare couch in the Burgomaster's house—no more music, no more friends, no more outings in the Grosser Garten!

"But even Dresden," she added, "is not the same since the war."

"Nothing is the same anywhere since the war!" He suddenly took fire. "Everybody has lost by the war! Nobody has anything to gain from war!—Nobody really wants it. I don't suppose you wanted it any more than we did!—And now that everybody knows they don't want it, there must never be another!—That's why America came into it—so that there should never be another war!"

"Yes," she looked up at him with strong soft eyes. "I don't think that the Americans hate us."

Of course not! How proud he felt that she knew it! He was aware of his cleanness, his blondness, his straightness—he was exalted to know himself an American: heir to the War of Independence, soldier of the American Republic! They had left the intrigues, the antagonisms, the greeds of the old world behind—and now they had come back to save it! *He* was not pledged to hate the Germans—he was pledged to Humanity and Justice. And he loved them all!—he loved Herr Hoffer, who had read through the whole of French literature in a French prison-camp and had found it polished but superficial; Sergeant Schwab, who had been stricken speechless by the sun and oleanders of Galveston; dear Bäbchen, who had liked to take breakfast out of doors and to feed the beautiful swans.

Everything in him that had been kicked and kept under during the months he had spent in the army—by the naggings and snubs of superiors, by the months of suffocating boredom, by the brutalities of the artillery school at Langres, by the intolerable horror of artillery itself: blowing people to shreds whom you had never seen, so that you had to try to occupy your mind with the mathematical and technical end, all culminating in Captain Scudder!—his spirit rose proudly to reject the army and everything that made it possible, to affirm human solidarity! Now forever there must be no more hatred, no more slaughter, among Christian peoples!—men who were moved by the same music, made gay by the same wine!

All about them, outside this room, the desolation of Europe opened: the starved fatigue of the living, the abyss—one could not look into it!—of the dead; that world which had been cursed for four years with the indictment of every natural instinct, the abortion of every kindly impulse. And tonight in this bright-lit room, where still the wine from Moselle grapes was yellow, where still Schubert's music swam in sun, the fellowship of men was reviving after the bitterness, the agony, the panic! Had young German girls like Bäbchen—and young French and young English and young Americans—been cheated of springtime and music and youth? Well, the Americans were there to see to it that the children of the future should never again be so cheated! . . . The Americans and Germans were much alike . . . they were all speaking that fine language, French. . . . He wondered whether he couldn't do something about that poor old man and his cow. It would make Bäbchen admire him. . . . What if he should marry her and take her home? . . .

He watched her lips, so good-natured and full, finishing words he had not heard her speak. A sudden utterance took shape in his thought: it demanded expression in German.

"*Sie sind sehr schön!*" he said suddenly, earnestly, and took her hand under the table.

"*Sie sind sehr freundlich das zu sagen,*" she answered with grave eyes, leaving her hand in his.

Herr Hoffer and the Sergeant had been driven by the wine to the toilet; Frau Hoffer, at the piano, had her back to them. He kissed Bäbchen's lips with grave tenderness.

A deep blush flooded her face and flooded her pretty round neck and spread under her plain blue beads and beneath the black border of her mourning.

IV

The next day Lieutenant Franklin received the general order against fraternizing with the Germans.

The scandal was now notorious: the Americans and the French, since the Armistice, had been getting to hate each other worse and worse; and the Americans were making buddies of the Germans. The situation had come to a head in a riot in the Trèves railroad station: some French soldiers had attempted to ride the Germans and some Americans had sided with the latter and beaten up the French.

He received also a special order informing him that he had been relieved of duty in Germany and was immediately to proceed to France.

He went in to see Colonel McCarthy. The Chief of Staff had just come into his office and was regarding the pile of papers which confronted him with the unconquerable hostility of a man who has never felt at ease with reading and writing. A regular army officer, like Major Bradley, he had, like him, risen inevitably to an important post on the staff.

"I simply thought," the Lieutenant suggested, not without a note of pleading, "that if it was on account of my not knowing German, I can really get along perfectly well out there because they all speak French. Besides, I've been taking German lessons lately—"

"We don't want somebody who's just learning it,"

interrupted Colonel McCarthy, "we want somebody who already knows it." He was a tall man with graying hair and a disagreeable sulky mouth: years of inaction at army posts with nothing to think about but promotion, imagined Lieutenant Franklin.

"Very well, sir," he assented sadly.

"—And we want somebody," pursued the Colonel, glaring at an intelligence report he had picked up, "who won't talk too much French or German or anything else! You had no instructions to take German lessons!"

On the stairway, he met Major Liggett stalking by with his hands in his ulster pockets.

"Well," Lieutenant Franklin accosted him, assuming a comic tone, "they're sending me back again!"

"That so?" replied Major Liggett. "Well, I guess we can all go home now—I see that Scudder's got his major's commission."

"How did he manage that?" asked the Lieutenant. "I thought that since the Armistice they weren't handing out any more promotions."

"Only for regular army officers," Major Liggett ironically explained, "or for close friends of regular army officers."

"How did he get such a drag with them?"

"Why, look at the service he's rendered! The very first thing he gets here, he puts all the papers out of business. And now since the frogs have been squealing about the Americans getting too intimate with the Germans, he's been a regular little Hawkshaw—watching to see that the Americans don't give any candy to German children. He tried some of that stuff on me—wanted to drop in on me in my billet some evening. But I told-um I got so exhausted with the work that I just went right home and went to bed. He saw me taking a Christmas present to my old woman that lives in the house and tried to intimate I was sleeping with her. Ninety years old, at least—the original German witch!"

Major Scudder marched briskly up, the gold oak-leaves gleaming on his shoulders.

"Well, old boy, I congratulate you!" he greeted Lieutenant Franklin. "I hear you're going back to France! We envy you, don't we, Major?"

"You may," replied Major Liggett, "but if I've got to be over here at all, give me the Germans every time. But there's only just one country to go back to—and to stay in and to never leave!"

———

[I finally succeeded in making it clear that I was of no use whatever in Germany and got myself returned to Chaumont. I travelled back on the train with the original of Major Liggett.]

———

Hecker met a classmate of his in the Intelligence Library and, after exchanging the usual commonplaces, parted from him and began to talk to someone else, expounding the corruption of American politics, etc. It afterwards appeared that the classmate had complained to Blankenhorn that Hecker had been indulging in utterances that bordered on the treasonable. Blankenhorn told Hecker about it and wound up with this terse comment: "Be careful how you talk in the presence of the deaf: remember they have tongues."

Hecker said that a common error, difficult to expel from the minds of young students, was that Ginn and Company wrote the *Aeneid,* and [William J.] Rolfe

Macbeth.—He said that, in politics, he was a Bolshevik of the extreme Left.

He said that the motto seemed to be: When you are in France, do as the Americans do.

———

The Seine had overflowed its banks and turned the fields into a lake of gray silver, where the trees were reflected as black skeletons.

———

"It is now not uncommon to date the time when species that could fairly be called human first began to appear at about two million years back, of which the brief period we call historical is but an insignificant fraction. . . . The geological evidence tends to indicate that Chellean man, who first made tools that were both permanent and undoubtedly human, may have lived somewhere about twenty-seven thousand years ago, so that, of the continuous history of human culture, as distinguished from the history of man, our historical period is little more than a tenth part."—Havelock Ellis.

———

In the barracks [where we slept in bunks and I overheard a great deal of conversation]:
"Aw, they'll always have wars over here! As soon as a kid's born, they give him guns an' that!

"Why, sure! When Germany gets so strong that they can't beat her, they just call over America to help them."

"Aw, well, let 'em fight; I don't care."

"Why, you ———, I do, though, I got three kids over home."

"Did you ever screw any old people?"
"No: what's it like?"
"They think it's the last piece of tail they're ever going to get in their lives."

"We were wonderin' whether it's possible to screw and piss at the same time. So she got up on top of me and tried."
"What happened?"
"She fainted away up there."

———

Métivier explained that it was forbidden by law to kill fish with hand grenades [we had seen someone doing this]. "It ought to be abolished," he said, and then, after a moment's reflection, "and I'll tell you another thing: it ought to be forbidden to kill people with them, too!"

[Métivier was a French soldier friend of mine. His father had been a manufacturer of Aubusson tapestries. He contradicted the popular belief that Frenchmen never have you in their homes by inviting me to dinner at his mother's house in Paris. He was the kind of frank, honest and humorous Frenchman that I get along with best. I regret that, on a recent visit to Paris, I was unable to find any trace of him.]

———

After a week of snow and rain in the first part of May, the sun cleared up the damp wet weather and disclosed a sudden world of blue and gold and green. Long days of sun rested steadily on the earth and, quickly drying up the first moistures of the morning, unrolled their even course through steady sunny hours, till the slow twilight of evening. The thin-ribbed poplar screens that glinted with silver in the wind, from a distance seemed steeped with gold above a canal of jade, which mirrored the clouds and the blue sky with a light film of green. The ducks could float at ease again among the little green islands of the Marne, and the limaçons crawled by the moist brim with its tints of fresh clay flower-pots. On some days, the lightly troubled sky dotted the green water with little circles and clouded the hanging reflections of the poplars, already clouded with tempered green and yellow leaves that the water tempered again. It was like a divine benediction after those four years of horror and suffering.

The surface a silver mirror which the breezes glazed.

[At GHQ, I composed a statement, a kind of tentative manifesto, which I sent to several friends. I have been doing this kind of thing periodically all my life. I had already published one such in the *Nassau Lit,* an editorial called *The Fettered College;* and my latest has been my pamphlet, published in 1964, called *The Cold War and the Income Tax: A Protest.* All these statements of mine have been protests. In this one written after the Armistice, I indicted the institutions of the Western world and suggested a way out in the direction of socialism. None of my friends seemed to take it seriously—almost all of them were officers on active duty—with the exception of Stanley Dell, who wrote me an intelligent letter.]

[After the Armistice, it was easy enough to get leave. I made my first extended visit to Paris. I had already, on a

previous visit, contemplated availing myself of the prostitutes, and I remember sitting in my room at the University Club and considering this step. But I was full of
social morality. I thought I shouldn't encourage this evil,
and I finally decided not to yield. One day Kenneth
Simpson turned up and immediately requested me to
take him on a tour of the city. In his fast-talking fast-
moving way, he accompanied me to some of the more
obvious and less time-consuming sights such as Notre-
Dame, after every one of which he would say, "Well,
we've got that under control!" As soon as we got out of
the cab at the club, he accosted a woman on the pavement, exchanged a few words, and without further ceremony walked off with her. I was much surprised by this.
The woman looked so respectable that I could not understand how Kenneth knew that she would be so easily
accessible.

I also made a journey south to Toulouse and Perpignan
with an intelligent young Swede who stood at a desk and
made architectural drawings in the room in which I
worked at GHQ. Toulouse, when we got out of the train,
reminded me of Charlottesville, Virginia: the hot summer
climate, the leisurely tempo, the row of open hacks drawn
up at the station in the heavy but dry southern night. I
found there one or two men I knew, who were availing
themselves of the special arrangements by which soldiers
who had not been sent home were allowed to study at the
universities. I attended only one lecture, by a follower of
the sociologist Émile Durkheim. It was curious to contrast
his intellectual enthusiasm and his lucid abstract formulations with the lumbering rather obvious lectures that I
had heard at Columbia summer school, delivered by
Franklin H. Giddings, the American pioneer in this field
for whom had been created the first chair of sociology in

the United States. I have never since listened to a lecture on this subject.]

———

[I visited my friends at Vittel just as they were leaving for home and travelled with them on the train as far as Chaumont. The combat troops were sent home first, and the medical personnel fairly early; but we bureaucrats at GHQ were among the last to go, and I was not mustered out in the United States till after the 4th of July.]

Just as he was leaving, Leo (Rabbette) pulled out a volume of *Les Fleurs du Mal* from his pack and showed it to me. "They haven't beaten me yet!" he said, as he went off. "I never surrender! I never surrender!"

———

As one looks down the river at Paris or even at Épinal, one sees that every window of the buildings that line the water-front has been touched by the finger of beauty.

———

At the museum in Toulouse, the detached gargoyles had been set up on end in the cloister, with their heads thrown backward and to the side, as if they were sea-lions being fed with fish.

———

When the orange of the sunset had disappeared, one saw one star of liquid silver wavering behind the wind-swept leaves.

———

"That locomotive busted out like a bat outa hell."

———

List of books and pamphlets read,
beginning last of August, 1917

The Fruit of the Tree: Edith Wharton
Souls on Fifth: Granville Barker
Sea Warfare: Rudyard Kipling
Gallipoli: John Masefield
John Millington Synge: John Masefield
Holy Dying: Jeremy Taylor
Le Jardin d'Épicure: Anatole France
Dominique: Eugène Fromentin
Introduction and Catullus in the *Oxford Book of Latin
   Verse*
The Soul of a Bishop: H. G. Wells
Seven Great Statesmen: Andrew D. White (one of
   the books, and one of the best, that Alfred Bellinger
   had given me in our annual exchange)
George Bernard Shaw: His plays: H. L. Mencken
A Book of Prefaces: H. L. Mencken
Dubliners: James Joyce
Ixion in Heaven: Benjamin D'Israeli
A Change of Air: Katherine Fullerton Gerould
La Révolte des Anges: Anatole France
A Midsummer Night's Dream
Two Gentlemen of Verona
The Merry Wives of Windsor ⎫ William Shakespeare
Measure for Measure
A Short History of England: G. K. Chesterton
The Soul of Man Under Socialism: Oscar Wilde
The Sense of the Past: Henry James
Audessus de la Mêlée: Henri Barbusse
Love Songs: Sara Teasdale
Les Soirées de Médan: Zola, Maupassant, Huys-
   mans, Céard, Hennique, Alexis
Sébastian Roch: Octave Mirbeau

Six of One and Half a Dozen of the Other: Colour Blind Neutrality: William Archer

Les Affaires Sont les Affaires: Octave Mirbeau

Le Portefeuille: Octave Mirbeau

Books and Persons: Arnold Bennett

Vers les Meilleurs Temps: Anatole France

The Middle Years: Henry James

Histoire Contemporaine: Anatole France (L'Orme du Mail, Le Mannequin d'Osier, L'Anneau d'Améthyste, Monsieur Bergeret à Paris)

Renascence: Edna St. Vincent Millay [My cousin Carolyn Wilson sent me this. She had known Edna Millay at Vassar. This volume later disappeared. I imagine it was stolen in New York, when the first edition had become a rarity.]

How the English Take the War: William Hard

The German Soul: Baron Frederick von Hügel [Kemp Smith sent me this.]

La Paix par la Diplomatie: Lord Lansdowne

The New Freedom: Woodrow Wilson

Vers et Prose: Morceaux Choisis: Stéphane Mallarmé

The Foreign Policy of Sir Edward Grey: Gilbert Murray

Plain Tales from the Hills: Rudyard Kipling

Madame Sand: Philip Moeller

Adolphe: Benjamin Constant

Recollections: John Morley

The Acts of the Apostles: Saint Luke

The Return of the Soldier: Rebecca West

Mimi Pimson, Le Fils du Titien, L'Histoire d'un Merle Blanc, Croisilles, Frédéric et Bernerette, La Mouche, Le Secret de Javotte: Alfred de Musset

Le Génie Latin: Anatole France

La Rôtisserie de la Reine Pédauque: Anatole France

Les Mauvais Bergers: Octave Mirbeau

Les Vingt et Un Jours d'un Neurasthénique: Octave Mirbeau

L'Étui de Nacre: Anatole France

My Mission to London, 1912–1914: Prince Lichnowsky

Green Fruit: John Peale Bishop

The Nemesis of Mediocrity: Ralph Adams Cram

Balthasar: Anatole France

Au Petit Bonheur: Anatole France

Discours de Réception par l'Académie Française: Anatole France

La Société Historique d'Auteuil et de Passy: Anatole France

Sur la Pierre Blanche: Anatole France

Poems: Anatole France

Poems: José-Maria de Heredia

Le Jardin des Supplices: Octave Mirbeau

What Every Woman Knows: J. M. Barrie

John Redmond: L. G. Redmond

Le Foyer: Octave Mirbeau and Thadée Natanson

L'Epidémie: Octave Mirbeau

Le Puits de Sainte-Claire: Anatole France

Damn! A Book of Calumny: H. L. Mencken

Les Évangiles: Ernest Renan

Jacques Callot: Edmond Bruwaert

Vieux Ménages: Octave Mirbeau

Une Nuit au Luxembourg: Remy de Gourmont

A League of Nations: Viscount Grey

The Admirable Crichton: J. M. Barrie

Sylvia Scarlett: Compton Mackenzie

Manon Lescaut: L'Abbé Prévost

Brochures on Anders Zorn and Félicien Rops

Eminent Victorians: Lytton Strachey

Leaves of Grass
Democratic Vistas } Walt Whitman

[I had more leisure for reading after the Armistice and got through the rest of Renan's *Origines du Christianisme* and a good deal of Michelet's *Histoire de France,* a Lemerre edition of which, in very small and easily portable volumes, I had bought in a bookshop in the Parc at Vittel. In the Trier barracks, I read Wells's *Peter and Joan;* the color and vitality and optimism of Wells seemed incongruous in that formidable abandoned place.]

———

"Γλυκὺ ἀπείροις πόλεμος." Πίνδαρος

———

Colloquial

Oftentimes: most of the doctors
Elizabeth Herbert [David Hamilton's sister]:
"Elsie's homelife was awfully stuffy. She always calls her husband 'Mr.—', and he calls her 'little friend.' "
Western: *school* for *college* always
Imagine that!—I'll say!
What I mean!
Where do you get that stuff?

Army

Where d'ye think yuh are, *home?*
It's a great life if you don't weaken.
The first ten years are the hardest.
How d'ye get that way?
One-way ticket to France.
The ass-hole of the Army
A kiss-ass attitude; you can kiss ass.
Haul ass!: Hurry up!
Some shit!

[I compiled a glossary of war slang, after the war. Larry Noyes compiled and sent me a list of navy slang. Mencken borrowed and used my glossary in one of the later editions of *The American Language*; then I lent it to someone else, who never sent it back. Foolishly, I had made only one copy.]

Songs: Keep your head down, Alleman; Some day I'm going to murder the Bugler; Beautiful Katy; Parlez-vous; Beautiful Paris;* Bastard King of England; Joan of Arc; If you want to find the captains, I know where they are; Madelon; Tout le long de la Tamise;† Sambre-et Meuse; Le Père de la Victoire; I want to go home; Good-by-ee, don't cry-ee; When your balls hang low;‡ Here's to good old beer, drink 'er down; Will Yankee Doodle parlez-vous français?; Where do we go from here?; Over There.

Poor Butterfly was one of the most popular songs when the United States went into the war.

*And when I woke up in the morning,
  My mind and purse were blanks.
  She stole my identification tags—
  She thought that they were francs.
      Oh, Paris, beautiful Paris!
      I'll never go there, I'll never go there, I'll never go there any more!

  †*Tout le long de la Tamise*
  Ils sont allés tous les deux,
  Gouter l'heure exquise
  Du printemps qui grise
  Et des près fleuris semés de coins ombreux.
  Et dans un doux badinage,
  S'appelant "Darling" and "Lulu."
  Sous le vert feuillage,

Chacun d'eux s'engage,
Et le vent repète, "I love you."

There was also a parody of this, which began:
Tout le long de la chemise
l' ya d' la dentelle et des rubans . . .

[Before I had left Vittel, the flu epidemic of 1918 had taken, I think, as heavy a toll of our troops as any battle with the Germans had done. The hospitals were crowded with flu patients, many of whom died. I was on night duty and on my feet most of the time. The other night orderly was an elderly undertaker, who went around in felt slippers, with a lantern and a kind of nightcap on his head. He knew just how to handle dead bodies. We would put them on a stretcher and carry them down to a basement room, where we sometimes had to pile them up like logs. They were buried in big common ditches.

This was much the busiest time in our hospitals. We never had a chance to think—though doctors and nurses also died—about catching the disease ourselves. When the worst of it was over, I did collapse, although I had not caught the flu. I was allowed to go to bed for a day or so in a hospital room by myself. I found some copies of the magazine *Vanity Fair*, which I had never seen before but of which I was to become managing editor very soon

‡When your balls hang low,
  You can swing 'em to and fro-
  You can tie 'em in a knot,
  You can tie 'em in a bow-
  You can fling 'em on your shoulder,
  Like a bloody British soldier.
  You can do this evolution when your balls hang
    low.

after the war. I also had leisure to think, and it suddenly became very clear to me that I could never go back to my former life—that is, that I could never go back to the habits and standards of even the most cultivated elements of the world in which I had lived. I felt now that I had never quite believed in that world, that I had never, in fact, quite belonged to it. It now appeared to me too narrowly limited by its governing principles and prejudices. My experience of the army had had on me a liberating effect. I could now get on with all kinds of people and could satisfy my curiosity about aspects of life that otherwise I should not perhaps so soon have known. I had been already something of a Francophile and ready to accept any Frenchman; but many of my friends in the American army had been born in other countries than America: they had been Irishmen, Swedes, Danes, Swiss, Belgians and cockneys. I had spent my Christmas in Trier with the only other occupant of the barracks, an Italian boy, when we had had a good dinner with Moselle wine and gone to the opera at the Stadttheater. My association with all these had given me a strong contempt for the complaints about the "foreign" immigrants on the part of the old-line Americans and for the talk about the necessity for getting them "Americanized" that was evoked by the enthusiastic response of many emigrants from Russia and Eastern Europe to the Russian Revolution. I had been struck by the differences that, by natural processes, had been made for some of these immigrants by their having come from Europe to America. John Andersen told me that the United States had afforded him a freedom and an opportunity that, as even an educated peasant, he could never have known in Denmark. The family of Roy Gamble's father had been hereditary farriers in the family of some English nobleman. Roy had once gone to see them and had realized that the distance between him as an independent American and his English relatives who "knew their place" was too great now ever to be bridged. And the experience of military discipline, with its many injustices and absurdities, had given me a sympathy with the victims of any sort of power machine that I was afterwards never to lose.

When I was back in New York at first, my habits did not change very much, but my life began soon to take a different direction in a way that, I think, otherwise it would hardly have done. But such speculations are futile. I was by that time as much a product of the world of the war as of that of my earlier years, and I had to live now in the world in which I found myself after the war.]